Machine Learning Projects for .NET Developers

Mathias Brandewinder

Apress®

Machine Learning Projects for .NET Developers

ISBN-13 (pbk): 978-1-4302-6767-6

ISBN-13 (electronic): 978-1-4302-6766-9

Managing Director: Welmoed Spahr
Lead Editor: Gwenan Spearing
Technical Reviewer: Scott Wlaschin
Editorial Board: Steve Anglin, Mark Beckner, Gary Cornell, Louise Corrigan, Jim DeWolf, Jonathan Gennick, Robert Hutchinson, Michelle Lowman, James Markham, Susan McDermott, Matthew Moodie, Jeffrey Pepper, Douglas Pundick, Ben Renow-Clarke, Gwenan Spearing, Matt Wade, Steve Weiss
Coordinating Editor: Melissa Maldonado and Christine Ricketts
Copy Editor: Kimberly Burton-Weisman and April Rondeau
Compositor: SPi Global
Indexer: SPi Global
Artist: SPi Global

Distributed to the book trade worldwide by Springer Science+Business Media New York, 233 Spring Street, 6th Floor, New York, NY 10013. Phone 1-800-SPRINGER, fax (201) 348-4505, e-mail orders-ny@springer-sbm.com, or visit www.springeronline.com. Apress Media, LLC is a California LLC and the sole member (owner) is Springer Science + Business Media Finance Inc (SSBM Finance Inc). SSBM Finance Inc is a Delaware corporation.

For information on translations, please e-mail rights@apress.com, or visit www.apress.com.

Apress and friends of ED books may be purchased in bulk for academic, corporate, or promotional use. eBook versions and licenses are also available for most titles. For more information, reference our Special Bulk Sales–eBook Licensing web page at www.apress.com/bulk-sales.

Any source code or other supplementary material referenced by the author in this text is available to readers at www.apress.com. For detailed information about how to locate your book's source code, go to www.apress.com/source-code/.

Contents at a Glance

Contents

About the Author

Mathias Brandewinder is a Microsoft MVP for F# and is based in San Francisco, California, where he works for Clear Lines Consulting. An unashamed math geek, he became interested early on in building models to help others make better decisions using data. He collected graduate degrees in business, economics, and operations research, and fell in love with programming shortly after arriving in the Silicon Valley. He has been developing software professionally since the early days of .NET, developing business applications for a variety of industries, with a focus on predictive models and risk analysis.

About the Technical Reviewer

Scott Wlaschin is a .NET developer, architect, and author. He has over 20 years of experience in a wide variety of areas from high-level UX/UI to low-level database implementations.

He has written serious code in many languages, his favorites being Smalltalk, Python, and more recently F#, which he blogs about at fsharpforfunandprofit.com.

Acknowledgments

Thanks to my parents, I grew up in a house full of books; books have profoundly influenced who I am today. My love for them is in part what lead me to embark on this crazy project, trying to write one of my own, despite numerous warnings that the journey would be a rough one. The journey was rough, but totally worth it, and I am incredibly proud: I wrote a book, too! For this, and much more, I'd like to thank my parents.

Going on a journey alone is no fun, and I was very fortunate to have three great companions along the way: Gwenan the Fearless, Scott the Wise, and Petar the Rock. Gwenan Spearing and Scott Wlaschin have relentlessly reviewed the manuscript and given me invaluable feedback, and have kept this project on course. The end result has turned into something much better than it would have been otherwise. You have them to thank for the best parts, and me to blame for whatever problems you might find!

I owe a huge, heartfelt thanks to Petar Vucetin. I am lucky to have him as a business partner and as a friend. He is the one who had to bear the brunt of my moods and darker moments, and still encouraged me and gave me time and space to complete this. Thanks, dude—you are a true friend.

Many others helped me out on this journey, too many to mention them all in here. To everyone who made this possible, be it with code, advice, or simply kind words, thank you—you know who you are! And, in particular, a big shoutout to the F# community. It is vocal (apparently sometimes annoyingly so), but more important, it has been a tremendous source of joy and inspiration to get to know many of you. Keep being awesome!

Finally, no journey goes very far without fuel. This particular journey was heavily powered by caffeine, and Coffee Bar, in San Francisco, has been the place where I found a perfect macchiato to start my day on the right foot for the past year and a half.

Introduction

If you are holding this book, I have to assume that you are a .NET developer interested in machine learning. You are probably comfortable with writing applications in C#, most likely line-of-business applications. Maybe you have encountered F# before, maybe not. And you are very probably curious about machine learning. The topic is getting more press every day, as it has a strong connection to software engineering, but it also uses unfamiliar methods and seemingly abstract mathematical concepts. In short, machine learning looks like an interesting topic, and a useful skill to learn, but it's difficult to figure out where to start.

This book is intended as an introduction to machine learning for developers. My main goal in writing it was to make the topic accessible to a reader who is comfortable writing code, and is not a mathematician. A taste for mathematics certainly doesn't hurt, but this book is about learning some of the core concepts through code by using practical examples that illustrate how and why things work.

But first, what is machine learning? Machine learning is the art of writing computer programs that get better at performing a task as more data becomes available, without requiring you, the developer, to change the code.

This is a fairly broad definition, which reflects the fact that machine learning applies to a very broad range of domains. However, some specific aspects of that definition are worth pointing out more closely. Machine learning is about writing programs—code that runs in production and performs a task—which makes it different from statistics, for instance. Machine learning is a cross-disciplinary area, and is a topic relevant to both the mathematically-inclined researcher and the software engineer.

The other interesting piece in that definition is data. Machine learning is about solving practical problems using the data you have available. Working with data is a key part of machine learning; understanding your data and learning how to extract useful information from it are quite often more important than the specific algorithm you will use. For that reason, we will approach machine learning starting with data. Each chapter will begin with a real dataset, with all its real-world imperfections and surprises, and a specific problem we want to address. And, starting from there, we will build a solution to the problem from the ground up, introducing ideas as we need them, in context. As we do so, we will create a foundation that will help you understand how different ideas work together, and will make it easy later on to productively use libraries or frameworks, if you need them.

Our exploration will start in the familiar grounds of C# and Visual Studio, but as we progress we will introduce F#, a .NET language that is particularly suited for machine learning problems. Just like machine learning, programming in a functional style can be intimidating at first. However, once you get the hang of it, F# is both simple and extremely productive. If you are a complete F# beginner, this book will walk you through what you need to know about the language, and you will learn how to use it productively on real-world, interesting problems.

Along the way, we will explore a whole range of diverse problems, which will give you a sense for the many places and perhaps unexpected ways that machine learning can make your applications better. We will explore image recognition, spam filters, and a self-learning game, and much more. And, as we take that journey together, you will see that machine learning is not all that complicated, and that fairly simple models can produce surprisingly good results. And, last but not least, you will see that machine learning is a lot of fun! So, without further ado, let's start hacking on our first machine learning problem.

CHAPTER 1

■ ■ ■

256 Shades of Gray

Building a Program to Automatically Recognize Images of Numbers

If you were to create a list of current hot topics in technology, machine learning would certainly be somewhere among the top spots. And yet, while the term shows up everywhere, what it means exactly is often shrouded in confusion. Is it the same thing as "big data," or perhaps "data science"? How is it different from statistics? On the surface, machine learning might appear to be an exotic and intimidating specialty that uses fancy mathematics and algorithms, with little in common with the daily activities of a software engineer.

In this chapter, and in the rest of this book, my goal will be to demystify machine learning by working through real-world projects together. We will solve problems step by step, primarily writing code from the ground up. By taking this approach, we will be able to understand the nuts and bolts of how things work, illustrating along the way core ideas and methods that are broadly applicable, and giving you a solid foundation on which to build specialized libraries later on. In our first chapter, we will dive right in with a classic problem—recognizing hand-written digits—doing a couple of things along the way:

- Establish a methodology applicable across most machine learning problems. Developing a machine learning model is subtly different from writing standard line-of-business applications, and it comes with specific challenges. At the end of this chapter, you will understand the notion of cross-validation, why it matters, and how to use it.

- Get you to understand how to "think machine learning" and how to look at ML problems. We will discuss ideas like similarity and distance, which are central to most algorithms. We will also show that while mathematics is an important ingredient of machine learning, that aspect tends to be over-emphasized, and some of the core ideas are actually fairly simple. We will start with a rather straightforward algorithm and see that it actually works pretty well!

- Know how to approach the problem in C# and F#. We'll begin with implementing the solution in C# and then present the equivalent solution in F#, a .NET language that is uniquely suited for machine learning and data science.

Tackling such a problem head on in the first chapter might sound like a daunting task at first—but don't be intimidated! It is a hard problem on the surface, but as you will see, we will be able to create a pretty effective solution using only fairly simple methods. Besides, where would be the fun in solving trivial toy problems?

1

What Is Machine Learning?

But first, what is machine learning? At its core, machine learning is writing programs that learn how to perform a task from experience, without being explicitly programmed to do so. This is still a fuzzy definition, and begs the question: How do you define learning, exactly? A somewhat dry definition is the following: A program is learning if, as it is given more data points, it becomes automatically better at performing a given task. Another way to look at it is by flipping around the definition: If you keep doing the same thing over and over again, regardless of the results you observe, you are certainly not learning.

This definition summarizes fairly well what "doing machine learning" is about. Your goal is to write a program that will perform some task automatically. The program should be able to learn from experience, either in the form of a pre-existing dataset of past observations, or in the form of data accumulated by the program itself as it performs its job (what's known as "online learning"). As more data becomes available, the program should become better at the task without your having to modify the code of the program itself.

Your job in writing such a program involves a couple of ingredients. First, your program will need data it can learn from. A significant part of machine learning revolves around gathering and preparing data to be in a form your program will be able to use. This process of reorganizing raw data into a format that better represents the problem domain and that can be understood by your program is called **feature extraction**.

Then, your program needs to be able to understand how well it is performing its task, so that it can adjust and learn from experience. Thus, it is crucial to define a measure that properly captures what it means to "do the task" well or badly.

Finally, machine learning requires some patience, an inquisitive mind, and a lot of creativity! You will need to pick an algorithm, feed it data to train a predictive model, validate how well the model performs, and potentially refine and iterate, maybe by defining new features, or maybe by picking a new algorithm. This cycle—learning from training data, evaluating from validation data, and refining—is at the heart of the machine learning process. This is the scientific method in action: You are trying to identify a model that adequately predicts the world by formulating hypotheses and conducting a series of validation experiments to decide how to move forward.

Before we dive into our first problem, two quick comments. First, this might sound like a broad description, and it is. Machine learning applies to a large spectrum of problems, ranging all the way from detecting spam email and self-driving cars to recommending movies you might enjoy, automatic translation, or using medical data to help with diagnostics. While each domain has its specificities and needs to be well understood in order to successfully apply machine learning techniques, the principles and methods remain largely the same.

Then, note how our machine learning definition explicitly mentions "writing programs." Unlike with statistics, which is mostly concerned with validating whether or not a model is correct, the end goal of machine learning is to create a program that runs in production. As such, it makes it a very interesting area to work in, first because it is by nature cross-disciplinary (it is difficult to be an expert in both statistical methods and software engineering), and then because it opens up a very exciting new field for software engineers.

Now that we have a basic definition in place, let's dive into our first problem.

A Classic Machine Learning Problem: Classifying Images

Recognizing images, and human handwriting in particular, is a classic problem in machine learning. First, it is a problem with extremely useful applications. Automatically recognizing addresses or zip codes on letters allows the post office to efficiently dispatch letters, sparing someone the tedious task of sorting them manually; being able to deposit a check in an ATM machine, which recognizes amounts, speeds up the process of getting the funds into your account, and reduces the need to wait in line at the bank. And just imagine how much easier it would be to search and explore information if all the documents written by mankind were digitized! It is also a difficult problem: Human handwriting, and even print, comes with all sorts of variations (size, shape, slant, you name it); while humans have no problem recognizing letters and digits written by various people, computers have a hard time dealing with that task. This is the reason CAPTCHAs are such a simple and effective way to figure out whether someone is an actual human being or a bot. The human brain has this amazing ability to recognize letters and digits, even when they are heavily distorted.

FUN FACT: CAPTCHA AND RECAPTCHA

CAPTCHA ("Completely Automated Public Turing test to tell Computers and Humans Apart") is a mechanism devised to filter out computer bots from humans. To make sure a user is an actual human being, CAPTCHA displays a piece of text purposefully obfuscated to make automatic computer recognition difficult. In an intriguing twist, the idea has been extended with reCAPTCHA. reCAPTCHA displays two images instead of just one: one of them is used to filter out bots, while the other is an actual digitized piece of text (see Figure 1-1). Every time a human logs in that way, he also helps digitize archive documents, such as back issues of the *New York Times*, one word at a time.

Figure 1-1. A reCAPTCHA example

Our Challenge: Build a Digit Recognizer

The problem we will tackle is known as the "Digit Recognizer," and it is directly borrowed from a Kaggle.com machine learning competition. You can find all the information about it here: `http://www.kaggle.com/c/digit-recognizer`.

Here is the challenge: What we have is a dataset of 50,000 images. Each image is a single digit, written down by a human, and scanned in 28 × 28 pixels resolution, encoded in grayscale, with each pixel taking one of 256 possible shades of gray, from full white to full black. For each scan, we also know the correct answer, that is, what number the human wrote down. This dataset is known as the **training set**. Our goal now is to write a program that will learn from the training set and use that information to make predictions for images it has never seen before: is it a zero, a one, and so on.

Technically, this is known as a **classification** problem: Our goal is to separate images between known "categories," a.k.a. the classes (hence the word "classification"). In this case, we have ten classes, one for each single digit from 0 to 9. Machine learning comes in different flavors depending on the type of question you are trying to resolve, and classification is only one of them. However, it's also perhaps the most emblematic one. We'll cover many more in this book!

So, how could we approach this problem? Let's start with a different question first. Imagine that we have just two images, a zero and a one (see Figure 1-2):

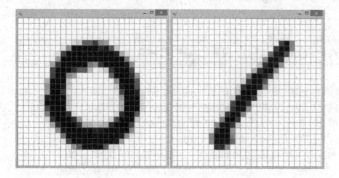

Figure 1-2. Sample digitized 0 and 1

Suppose now that I gave you the image in Figure 1-3 and asked you the following question: Which of the two images displayed in Figure 1-2 is it most similar to?

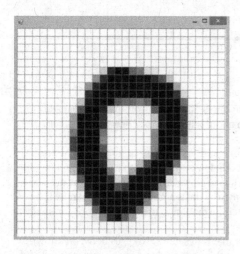

Figure 1-3. Unknown image to classify

As a human, I suspect you found the question trivial and answered "obviously, the first one." For that matter, I suspect that a two-year old would also find this a fairly simple game. The real question is, how could you translate into code the magic that your brain performed?

One way to approach the problem is to rephrase the question by flipping it around: The most similar image is the one that is the *least different*. In that frame, you could start playing "spot the differences," comparing the images pixel by pixel. The images in Figure 1-4 show a "heat map" of the differences: The more two pixels differ, the darker the color is.

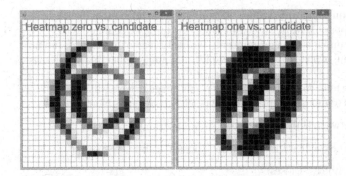

Figure 1-4. *"Heat map" highlighting differences between Figure 1-2 and Figure 1-3*

In our example, this approach seems to be working quite well; the second image, which is "very different," has a large black area in the middle, while the first one, which plots the differences between two zeroes, is mostly white, with some thin dark areas.

Distance Functions in Machine Learning

We could now summarize how different two images are with a single number, by summing up the differences across pixels. Doing this gives us a small number for similar images, and a large one for dissimilar ones. What we managed to define here is a "**distance**" between images, describing how close they are. Two images that are absolutely identical have a distance of zero, and the more the pixels differ, the larger the distance will be. On the one hand, we know that a distance of zero means a perfect match, and is the best we can hope for. On the other hand, our similarity measure has limitations. As an example, if you took one image and simply cloned it, but shifted it (for instance) by one pixel to the left, their distance pixel-by-pixel might end up being quite large, even though the images are essentially the same.

The notion of distance is quite important in machine learning, and appears in most models in one form or another. A distance function is how you translate what you are trying to achieve into a form a machine can work with. By reducing something complex, like two images, into a single number, you make it possible for an algorithm to take action—in this case, deciding whether two images are similar. At the same time, by reducing complexity to a single number, you incur the risk that some subtleties will be "lost in translation," as was the case with our shifted images scenario.

Distance functions also often appear in machine learning under another name: **cost functions.** They are essentially the same thing, but look at the problem from a different angle. For instance, if we are trying to predict a number, our prediction error—that is, how far our prediction is from the actual number—is a distance. However, an equivalent way to describe this is in terms of cost: a larger error is "costly," and improving the model translates to reducing its cost.

Start with Something Simple

But for the moment, let's go ahead and happily ignore that problem, and follow a method that has worked wonders for me, both in writing software and developing predictive models—what is the easiest thing that could possibly work? Start simple first, and see what happens. If it works great, you won't have to build anything complicated, and you will be done faster. If it doesn't work, then you have spent very little time building a simple proof-of-concept, and usually learned a lot about the problem space in the process. Either way, this is a win.

So for now, let's refrain from over-thinking and over-engineering; our goal is to implement the least complicated approach that we think could possibly work, and refine later. One thing we could do is the following: When we have to identify what number an image represents, we could search for the most similar (or least different) image in our known library of 50,000 training examples, and predict what that image says. If it looks like a five, surely, it must be a five!

The outline of our algorithm will be the following. Given a 28 × 28 pixels image that we will try to recognize (the "Unknown"), and our 50,000 training examples (28 × 28 pixels images and a label), we will:

- compute the total difference between Unknown and each training example;

- find the training example with the smallest difference (the "Closest"); and

- predict that "Unknown" is the same as "Closest."

Let's get cracking!

Our First Model, C# Version

To get warmed up, let's begin with a C# implementation, which should be familiar territory, and create a C# console application in Visual Studio. I called my solution DigitsRecognizer, and the C# console application CSharp— feel free to be more creative than I was!

Dataset Organization

The first thing we need is obviously data. Let's download the dataset trainingsample.csv from http://1drv.ms/1sDThtz and save it somewhere on your machine. While we are at it, there is a second file in the same location, validationsample.csv, that we will be using a bit later on, but let's grab it now and be done with it. The file is in CSV format (Comma-Separated Values), and its structure is displayed in Figure 1-5. The first row is a header, and each row afterward represents an individual image. The first column ("label"), indicates what number the image represents, and the 784 columns that follow ("pixel0", "pixel1", ...) represent each pixel of the original image, encoded in grayscale, from 0 to 255 (a 0 represents pure black, 255 pure white, and anything in between is a level of gray).

```
1  label,pixel0,pixel1,pixel2,pixel3,pixel4,pixel5,pix
2  1,0,0,0,0,0,0,0,0,0,0,0,0,0,0,0,0,0,0,0,0,0,0,0,0,(
3  0,0,0,0,0,0,0,0,0,0,0,0,0,0,0,0,0,0,0,0,0,0,0,0,0,(
4  1,0,0,0,0,0,0,0,0,0,0,0,0,0,0,0,0,0,0,0,0,0,0,0,0,(
5  4,0,0,0,0,0,0,0,0,0,0,0,0,0,0,0,0,0,0,0,0,0,0,0,0,(
6  0,0,0,0,0,0,0,0,0,0,0,0,0,0,0,0,0,0,0,0,0,0,0,0,0,(
7  0,0,0,0,0,0,0,0,0,0,0,0,0,0,0,0,0,0,0,0,0,0,0,0,0,(
8  7,0,0,0,0,0,0,0,0,0,0,0,0,0,0,0,0,0,0,0,0,0,0,0,(
```

Figure 1-5. *Structure of the training dataset*

6

For instance, the first row of data here represents number 1, and if we wanted to reconstruct the actual image from the row data, we would split the row into 28 "slices," each of them representing one line of the image: pixel0, pixel1, ..., pixel 27 encode the first line of the image, pixel28, pixel29, ..., pixel55 the second, and so on and so forth. That's how we end up with 785 columns total: one for the label, and 28 lines × 28 columns = 784 pixels. Figure 1-6 describes the encoding mechanism on a simplified 4 × 4 pixels image: The actual image is a 1 (the first column), followed by 16 columns representing each pixel's shade of gray.

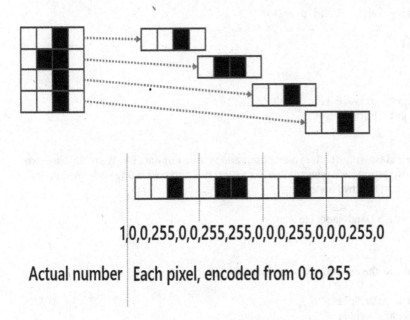

1,0,0,255,0,0,255,255,0,0,0,255,0,0,0,255,0

Actual number | Each pixel, encoded from 0 to 255

Figure 1-6. *Simplified encoding of an image into a CSV row*

■ **Note** If you look carefully, you will notice that the file trainingsample.csv contains only 5,000 lines, instead of the 50,000 I mentioned earlier. I created this smaller file for convenience, keeping only the top part of the original. 50,000 lines is not a huge number, but it is large enough to unpleasantly slow down our progress, and working on a larger dataset at this point doesn't add much value.

Reading the Data

In typical C# fashion, we will structure our code around a couple of classes and interfaces representing our domain. We will store each image's data in an Observation class, and represent the algorithm with an interface, IClassifier, so that we can later create model variations.

As a first step, we need to read the data from the CSV file into a collection of observations. Let's go to our solution and add a class in the CSharp console project in which to store our observations:

Listing 1-1. Storing data in an Observation class

```
public class Observation
{
    public Observation(string label, int[] pixels)
    {
        this.Label = label;
        this.Pixels = pixels;
    }

    public string Label { get; private set; }
    public int[] Pixels { get; private set; }
}
```

Next, let's add a DataReader class with which to read observations from our data file. We really have two distinct tasks to perform here: extracting each relevant line from a text file, and converting each line into our observation type. Let's separate that into two methods:

Listing 1-2. Reading from file with a DataReader class

```
public class DataReader
{
    private static Observation ObservationFactory(string data)
    {
        var commaSeparated = data.Split(',');
        var label = commaSeparated[0];
        var pixels =
            commaSeparated
            .Skip(1)
            .Select(x => Convert.ToInt32(x))
            .ToArray();

        return new Observation(label, pixels);
    }

    public static Observation[] ReadObservations(string dataPath)
    {
        var data =
            File.ReadAllLines(dataPath)
            .Skip(1)
            .Select(ObservationFactory)
            .ToArray();

        return data;
    }
}
```

Note how our code here is mainly LINQ expressions! Expression-oriented code, like LINQ (or, as you'll see later, F#), helps you write very clear code that conveys intent in a straightforward manner, typically much more so than procedural code does. It reads pretty much like English: "read all the lines, skip the headers, split each line around the commas, parse as integers, and give me new observations." This is how I would describe what I was trying to do, if I were talking to a colleague, and that intention is very clearly reflected in the code. It also fits particularly well with data manipulation tasks, as it gives a natural way to describe data transformation workflows, which are the bread and butter of machine learning. After all, this is what LINQ was designed for—"Language Integrated Queries!"

We have data, a reader, and a structure in which to store them—let's put that together in our console app and try this out, replacing PATH-ON-YOUR-MACHINE in trainingPath with the path to the actual data file on your local machine:

Listing 1-3. Console application

```
class Program
{
    static void Main(string[] args)
    {
        var trainingPath = @"PATH-ON-YOUR-MACHINE\trainingsample.csv";
        var training = DataReader.ReadObservations(trainingPath);

        Console.ReadLine();
    }
}
```

If you place a breakpoint at the end of this code block, and then run it in debug mode, you should see that training is an array containing 5,000 observations. Good—everything appears to be working.

Our next task is to write a Classifier, which, when passed an Image, will compare it to each Observation in the dataset, find the most similar one, and return its label. To do that, we need two elements: a Distance and a Classifier.

Computing Distance between Images

Let's start with the distance. What we want is a method that takes two arrays of pixels and returns a number that describes how different they are. Distance is an area of volatility in our algorithm; it is very likely that we will want to experiment with different ways of comparing images to figure out what works best, so putting in place a design that allows us to easily substitute various distance definitions without requiring too many code changes is highly desirable. An interface gives us a convenient mechanism by which to avoid tight coupling, and to make sure that when we decide to change the distance code later, we won't run into annoying refactoring issues. So, let's extract an interface from the get-go:

Listing 1-4. IDistance interface

```
public interface IDistance
{
    double Between(int[] pixels1, int[] pixels2);
}
```

Now that we have an interface, we need an implementation. Again, we will go for the easiest thing that could work for now. If what we want is to measure how different two images are, why not, for instance, compare them pixel by pixel, compute each difference, and add up their absolute values? Identical images will have a distance of zero, and the further apart two pixels are, the higher the distance between the two images will be. As it happens, that distance has a name, the "**Manhattan distance,**" and implementing it is fairly straightforward, as shown in Listing 1-5:

Listing 1-5. Computing the Manhattan distance between images

```
public class ManhattanDistance : IDistance
{
    public double Between(int[] pixels1, int[] pixels2)
    {
        if (pixels1.Length != pixels2.Length)
        {
            throw new ArgumentException("Inconsistent image sizes.");
        }

        var length = pixels1.Length;

        var distance = 0;

        for (int i = 0; i < length; i++)
        {
            distance += Math.Abs(pixels1[i] - pixels2[i]);
        }

        return distance;
    }
}
```

FUN FACT: MANHATTAN DISTANCE

I previously mentioned that distances could be computed with multiple methods. The specific formulation we use here is known as the "Manhattan distance." The reason for that name is that if you were a cab driver in New York City, this is exactly how you would compute how far you have to drive between two points. Because all streets are organized in a perfect, rectangular grid, you would compute the absolute distance between the East/West locations, and North/South locations, which is precisely what we are doing in our code. This is also known as, much less poetically, the L1 Distance.

We take two images and compare them pixel by pixel, computing the difference and returning the total, which represents how far apart the two images are. Note that the code here uses a very procedural style, and doesn't use LINQ at all. I actually initially wrote that code using LINQ, but frankly didn't like the way the result looked. In my opinion, after a certain point (or for certain operations), LINQ code written in C# tends to look a bit over-complicated, in large part because of how verbose C# is, notably for functional constructs (Func<A,B,C>). This is also an interesting example that contrasts the two styles. Here, understanding what the code is trying to do does require reading it line by line and translating it into a "human description." It also uses mutation, a style that requires care and attention.

MATH.ABS()

You may be wondering why we are using the absolute value here. Why not simply compute the differences? To see why this would be an issue, consider the example below:

If we used just the "plain" difference between pixel colors, we would run into a subtle problem. Computing the difference between the first and second images would give me -255 + 255 – 255 + 255 = 0—exactly the same as the distance between the first image and itself. This is clearly not right: The first image is obviously identical to itself, and images one and two are as different as can possibly be, and yet, by that metric, they would appear equally similar! The reason we need to use the absolute value here is exactly that: without it, differences going in opposite directions end up compensating for each other, and as a result, completely different images could appear to have very high similarity. The absolute value guarantees that we won't have that issue: Any difference will be penalized based on its amplitude, regardless of its sign.

Writing a Classifier

Now that we have a way to compare images, let's write that classifier, starting with a general interface. In every situation, we expect a two-step process: We will train the classifier by feeding it a training set of known observations, and once that is done, we will expect to be able to predict the label of an image:

Listing 1-6. IClassifier interface

```
public interface IClassifier
{
    void Train(IEnumerable<Observation> trainingSet);
    string Predict(int[] pixels);
}
```

Here is one of the multiple ways in which we could implement the algorithm we described earlier:

Listing 1-7. Basic Classifier implementation

```
public class BasicClassifier : IClassifier
{
    private IEnumerable<Observation> data;

    private readonly IDistance distance;

    public BasicClassifier(IDistance distance)
    {
        this.distance = distance;
    }
```

```
    public void Train(IEnumerable<Observation> trainingSet)
    {
        this.data = trainingSet;
    }

    public string Predict(int[] pixels)
    {
        Observation currentBest = null;
        var shortest = Double.MaxValue;

        foreach (Observation obs in this.data)
        {
            var dist = this.distance.Between(obs.Pixels, pixels);
            if (dist < shortest)
            {
                shortest = dist;
                currentBest = obs;
            }
        }

        return currentBest.Label;
    }
}
```

The implementation is again very procedural, but shouldn't be too difficult to follow. The training phase simply stores the training observations inside the classifier. To predict what number an image represents, the algorithm looks up every single known observation from the training set, computes how similar it is to the image it is trying to recognize, and returns the label of the closest matching image. Pretty easy!

So, How Do We Know It Works?

Great—we have a classifier, a shiny piece of code that will classify images. We are done—ship it!

Not so fast! We have a bit of a problem here: We have absolutely no idea if our code works. As a software engineer, knowing whether "it works" is easy. You take your specs (everyone has specs, right?), you write tests (of course you do), you run them, and bam! You know if anything is broken. But what we care about here is not whether "it works" or "it's broken," but rather, "is our model any good at making predictions?"

Cross-validation

A natural place to start with this is to simply measure how well our model performs its task. In our case, this is actually fairly easy to do: We could feed images to the classifier, ask for a prediction, compare it to the true answer, and compute how many we got right. Of course, in order to do that, we would need to know what the right answer was. In other words, we would need a dataset of images with known labels, and we would use it to test the quality of our model. That dataset is known as a **validation set** (or sometimes simply as the "test data").

At that point, you might ask, why not use the training set itself, then? We could train our classifier, and then run it on each of our 5,000 examples. This is not a very good idea, and here's why: If you do this, what you will measure is how well your model learned the training set. What we are really interested in is something slightly different: How well can we expect the classifier to work, once we release it "in the wild," and start feeding it new images it has never encountered before? Giving it images that were used in training will likely give you an optimistic estimate. If you want a realistic one, feed the model data that hasn't been used yet.

■ **Note**   As a case in point, our current classifier is an interesting example of how using the training set for validation can go very wrong. If you try to do that, you will see that it gets every single image properly recognized. 100% accuracy! For such a simple model, this seems too good to be true. What happens is this: As our algorithm searches for the most similar image in the training set, it finds a perfect match every single time, because the images we are testing against belong to the training set. So, when results seem too good to be true, check twice!

The general approach used to resolve that issue is called **cross-validation**. Put aside part of the data you have available and split it into a training set and a validation set. Use the first one to train your model and the second one to evaluate the quality of your model.

Earlier on, you downloaded two files, trainingsample.csv and validationsample.csv. I prepared them for you so that you don't have to. The training set is a sample of 5,000 images from the full 50,000 original dataset, and the validation set is 500 other images from the same source. There are more fancy ways to proceed with cross-validation, and also some potential pitfalls to watch out for, as we will see in later chapters, but simply splitting the data you have into two separate samples, say 80%/20%, is a simple and effective way to get started.

Evaluating the Quality of Our Model

Let's write a class to evaluate our model (or any other model we want to try) by computing the proportion of classifications it gets right:

Listing 1-8. Evaluating the BasicClassifier quality

```
public class Evaluator
{
    public static double Correct(
        IEnumerable<Observation> validationSet,
        IClassifier classifier)
    {
        return validationSet
            .Select(obs => Score(obs, classifier))
            .Average();
    }

    private static double Score(
        Observation obs,
        IClassifier classifier)
    {
        if (classifier.Predict(obs.Pixels) == obs.Label)
            return 1.0;
        else
            return 0.0;
    }
}
```

We are using a small trick here: we pass the Evaluator an IClassifier and a dataset, and for each image, we "score" the prediction by comparing what the classifier predicts with the true value. If they match, we record a 1, otherwise we record a 0. By using numbers like this rather than true/false values, we can average this out to get the percentage correct.

So, let's put all of this together and see how our super-simple classifier is doing on the validation dataset supplied, validationsample.csv:

Listing 1-9. Training and validating a basic C# classifier

```
class Program
{
    static void Main(string[] args)
    {
        var distance = new ManhattanDistance();
        var classifier = new BasicClassifier(distance);

        var trainingPath = @"PATH-ON-YOUR-MACHINE\trainingsample.csv";
        var training = DataReader.ReadObservations(trainingPath);
        classifier.Train(training);

        var validationPath = @"PATH-ON-YOUR-MACHINE\validationsample.csv";
        var validation = DataReader.ReadObservations(validationPath);

        var correct = Evaluator.Correct(validation, classifier);
        Console.WriteLine("Correctly classified: {0:P2}", correct);

        Console.ReadLine();
    }
}
```

If you run this now, you should get 93.40% correct, on a problem that is far from trivial. I mean, we are automatically recognizing digits handwritten by humans, with decent reliability! Not bad, especially taking into account that this is our first attempt, and we are deliberately trying to keep things simple.

Improving Your Model

So, what's next? Well, our model is good, but why stop there? After all, we are still far from the Holy Grail of 100% correct—can we squeeze in some clever improvements and get better predictions?

This is where having a validation set is absolutely crucial. Just like unit tests give you a safeguard to warn you when your code is going off the rails, the validation set establishes a baseline for your model, which allows you to not to fly blind. You can now experiment with modeling ideas freely, and you can get a clear signal on whether the direction is promising or terrible.

At this stage, you would normally take one of two paths. If your model is good enough, you can call it a day—you're done. If it isn't good enough, you would start thinking about ways to improve predictions, create new models, and run them against the validation set, comparing the percentage correctly classified so as to evaluate whether your new models work any better, progressively refining your model until you are satisfied with it.

But before jumping in and starting experimenting with ways to improve our model, now seems like a perfect time to introduce F#. F# is a wonderful .NET language, and is uniquely suited for machine learning and data sciences; it will make our work experimenting with models much easier. So, now that we have a working C# version, let's dive in and rewrite it in F# so that we can compare and contrast the two and better understand the F# way.

Introducing F# for Machine Learning

Did you notice how much time it took to run our model? In order to see the quality of a model, after any code change, we need to rebuild the console app and run it, reload the data, and compute. That's a lot of steps, and if your dataset gets even moderately large, you will spend the better part of your day simply waiting for data to load. Not great.

Live Scripting and Data Exploration with F# Interactive

By contrast, F# comes with a very handy feature, called F# Interactive, in Visual Studio. F# Interactive is a REPL (Read-Evaluate-Print Loop), basically a live-scripting environment where you can play with code without having to go through the whole cycle I described before.

So, instead of a console application, we'll work in a script. Let's go into Visual Studio and add a new library project to our solution (see Figure 1-7), which we will name FSharp.

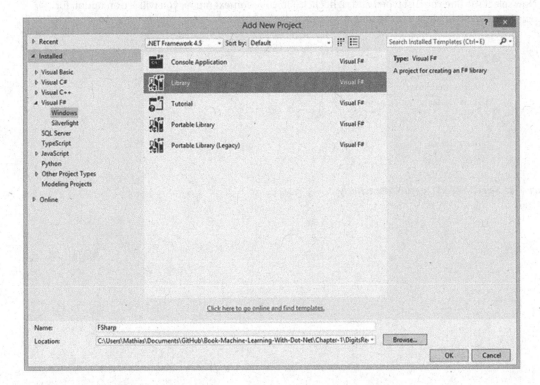

Figure 1-7. *Adding an F# library project*

■ **Tip**   If you are developing using Visual Studio Professional or higher, F# should be installed by default. For other situations, please check www.fsharp.org, the F# Software Foundation, which has comprehensive guidance on getting set up.

It's worth pointing that you have just added an F# project to a .NET solution with an existing C# project. F# and C# are completely interoperable and can talk to each other without problems—you don't have to restrict yourself to using one language for everything. Unfortunately, oftentimes people think of C# and F# as competing languages, which they aren't. They complement each other very nicely, so get the best of both worlds: Use C# for what C# is great at, and leverage the F# goodness for where F# shines!

In your new project, you should see now a file named Library1.fs; this is the F# equivalent of a .cs file. But did you also notice a file called script.fsx? .fsx files are script files; unlike .fs files, they are not part of the build. They can be used outside of Visual Studio as pure, free-standing scripts, which is very useful in its own right. In our current context, machine learning and data science, the usage I am particularly interested in is in Visual Studio: .fsx files constitute a wonderful "scratch pad" where you can experiment with code, with all the benefits of IntelliSense.

Let's go to Script.fsx, delete everything in there, and simply type the following anywhere:

```
let x = 42
```

Now select the line you just typed and right click. On your context menu, you will see an option for "Execute in Interactive," shown in Figure 1-8.

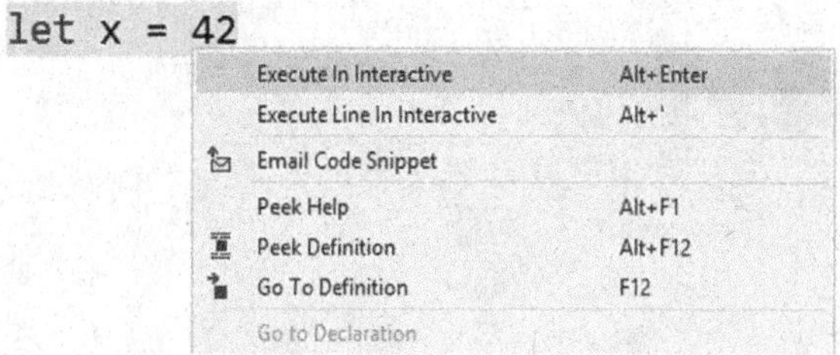

Figure 1-8. *Selecting code to run interactively*

Go ahead—you should see the results appear in a Window labeled "F# Interactive" (Figure 1-9).

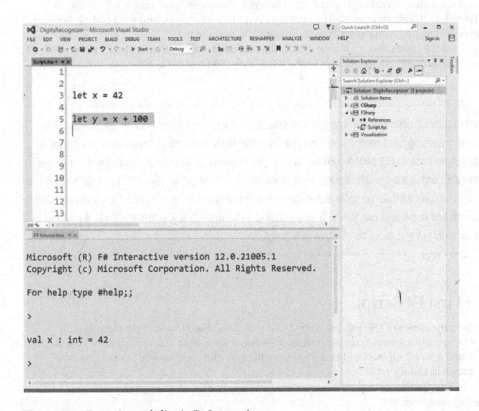

Figure 1-9. *Executing code live in F# Interactive*

■ **Tip**   You can also execute whatever code is selected in the script file by using the keyboard shortcut Alt + Enter. This is much faster than using the mouse and the context menu. A small warning to ReSharper users: Until recently, ReSharper had the nasty habit of resetting that shortcut, so if you are using a version older than 8.1, you will probably have to recreate that shortcut.

The F# Interactive window (which we will refer to as FSI most of the time, for the sake of brevity) runs as a session. That is, whatever you execute in the interactive window will remain in memory, available to you until you reset your session by right-clicking on the contents of the F# Interactive window and selecting "Reset Interactive Session."

In this example, we simply create a variable x, with value 42. As a first approximation, this is largely similar to the C# statement var x = 42; There are some subtle differences, but we'll discuss them later. Now that x "exists" in FSI, we can keep using it. For instance, you can type the following directly in FSI:

```
> x + 100;;
val it : int = 142
>
```

FSI "remembers" that x exists: you do not need to rerun the code you have in the .fsx file. Once it has been run once, it remains in memory. This is extremely convenient when you want to manipulate a somewhat large dataset. With FSI, you can load up your data once in the morning and keep coding, without having to reload every single time you have a change, as would be the case in C#.

You probably noted the mysterious ;; after x + 100. This indicates to FSI that whatever was typed until that point needs to be executed now. This is useful if the code you want to execute spans multiple lines, for instance.

■ **Tip**   If you tried to type F# code directly into FSI, you probably noticed that there was no IntelliSense. FSI is a somewhat primitive development environment compared to the full Visual Studio experience. My advice in terms of process is to type code in FSI only minimally. Instead, work primarily in an .fsx file. You will get all the benefits of a modern IDE, with auto-completion and syntax validation, for instance. This will naturally lead you to write complete scripts, which can then be replayed in the future. While scripts are not part of the solution build, they are part of the solution itself, and can (should) be versioned as well, so that you are always in a position to replicate whatever experiment you were conducting in a script.

Creating our First F# Script

Now that we have seen the basics of FSI, let's get started. We will convert our C# example, starting with reading the data. First, we will execute a complete block of F# code to see what it does, and then we will examine it in detail to see how it all works. Let's delete everything we currently have in `Script.fsx`, and write the F# code shown in Listing 1-10:

Listing 1-10. Reading data from file

```
open System.IO

type Observation = { Label:string; Pixels: int[] }

let toObservation (csvData:string) =
    let columns = csvData.Split(',')
    let label = columns.[0]
    let pixels = columns.[1..] |> Array.map int
    { Label = label; Pixels = pixels }

let reader path =
    let data = File.ReadAllLines path
    data.[1..]
    |> Array.map toObservation

let trainingPath = @"PATH-ON-YOUR-MACHINE\trainingsample.csv"
let trainingData = reader trainingPath
```

There is quite a bit of action going on in these few lines of F#. Before discussing how this all works, let's run it to see the result of our handiwork. Select the code, right click, and pick "Run in Interactive." After a couple of seconds, you should see something along these lines appear in the F# Interactive window:

```
>
type Observation =
  {Label: string;
   Pixels: int [];}
val observationFactory : csvData:string -> Observation
val reader : path:string -> Observation []
val trainingPath : string =
  "-"+[58 chars]
val trainingData : Observation [] =
  [|{Label = "1";
     Pixels =
      [|0; 0; 0; 0; 0; 0; 0; 0; 0; 0; 0; 0; 0; 0; 0; 0; 0; 0; 0; 0; 0; 0; 0;
        0; 0; 0; 0; 0; 0; 0; 0; 0; 0; 0; 0; 0; 0; 0; 0; 0; 0; 0; 0; 0; 0; 0;
        0; 0; 0; 0; 0; 0; 0; 0; 0; 0; 0; 0; 0; 0; 0; 0; 0; 0; 0; 0; 0; 0; 0;
        0; 0; 0; 0; 0; 0; 0; 0; 0; 0; 0; 0; 0; 0; 0; 0; 0; 0; 0; 0; 0; 0; 0;
        0; 0; 0; 0; ...|];};
    /// Output has been cut out for brevity here ///
    {Label = "3";
     Pixels =
      [|0; 0; 0; 0; 0; 0; 0; 0; 0; 0; 0; 0; 0; 0; 0; 0; 0; 0; 0; 0; 0; 0; 0;
        0; 0; 0; 0; 0; 0; 0; 0; 0; 0; 0; 0; 0; 0; 0; 0; 0; 0; 0; 0; 0; 0; 0;
        0; 0; 0; 0; 0; 0; 0; 0; 0; 0; 0; 0; 0; 0; 0; 0; 0; 0; ...|];};
    ...|]
>
```

Basically, in a dozen lines of F#, we got all the functionality of the DataReader and Observation classes. By running it in F# Interactive, we could immediately load the data and see how it looked. At that point, we loaded an array of Observations (the data) in the F# Interactive session, which will stay there for as long as you want. For instance, suppose that you wanted to know the label of Observation 100 in the training set. No need to reload or recompile anything: just type the following in the F# Interactive window, and execute:

```
let test = trainingData.[100].Label;;
```

And that's it. Because the data is already there in memory, it will just work.

This is extremely convenient, especially in situations in which your dataset is large, and loading it is time consuming. This is a significant benefit of using F# over C# for data-centric work: While any change in code in a C# console application requires rebuilding and reloading the data, once the data is loaded in F# Interactive, it's available for you to hack to your heart's content. You can change your code and experiment without the hassle of reloading.

Dissecting Our First F# Script

Now that we saw what these ten lines of code do, let's dive into how they work:

```
open System.IO
```

This line is straightforward—it is equivalent to the C# statement using System.IO. Every .NET library is accessible to F#, so all the knowledge you accumulated over the years learning the .NET namespaces jungle is not lost—you will be able to reuse all that and augment it with some of the F#-specific goodies made available to you!

In C#, we created an Observation class to hold the data. Let's do the same in F#, using a slightly different type:

```
type Observation = { Label:string; Pixels: int[] }
```

Boom—done. In one line, we created a *record* (a type specific to F#), something that is essentially an immutable class (and will appear as such if you call your F# code from C#), with two properties: Label and Pixels. To use a record is then as simple as this:

```
let myObs = { Label = "3"; Pixels = [| 1; 2; 3; 4; 5 |] }
```

We instantiate an Observation by simply opening curly braces and filling in all its properties. F# automatically infers that what we want is an Observation, because it is the only record type that has the correct properties. We create an array of integers for Pixels by simply opening and closing an array with the symbols [| |] and filling in the contents.

Now that we have a container for the data, let's read from the CSV file. In the C# example, we created a method, ReadObservations, and a DataReader class to hold it, but that class is honestly not doing much for us. So rather than creating a class, we'll simply write a function reader, which takes one argument, path, and uses an auxiliary function to extract an Observation from a csv line:

```
let toObservation (csvData:string) =
    let columns = csvData.Split(',')
    let label = columns.[0]
    let pixels = columns.[1..] |> Array.map int
    { Label = label; Pixels = pixels }

let reader path =
    let data = File.ReadAllLines path
    data.[1..]
    |> Array.map toFactory
```

We are using quite a few features of F# here—let's unpack them. It's a bit dense, but once you go through this, you'll know 80% of what you need to understand about F# in order to do data science productively with it!

Let's begin with a high-level overview. Here is how our equivalent C# code looked (Listing 1-2):

```
private static Observation ObservationFactory(string data)
{
    var commaSeparated = data.Split(',');
    var label = commaSeparated[0];
    var pixels =
        commaSeparated
        .Skip(1)
        .Select(x => Convert.ToInt32(x))
        .ToArray();

    return new Observation(label, pixels);
}

public static Observation[] ReadObservations(string dataPath)
{
    var data =
        File.ReadAllLines(dataPath)
        .Skip(1)
        .Select(ObservationFactory)
        .ToArray();

    return data;
}
```

There are a few obvious differences between C# and F#. First, F# doesn't have any curly braces; F#, like other languages such as Python, uses whitespace to mark code blocks. In other words, white space is significant in F# code: when you see code indented by whitespace, with the same depth, then it belongs to the same block, as if invisible curly braces were around it. In the case of the reader function in Listing 1-10, we can see that the body of the function starts at let data ... and ends with |> Array.map observationFactory.

Another obvious high-level difference is the missing return type, or type declaration, on the function argument. Does this mean that F# is a dynamic language? If you hover over reader in the .fsx file, you'll see the following hint show up: val reader : path:string -> Observation [], which denotes a function that takes a path, expected to be of type string, and returns an array of observations. F# is every bit as statically typed as C#, but uses a powerful type-inference engine, which will use every hint available to figure out all by itself what the correct types have to be. In this case, File.ReadAllLines has only two overloads, and the only possible match implies that path has to be a string.

In a way, this gives you the best of both worlds—you get all the benefits of having less code, just as you would with a dynamic language, but you also have a solid type system, with the compiler helping you avoid silly mistakes.

■ **Tip** The F# type-inference system is absolutely amazing at figuring out what you meant with the slightest of hints. However, at times you will need to help it, because it cannot figure it out by itself. In that case, you can simply annotate with the expected type, like this: let reader (path:string) = . In general, I recommend using type annotations in high-level components of your code, or crucial components, even when it is unnecessary. It helps make the intent of your code more directly obvious to others, without having to open an IDE to see what the inferred types are. It can also be useful in tracking down the origin of some issues, by making sure that when you are composing multiple functions together, each step is actually being passed the types it expects.

The other interesting difference between C# and F# is the missing return statement. Unlike C#, which is largely procedural, F# is expression oriented. An expression like let x = 2 + 3 * 5 binds the name x to an expression; when that expression is evaluated as (2 + 3 * 5 is 17), the value is bound to x. The same goes for a function: The function will evaluate to the value of the last expression. Here is a contrived example to illustrate what is happening:

```
let demo x y =
    let a = 2 * x
    let b = 3 * y
    let z = a + b
    z // this is the last expression:
    // therefore demo will evaluate to whatever z evaluates to.
```

Another difference you might have picked up on, too, is the lack of parentheses around the arguments. Let's ignore that point for a minute, but we'll come back to it a bit later in this chapter.

Creating Pipelines of Functions

Let's dive in to the body of the read function. let data = File.ReadAllLines path simply reads all the contents of the file located at path into an array of strings, one per line, all at once. There's no magic here, but it proves the point that we can indeed use anything made available in the .NET framework from F#, regardless of what language was used to write it.

data.[1..] illustrates the syntax for indexers in F#; myArray.[0] will return the first element of your array. Note the presence of a dot between myArray and the bracketed index! The other interesting bit of syntax here demonstrates array slicing; data.[1..] signifies "give me a new array, pulling elements from data starting at index 1 until the last one." Similarly, you could do things like data.[5..10] (give me all elements from indexes 5 to 10), or data.[..3] (give me all elements until index 3). This is incredibly convenient for data manipulation, and is one of the many reasons why F# is such a nice language for data science.

In our example, we kept every element starting at index 1, or in other words, we dropped the first element of the array—that is, the headers.

The next step in our C# code involved extracting an Observation from each line using the ObservationFactory method, which we did by using the following:

```
myData.Select(line => ObservationFactory(line));
```

The equivalent line in F# is as follows:

```
myData |> Array.map (fun line -> toObservation line)
```

At a very high level, you would read the statement as "take the array myData and pass it forward to a function that will apply a mapping to each array element, converting each line to an observation." There are two important differences with the C# code. First, while the Select statement appears as a method on the array we are manipulating, in F#, the logical owner of the function is not the array itself, but the Array module. The Array module acts in a fashion similar to the Enumerable class, which provides a collection of C# extension methods on IEnumerable.

■ **Note**   If you enjoy using LINQ in C#, I suspect you will really like F#. In many respects, LINQ is about importing concepts from functional programming into an object-oriented language, C#. F# offers a much deeper set of LINQ-like functions for you to play with. To get a sense for that, simply type "Array." in .fsx, and see how many functions you have at your disposal!

The second major difference is the mysterious symbol "|>". This is known as the *pipe-forward* operator. In a nutshell, it takes whatever the result of the previous expression was and passes it forward to the next function in the pipeline, which will use it as the last argument. For instance, consider the following code:

```
let double x = 2 * x
let a = 5
let b = double a
let c = double b
```

This could be rewritten as follows:

```
let double x = 2 * x
let c = 5 |> double |> double
```

double is a function expecting a single argument that is an integer, so we can "feed" a 5 directly into it through the pipe-forward operator. Because double also produces an integer, we can keep forwarding the result of the operation ahead. We can slightly rewrite this code to look this way:

```
let double x = 2 * x
let c =
    5
    |> double
    |> double
```

Our example with Array.map follows the same pattern. If we used the raw Array.map version, the code would look like this:

```
let transformed = Array.map (fun line -> toObservation line) data
```

Array.map expects two arguments: what transformation to apply to each array element, and what array to apply it to. Because the target array is the last argument of the function, we can use pipe-forward to "feed" an array to a map, like this:

```
data |> Array.map (fun line -> toObservation line)
```

If you are totally new to F#, this is probably a bit overwhelming. Don't worry! As we go, we will see a lot more examples of F# in action, and while understanding exactly why things work might take a bit, getting it to work is actually fairly easy. The pipe-forward operator is one of my favorite features in F#, because it makes workflows so straightforward to follow: take something and pass it through a pipeline of steps or operations until you are done.

Manipulating Data with Tuples and Pattern Matching

Now that we have data, we need to find the closest image from the training set. Just like in the C# example, we need a distance for that. Unlike C#, again, we won't create a class or interface, and will just use a function:

```
let manhattanDistance (pixels1,pixels2) =
    Array.zip pixels1 pixels2
    |> Array.map (fun (x,y) -> abs (x-y))
    |> Array.sum
```

Here we are using another central feature of F#: the combination of tuples and pattern matching. A *tuple* is a grouping of unnamed but ordered values, possibly of different types. Tuples exist in C# as well, but the lack of pattern matching in the language really cripples their usefulness, which is quite unfortunate, because it's a deadly combination for data manipulation.

There is much more to pattern matching than just tuples. In general, pattern matching is a mechanism with allows your code to simply recognize various shapes in the data, and to take action based on that. Here is a small example illustrating how pattern matching works on tuples:

```
let x = "Hello", 42 // create a tuple with 2 elements
let (a, b) = x // unpack the two elements of x by pattern matching
printfn "%s, %i" a b
printfn "%s, %i" (fst x) (snd x)
```

Here we "pack" within x two elements: a string "Hello" and an integer 42, separated by a comma. The comma typically indicates a tuple, so watch out for this in F# code, as this can be slightly confusing at first. The second line "unpacks" the tuple, retrieving its two elements into a and b. For tuples of two elements, a special syntax exists to access its first and second elements, using the fst and snd functions.

▓ **Tip**   You may have noticed that, unlike C#, F# does not use parentheses to define the list of arguments a function expects. As an example, add x y = x + y is how you would typically write an addition function. The following function tupleAdd (x, y) = x + y is perfectly valid F# code, but has a different meaning: It expects a single argument, which is a fully-formed tuple. As a result, while 1 |> add 2 is valid code, 1 |> tupleAdd 2 will fail to compile—but (1,2) |> tupleAdd will work.

This approach extends to tuples beyond two elements; the main difference is that they do not support fst and snd. Note the use of the wildcard _ below, which means "ignore the element in 2nd position":

```
let y = 1,2,3,4
let (c,_,d,e) = y
printfn "%i, %i, %i" c d e
```

Let's see how this works in the manhattanDistance function. We take the two arrays of pixels (the images) and apply Array.zip, creating a single array of tuples, where elements of the same index are paired up together. A quick example might help clarify:

```
let array1 = [| "A";"B";"C" |]
let array2 = [| 1 .. 3 |]
let zipped = Array.zip array1 array2
```

Running this in FSI should produce the following output, which is self-explanatory:

```
val zipped : (string * int) [] = [|("A", 1); ("B", 2); ("C", 3)|]
```

So what the Manhattan distance function does is take two arrays, pair up corresponding pixels, and for each pair it computes the absolute value of their difference and then sums them all up.

Training and Evaluating a Classifier Function

Now that we have a Manhattan distance function, let's search for the element in the training set that is closest to the image we want to classify:

```
let train (trainingset:Observation[]) =
    let classify (pixels:int[]) =
        trainingset
        |> Array.minBy (fun x -> manhattanDistance x.Pixels pixels)
        |> fun x -> x.Label
    classify

let classifier = train training
```

train is a function that expects an array of Observation. Inside that function, we create another function, classify, which takes an image, finds the image that has the smallest distance from the target, and returns the label of that closest candidate; train returns that function. Note also how while manhattanDistance is not part of the arguments list for the train function, we can still use it inside it; this is known as "capturing a variable into a closure," using within a function a variable whose scope is not defined inside that function. Note also the usage of minBy (which doesn't exist in C# or LINQ), which conveniently allows us to find the smallest element in an array, using any arbitrary function we want to compare items to each other.

Creating a model is now as simple as calling train training.

If you hover over classifier, you will see it has the following type:

```
val classifier : (int [] -> string)
```

What this tells you is that classifier is a function, which takes in an array of integers (the pixels of the image you are trying to classify), and returns a string (the predicted label). In general, I highly recommend taking some time hovering over your code and making sure the types are what you think they are. The F# type inference system is fantastic, but at times it is almost too smart, and it will manage to figure out a way to make your code work, just not always in the way you anticipated.

And we are pretty much done. Let's now validate our classifier:

```
let validationPath = @" PATH-ON-YOUR-MACHINE\validationsample.csv"
let validationData = reader validationPath

validationData
|> Array.averageBy (fun x -> if model x.Pixels = x.Label then 1. else 0.)
|> printfn "Correct: %.3f"
```

This is a pretty straightforward conversion of our C# code: We read the validation data, mark every correct prediction by a 1, and compute the average. Done.

And that's it. In thirty-ish lines of code, in a single file, we have all of the required code in its full glory.

There is obviously much more to F# than what we just saw in this short crash course. However, at this point, you should have a better sense of what F# is about and why it is such a great fit for machine learning and data science. The code is short but readable, and works great for composing data-transformation pipelines, which are an essential activity in machine learning. The F# Interactive window allows you to load your data in memory, once, and then explore the data and modeling ideas, without wasting time reloading and recompiling. That alone is a huge benefit—but we'll see much more about F#, and how to combine its power with C#, as we go further along in the book!

Improving Our Model

We implemented the Dumbest Model That Could Possibly Work, and it is actually performing pretty well—93.4% correct. Can we make this better?

Unfortunately, there is no general answer to that. Unless your model is already 100% correct in its predictions, there is always the possibility of making improvements, and there is only one way to know: try things out and see if it works. Building a good predictive model involves a lot of trial and error, and being properly set up to iterate rapidly, experiment, and validate ideas is crucial.

What directions could we explore? Off the top of my head, I can think of a few. We could

- tweak the distance function. The Manhattan distance we are using here is just one of many possibilities, and picking the "right" distance function is usually a key element in having a good model. The distance function (or cost function) is essentially how you convey to the machine what it should consider to be similar or different items in its world, so thinking this through carefully is very important.

- search for a number of closest points instead of considering just the one closest point, and take a "majority vote." This could make the model more robust; looking at more candidates could reduce the chance that we accidentally picked a bad one. This approach has a name—the algorithm is called "K Nearest Neighbors," and is a classic of machine learning.

- do some clever trickery on the images; for instance, imagine taking a picture, but shifting it by one pixel to the right. If you compared that image to the original version, the distance could be huge, even though they ARE the same image. One way we could compensate for that problem is, for instance, by using some blurring. Replacing each pixel with the average color of its neighbors could mitigate "image misalignment" problems.

I am sure you could think of other ideas, too. Let's explore the first one together.

Experimenting with Another Definition of Distance

Let's begin with the distance. How about trying out the distance you probably have seen in high school, pedantically known as the **Euclidean distance**? Here is the math for that distance:

$$Dist(X,Y) = \sqrt{(x_1 - y_1)^2 + (x_2 - y_2)^2 + \cdots + (x_n - y_n)^2}$$

This simply states that the distance between two points X and Y is the square root of the sum of the difference between each of their coordinates, squared up. You have probably seen a simplified version of this formula, stating that if you take two points on a plane, X = (x1, x2) and Y = (y1, y2), their Euclidean distance is:

$$Dist(X,Y) = \sqrt{\left(x_1 - y_1\right)^2 + \left(x_2 - y_2\right)^2}$$

In case you are more comfortable with code than with math, here is how it would look in F#:

```
let euclideanDistance (X,Y) =
    Array.zip X Y
    |> Array.map (fun (x,y) -> pown (x-y) 2)
    |> Array.sum
    |> sqrt
```

We take two arrays of floats as input (each representing the coordinates of a point), compute the difference for each of their elements and square that, sum, and take the square root. Not very hard, and pretty clear!

A few technical details should be mentioned here. First, F# has a lot of nice mathematical functions built in, which you would typically look for in the System.Math class. sqrt is such a function—isn't it nice to be able to write let x = sqrt 16.0 instead of var x = Math.Sqrt(16)? pown is another such function; it is a specialized version of "raise to the nth power" for cases when the exponent is an integer. The general version is the ** operator, as in let x = 2.0 ** 4.0; pown will give you significant performance boosts when you know the exponent is an integer.

Another detail: The distance function we have here is correct, but technically, for our purposes, we can actually drop the sqrt from there. What we need is the closest point, and if 0 <= A < B, then sqrt A < sqrt B. So rather than incur the cost of that operation, let's drop it. This also allows us to operate on integers, which is much faster than doubles or floats.

Factoring Out the Distance Function

If our goal is to experiment with different models, it's probably a good time to do some refactoring. We want to swap out different pieces in our code and see what the impact is on the prediction quality. Specifically, we want to switch distances. The typical object-oriented way to do that would be to extract an interface, say IDistance, and inject that into the training (which is exactly what we did in the C# sample). However, if you really think about it, the interface is total overkill—the only thing we need is a function, which takes two points as an input and returns an integer, their distance from each other. Here is how we could do it:

Listing 1-11. Refactoring the distance

```
type Distance = int[] * int[] -> int

let manhattanDistance (pixels1,pixels2) =
    Array.zip pixels1 pixels2
    |> Array.map (fun (x,y) -> abs (x-y))
    |> Array.sum

let euclideanDistance (pixels1,pixels2) =
    Array.zip pixels1 pixels2
    |> Array.map (fun (x,y) -> pown (x-y) 2)
    |> Array.sum
```

```
let train (trainingset:Observation[]) (dist:Distance) =
    let classify (pixels:int[]) =
        trainingset
        |> Array.minBy (fun x -> dist (x.Pixels, pixels))
        |> fun x -> x.Label
    classify
```

Instead of an interface, we create a type `Distance`, which is a function signature that expects a pair of pixels and returns an integer. We can now pass any `Distance` we want as an argument to the train function, which will return a classifier using that particular distance. For instance, we can train a classifier with the `manhattanDistance` function, or the `euclideanDistance` function (or any other arbitrary distance function, in case we want to experiment further), and compare how well they perform. Note that this would all be perfectly possible in C# too: Instead of creating an interface `IDistance`, we could simply use `Func<int[],int[],int>`. This is how our code would look:

Listing 1-12. Functional C# example

```
public class FunctionalExample
{
    private IEnumerable<Observation> data;

    private readonly Func<int[], int[], int> distance;

    public FunctionalExample(Func<int[], int[], int> distance)
    {
        this.distance = distance;
    }

    public Func<int[], int[], int> Distance
    {
        get { return this.distance; }
    }

    public void Train(IEnumerable<Observation> trainingSet)
    {
        this.data = trainingSet;
    }

    public string Predict(int[] pixels)
    {
        Observation currentBest = null;
        var shortest = Double.MaxValue;

        foreach (Observation obs in this.data)
        {
            var dist = this.Distance(obs.Pixels, pixels);
            if (dist < shortest)
```

```
            {
                shortest = dist;
                currentBest = obs;
            }
        }

        return currentBest.Label;
    }
}
```

This approach, which focuses on composing functions instead of objects, is typical of what's called a functional style of programming. C#, while coming from object-oriented roots, supports a lot of functional idioms. Arguably, pretty much every feature and innovation that has made its way into C# since version 3.5 (LINQ, Async, ...) has been borrowed from functional programming. At this point, one could describe C# as a language that is object oriented first, but supports functional idioms, whereas F# is a functional programming language first, but can accommodate an object-oriented style as well. Throughout this book, we will in general emphasize a functional style over an object-oriented one, because in our opinion it fits much better with machine learning algorithms than an object-oriented style does, and also because, more generally, code written in a functional style offers serious benefits.

In any case, we are set up to see whether our idea is a good one. We can now create two models and compare their performance:

```
let manhattanClassifier = train trainingData manhattanDistance
let euclideanClassifier = train trainingData euclideanDistance

printfn "Manhattan"
evaluate validationData manhattanClassifier
printfn "Euclidean"
evaluate validationData euclideanClassifier
```

The nice thing here is that we don't have to reload the dataset in memory; we simply modify the script file, select the section that contains new code we want to run, and run it. If we do that, we should see that the new model, euclideanModel, correctly classifies 94.4% of the images, instead of 93.4% for the manhattanModel. Nice! We just squeezed in a 1% improvement. 1% might not sound like much, but if you are already at 93.4%, you just reduced your error from 6.6% to 5.6%, a gain of around 15%.

From a small change in the distance function, we obtained a very significant improvement. This seems to be a promising direction, and it might be worth experimenting with more complicated distance functions, or trying out some of the other directions mentioned earlier. One thing that will probably happen to you if you don't pay attention is that you'll have a big bowl of messy code, with lots of experimentations. Just as version control and automation are essential for classic software development, they are your friends when you develop a predictive model, too. The details and rhythm of the process might differ, but the overall idea is the same: You want to be in a position where you can make changes to code without being worried you will break anything, and "it works on my machine" is not good enough. At any time, anyone should be able to just grab your code and replicate your results with no manual intervention. This approach is known as "reproducible research." I strongly encourage you to go that direction and use scripting and source control everywhere you can; I have experienced myself the horrible scenario in which you know you had a model yesterday that worked better, but because you haven't bothered to save things cleanly, you just can't remember how exactly you did it, and that model is gone. Don't be that person! Especially in this day and age when creating branches with DVCS like Git or Mercurial is so easy, there is no excuse to have that type of issue. When you have a new idea for a model, create a branch and save the steps you execute in your script.

So, What Have We Learned?

We covered quite a bit of ground in this chapter! On the machine learning front, you are now familiar with a few key concepts, as well as with the methodology. And if you are new to F#, you have now written your first piece of F# code!

Let's review some of the main points, starting with the machine learning side.

First, we discussed cross-validation, the process of using separate datasets for training and validation, setting apart some of the data to evaluate the quality of your prediction model. This is a crucial process on many levels. First, it provides you with a baseline, a "ground truth" that guides your experimentation. Without a validation set, you cannot make judgments on whether a particular model is better than another. Cross-validation allows you to measure quality scientifically. It plays a role somewhat analogous to an automated test suite, warning you when your development efforts are going off the rails.

Once your cross-validation setup is in place, you can try to experiment, selecting models or directions to investigate on quantifiable grounds. The trial-and-error approach is an essential part of "doing machine learning." There is no way to know beforehand if a particular approach will work well, so you will have to try it out on the data to see by yourself, which makes it very important to set yourself up for success and embrace "reproducible research" ideas. Automate your process as much as possible with scripts, and use source control liberally so that at any given point you can replicate every step of your model without human intervention. In general, set yourself up so that you can easily change and run code.

What to Look for in a Good Distance Function

In our digit-recognizer exploration, we saw that a small change in what distance we used significantly improved our model. At the heart of most (every?) machine learning models, there is a distance function. All the learning process boils down to is the computer attempting to find the best way possible to fit known data to a particular problem – and the definition of "best fit" is entirely encapsulated in the distance function. In a way, it is the translation of your goals from a human form into a statement that is understandable by a machine, stated using mathematics. The distance function is also frequently called the cost function; thinking in cost emphasizes more what makes a bad solution bad, and what penalty to use so as to avoid selecting bad solutions.

In my experience, it is always worthwhile to take the time to think through your cost function. No matter how clever an algorithm you use, if the cost function is flawed, the results will be terrible. Imagine a dataset of individuals that includes two measurements: height in feet and weight in pounds. If we were to search for the "most similar" individuals in our dataset, along the lines of what we did for images, here is what will happen: While heights are typically in the 5 to 6 feet range, weights are on a wider and higher scale, say, 100 to 200 pounds. As a result, directly computing a distance based on these two measurements will essentially ignore differences in height, because a 1 foot difference will be equivalent to a 1 pound difference. One way to address this is to transform all features to make sure they are on consistent scales, a process known as "normalization," a topic we'll discuss in more detail later. Fortunately, all pixels are encoded on an identical scale, and we could ignore that problem here, but I hope this example of "Distance Gone Wrong" gives you a sense of why it is worth giving your distance function some thought!

This is also one of those cases where the proper mathematical definitions are actually useful. If you dig back your math notes from way back in school, you'll see that a distance function (sometimes also called a metric by mathematicians) is defined by a few properties:

- Distance(A,B) > 0 (there is no negative distance)

- Distance(A,B) = 0 if and only if A = B (the only element with 0 distance to A is A itself)

- Distance(A,B) = Distance(B,A) (symmetry: going from A to B should be the same length as going from B to A)

- Distance(A,B) <= Distance(A,C) + Distance(C,B) ("Triangle inequality": there is no shorter distance between two points than direct travel)

We just looked at two distances in this chapter, but there is a wide variety of functions that satisfy these properties, each of which defines similarity in a different manner. For that matter, the cost function in a model doesn't need to satisfy all these properties, but in general, if it doesn't, you might want to ask yourself what unintended side effects could arise because of it. For instance, in the initial example with the Manhattan distance, if we had omitted the absolute value, we would be blatantly violating both rule 1 (non-negative distance) and rule 3 (symmetry). In some case, there are good reasons to take liberties and use a function that is not a metric, but when that happens, take an extra minute to think through what could possibly go wrong!

Models Don't Have to Be Complicated

Finally, I hope what came through is that effective models don't have to be complicated! Whether in C# or F#, both classifiers were small and used fairly simple math. Of course, some complex models may give you amazing results, too, but if you can get the same result with a simple model that you can understand and modify easily, then why not go for easy?

This is known as Occam's Razor, named after William of Ockham, a medieval philosopher. Occam's Razor follows a principle of economy. When trying to explain something, when choosing between multiple models that could fit, pick the simplest one. Only when no simple explanation works should you go for complicated models.

In the same vein, we implemented first "the simplest thing that could possibly work" here, and I strongly encourage you to follow that approach. If you don't, here is what will probably happen: You will start implementing a few ideas that could work; they will spark new ideas, so you will soon have a bunch of half-baked prototypes, and will go deeper and deeper in the jungle, without a clear process or method. Suddenly, you will realize you have spent a couple of weeks coding away, and you are not quite sure whether anything works or where to go from there. This is not a good feeling. Time box yourself and spend one day (or one week, or one hour, whatever is realistic given your problem) and build an end-to-end model with the dumbest, simplest possible prediction model you can think of. It might actually turn out to be good enough, in which case you won't have wasted any time. And if it isn't good enough, by that point you will have a proper harness, with data integration and cross-validation in place, and you will also likely have uncovered whatever unexpected nastiness might exist in your dataset. You will be in a great place to enter the jungle.

Why F#?

If this was your first exposure to F#, you might have wondered initially why I would introduce that language, and not stick with C#. I hope that the example made clear why I did! In my opinion, while C# is a great language, F# is a fantastic fit for machine learning and data exploration. We will see more of F# in further chapters, but I hope some of these reasons became clear in this chapter.

First, the F# Interactive and Scripting environments are absolute time savers. When developing a machine learning model, it is crucial to be able to experiment, change code, and see the impact, fast, and you need a scripting environment for that. My typical F# workflow is to load whatever data I need in the Interactive environment when I begin the day. Once that is done, I don't need to reload it again—the data is there, in memory, and I can freely play with models. By contrast, testing out a new idea in C# forces me to rebuild the code and reload the data, which will end up being a big time sink.

Also, some of the language features of F# make it a great fit for data manipulation. Its focus on functions, rather than objects, works great for applying functions to data and shaping them any way you need. The pipe-forward operator |> is very convenient for combining such transformations and creating a pipeline that represents in a very readable way data transformation workflows. Combine this with the ability to pack data into tuples and unpack it with pattern matching, and the huge choice of built-in functions in the Array, List, and Seq modules, and you've got something like LINQ on steroids with which to transform and reshape your data any which way you want.

Going Further

One reaction I often get from people who see the algorithm for the first time is "but... this is pretty dumb." What they really mean is, "but... where is the learning?" Formally, machine learning is defined as "writing a program that performs a task better when it gets more data." Our model, the 1 Nearest Neighbor, fits that definition perfectly: You would expect larger samples to "work better" (or conversely, you would expect the performance to degrade if you reduced the sample). On the other hand, it doesn't quite fit our intuitive understanding of learning. Our model really memorizes everything it has seen, whereas humans tend to think of learning as identifying higher-level abstractions, which provide a more compact representation of our experience. When you see the picture of a number, you don't go over every picture you have ever seen in your entire life to decide whether this is a match—you know higher-level concepts that allow you to filter and recognize ("A zero looks like a circle").

More advanced algorithms, such as Support Vector Machines or Neural Networks, could be used on our problem (we will do that in Chapter 8), and their behavior is more in line with this conception of "learning": They process the data during the training phase and extract a reduced representation. The obvious downside is that the training phase will actually be much more involved; the upside is that the resulting model will be both smaller and faster.

So, should you use a Support Vector Machine, a Neural Network, or something else? As is often the case, the answer is "it depends." First, it depends on what your ultimate goal is. Your goal might be to be more accurate; if your code were to be deployed in a real production environment, it might also be to be faster, to use less memory, or something else.

As we discussed earlier, there is really no way to know whether a model will be better than another one—you have to try it out, and that can be expensive. So, before embarking on a quest to make your model better, think twice about it: Is your current model good enough? Are you focusing your efforts on the right question? As the French proverb says, "le mieux est l'ennemi du bien"—"the better is the enemy of the good." Our simple algorithm achieves around 95% correct classification, which is pretty good. If this is enough, don't waste time; move on to your next interesting problem. Machine learning problems have a way of taking on a life of their own: unless you got a perfect model that is fast and 100% accurate, you are never completely done, and it is tempting to go back and try to improve it and squeeze out a little more accuracy. So think ahead of time what is "good enough," otherwise you may end up in a long quest for perfection!

USEFUL LINKS

- The F# Software Foundation, at www.fsharp.org, offers plenty of information on how to get set up and started with F#.

- The full dataset for the Kaggle Digit Recognizer competition can be found at www.kaggle.com/c/digit-recognizer. You can even enter the competition and see how you fare—it's a lot of fun, and a great learning experience!

CHAPTER 2

■ ■ ■

Spam or Ham?

Automatically Detect spam in Text Using Bayes' Theorem

If you use email (I suspect you do!), chances are that you see machine learning at work on a daily basis. Your email client probably includes some spam filter mechanism, which automatically identifies blatantly unwanted promotional materials in your incoming messages and discreetly sends them into oblivion in a "spam folder." It spares you the annoyance of having to delete these messages manually one by one; it will also save you from inadvertently clicking potentially harmful links. This is typical of how machine learning, when well done, can make human life better. Computers are great at performing repetitive tasks and being thorough about it; by automatically taking care of tedious activities and saving us from mistakes, they enable us humans to focus on more interesting, thought-engaging activities.

Spam detection is a great illustration of machine learning in action, and is the canonical example of what classification is about. Given a collection of email messages, we need to classify them into two categories, or classes: Spam (an unwanted message that should go directly to the trash) or Ham (a valid message that we do want to read). It is also interesting for another reason: Unlike the digit-recognition problem we tackled in Chapter 1, where the data was in numeric form, spam detection is all about text. A major part of the material available in the digital universe is text rather than well-organized tables of numbers, so understanding how to work with it is important.

In this chapter, we will build a spam-detection engine from scratch, and then use that example to illustrate a couple of useful techniques and ideas. We will

- establish an approach to working with text. From the computer standpoint, a raw text document is just a random collection of characters. We will see how we can extract features (that is, convert the original data into new and more informative or usable properties, the "features") from a block of text by transforming it into tokens that can be processed by a computer.

- look at Bayes' Theorem, a simple yet powerful mathematical formula that quantifies how new information can be incorporated so as to update our assessment of uncertain events. As a direct application, we will implement a naïve Bayes classifier, an algorithm that uses vocabulary frequency to determine document types.

- discuss the importance of understanding your data for properly interpreting your results and their quality, and illustrate how extracting new features from a dataset can significantly enhance the predictive power of a model, without modifying the algorithm itself.

We will focus first on implementing a general algorithm to analyze text documents and decide what category they belong to. Once we have that tool in place, we will turn our attention back to our dataset and see how carefully inspecting the data we have available will allow us to craft new features and improve the quality of our predictions quite significantly.

Our Challenge: Build a Spam-Detection Engine

The documents we will be working with here won't be email. Instead, we will be dealing with text messages. Our goal will be to recognize spam, using a dataset of real SMS (Short Message Service) messages from the United Kingdom, which we found in the wonderful University of California–Irvine Machine Learning Repository.

■ **Side note**   The UCI Machine Learning Repository was started in 1987 by the Center for Machine Learning and Intelligent Systems at University of California Irvine. You can find the Machine Learning Repository at http://archive.ics.uci.edu/ml/. It is a library of nearly 300 clean and well-documented datasets, searchable and organized by criteria such as size, type of features, and more. It is a fantastic resource for learning machine learning, and it contains a number of "classic" datasets that are often used as benchmarks to evaluate the performance of algorithms.

Getting to Know Our Dataset

Before discussing what model we could use, let's first take a look at the data. The dataset can be downloaded from http://1drv.ms/1uzMplL (it is simply a duplicate of the original file from the UCI repository, which can be found at http://archive.ics.uci.edu/ml/datasets/SMS+Spam+Collection). It is stored as a single text file, named SMSSpamCollection, with no file extension, and contains 5,574 real text messages. Each line is an individual SMS, identified as either "ham" or "spam." Here is what the first lines look like:

```
ham    Go until jurong point, crazy.. Available only in bugis n great world la e buffet...
       Cine there got amore wat...
ham    Ok lar... Joking wif u oni...
spam   Free entry in 2 a wkly comp to win FA Cup final tkts 21st May 2005. Text FA to 87121
       to receive entry question(std txt rate)T&C's apply 08452810075over18's
ham    U dun say so early hor... U c already then say...
ham    Nah I don't think he goes to usf, he lives around here though
spam   FreeMsg Hey there darling it's been 3 week's now and no word back! I'd like some fun
       you up for it still? Tb ok! XxX std chgs to send, £1.50 to rcv
```

The first thing that jumps out at me is that the language people use in text messages is clearly different from "standard proper English!" This is something we want to keep in mind, because it might have implications for our analysis. For instance, a fragment like "U c," short for "You see," will likely not be found in a normal dictionary.

With that in mind, my first step would be to try and get an informal "gut feeling" for how these two groups differ. Are there words that appear more frequently in spam, or in ham? This can help guide us in building a smart engine to automatically differentiate ham from spam. Let's start by breaking the dataset by class ("ham" versus "spam") and counting word frequency in each. Given the exploratory nature of this activity, it seems like a good place to use an F# script.

■ **Tip**   Spend time exploring your data! Blindly applying algorithms to datasets can work decently well, but will bring you only that far. Just as it pays to learn the domain model when developing an application, a deeper understanding of the data will help you build smarter predictive models.

Using Discriminated Unions to Model Labels

The first thing we need is data. We will proceed along the same lines as the previous chapter, with one variation. While the entire digits dataset consisted of numbers (both the pixels encoding as well as the label), here we have one feature (the text message itself) and a label that is either Ham or Spam. How should we represent that?

One possibility would be to encode labels as Booleans, say, `true` for Ham and `false` for Spam. This would work perfectly fine; however, there is a bit of a drawback: It doesn't make the meaning of the field self-evident. If I just showed you one record from the dataset encoded that way—for instance:

```
True    Ok lar... Joking wif u oni... ,
```

How could you possibly guess what `true` stands for? Another potential issue is that a Boolean will not extend well if the need ever arises for more categories—say, Ham, Spam, and Ambiguous messages.

Machine learning is hard enough as it stands without adding extra, unnecessary complexity. For that reason, we will represent the label as an F# **discriminated union** (which I will also refer to at times as DU). If you have never seen discriminated unions before, as a first approximation, think of them as being somewhat similar to C# enums, in that they define a set of exclusive cases, but these are much more powerful. While this doesn't do DUs justice at all, the analogy will be good enough to get us started.

Let's illustrate briefly how DUs work, with an example you can run in FSI. Defining a DU is as simple as defining a type:

```
type DocType =
    | Ham
    | Spam
```

Running this in the F# Interactive window (adding ;; at the end to trigger evaluation), you should see the following:

```
type DocType =
    | Ham
    | Spam
```

This defines a simple type, DocType, which can be one of two things, and nothing else: Spam or Ham. One of the main reasons why I love discriminated unions is because they work so well with pattern matching and allow you to write code that describes your business domain in a very clear fashion. For instance, in our case, each example in our training set is either Ham or Spam and contains text, the contents of the actual message. We could represent this as a tuple, where each example is a DocType and a string, and process examples along these lines, which you can try out in the F# Interactive window:

```
let identify (example:DocType*string) =
    let docType,content = example
    match docType with
    | Ham -> printfn "'%s' is ham" content
    | Spam -> printfn "'%s' is spam" content
```

This example is strictly for illustration purposes, but shows the pattern we are going to follow later on. In this case, we created a small function that took in an example and printed out its contents, and whether it was Ham or Spam. We first separated the example into its two parts (DocType and content) by pattern matching the tuple, and then we used pattern matching on the two possible cases for DocType, handling each case in a separate "branch." Try typing this in FSI:

```
identify (Ham,"good message");;
```

... and you should see the following result:

```
'good message' is ham
```

Until we can better determine what we want to do with the actual SMS contents, this is how we will model our data. Let's get started with loading our dataset!

Reading Our Dataset

Just like in Chapter 1, we will be spending most of our time live hacking at our dataset, progressively building and refining a model from the scripting environment. Let's fire up Visual Studio and create a new F# library project, which we will name HamOrSpam. For convenience, let's also use the file system from outside of Visual Studio to add a folder called Data in the solution, and drop the data file SMSSpamCollection (downloaded as is, without any file extension, from the link mentioned earlier) in there. See Figure 2-1.

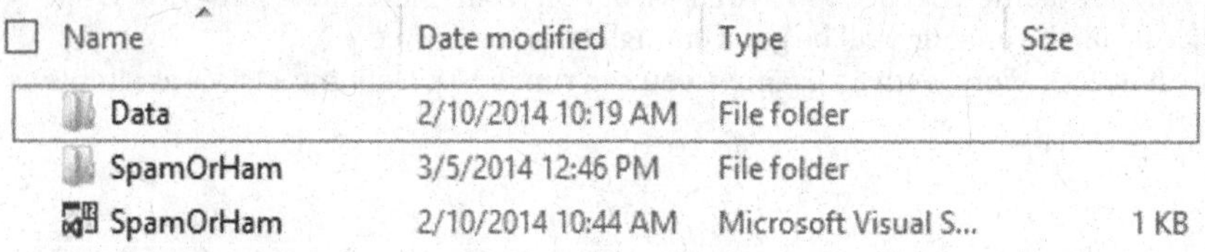

Name	Date modified	Type	Size
Data	2/10/2014 10:19 AM	File folder	
SpamOrHam	3/5/2014 12:46 PM	File folder	
SpamOrHam	2/10/2014 10:44 AM	Microsoft Visual S...	1 KB

Figure 2-1. *Folder organization*

This will allow us to use a small trick to access the data file in a cleaner fashion than what we did in Chapter 1. F# has a couple of handy built-in constants, __SOURCE_DIRECTORY__ and __SOURCE_FILE__, which greatly simplify working with files from scripts, and allow us to refer to the data file location without having to hard-code a path that would depend on our local machine. As you probably have guessed from their names, the first one evaluates to the full path of the directory containing the file itself, and the second returns the full path to the file itself, including the file name.

It's time to get to the script itself. The main difference between this and the digit-recognizer dataset is that we have no headers, and just two columns, which are not comma separated, but rather are tab delimited. Otherwise, the problem is mostly the same: We have a file containing examples, which we want to extract into an array. Not surprisingly, our solution will look very similar, too: Read the file and apply a function to each line in order to parse it into label and content, splitting it around '\t', the tab symbol.

Let's go straight to the Script.fsx file in our project. Delete the code that is there by default and paste the following code in:

Listing 2-1. Reading the SMS dataset from the file

```fsharp
open System.IO

type DocType =
    | Ham
    | Spam

let parseDocType (label:string) =
    match label with
    | "ham"  -> Ham
    | "spam" -> Spam
    | _      -> failwith "Unknown label"

let parseLine (line:string) =
    let split = line.Split('\t')
    let label = split.[0] |> parseDocType
    let message = split.[1]
    (label, message)

Let fileName = "SMSSpamCollection"
let path = __SOURCE_DIRECTORY__ + @"..\..\Data\" + fileName

let dataset =
    File.ReadAllLines path
    |> Array.map parseLine
```

At this point, you should be able to select the entire code you just wrote in the script file and execute it in F# Interactive, which will produce the following:

```fsharp
val dataset : (DocType * string) [] =
  [|(Ham,
     "Go until jurong point, crazy.. Available only in bugis n grea"+[50 chars]);
    (Ham, "Ok lar... Joking wif u oni...");
    (Spam,
     "Free entry in 2 a wkly comp to win FA Cup final tkts 21st May"+[94 chars]);
    // Snipped for brevity
    (Ham,
     "Hi. Wk been ok - on hols now! Yes on for a bit of a run. Forg"+[117 chars]);
    (Ham, "I see a cup of coffee animation"); ...|]
```

We now have a dataset of examples, each of which is identified as Spam or Ham. We can start getting to work on the question we are really interested in: What features can we use to distinguish between Ham and Spam messages?

■ **Tip**   Using `File.ReadAllLines` to read the contents of the dataset may not always be the best idea. We are loading everything in memory at once into an array, and then creating another array to store the result of the `Array.map` transformation. This particular dataset contains around 5,000 lines, which is fairly small, but when dealing with larger datasets, you can use a streaming version (such as `System.IO.StreamReader.ReadLine()`) to load the dataset one line at a time into memory.

Deciding on a Single Word

Now that we have data, we can begin the analysis. Our end goal is to recognize Spam from Ham, but, unlike in the digit-recognizer case, we don't have a clear set of features yet; the only material we have available is a raw chunk of text, the SMS itself. At the same time, one would suspect that there is a lot of information to be leveraged in the text. We just need to find a way to transform these strings into features we can work with.

Using Words as Clues

If you looked through the dataset we just loaded, you probably noticed that Spam messages look a bit different from Ham. Scanning through messages, your eyes can easily pick some clues that raise a red flag, and suggest that a message is more likely to be Spam. As an example, the word "FREE" (all caps!) appears early on in a couple of Spam items, and doesn't seem to pop up often in Ham.

This suggests a possible approach: using individual words from the entire message to recognize which category it belongs to. Let's first try to confirm that our intuition is correct by counting how many Spam messages contain that particular string and comparing it with the Ham messages. We can test this out by typing a couple of lines of F# in our script. First, let's filter our dataset so as to keep only Spam, then filter again, this time retaining only messages that contain "FREE," and finally count how many items are left:

```
let spamWithFREE =
    dataset
    |> Array.filter (fun (docType,_) -> docType = Spam)
    |> Array.filter (fun (_,sms) -> sms.Contains("FREE"))
    |> Array.length
```

Select the code above and run it in F# Interactive—you should see the following result:

```
val spamWithFREE : int = 112
```

Now let's do the same thing for Ham:

```
let hamWithFREE =
    dataset
    |> Array.filter (fun (docType,_) -> docType = Ham)
    |> Array.filter (fun (_,sms) -> sms.Contains("FREE"))
    |> Array.length
```

This should produce the following:

```
val hamWithFREE : int = 1
```

The numbers confirm our intuition: "FREE" is indeed used much more frequently in Spam than in Ham, and seems like a good flag to use for differentiating the two categories. We could use this to build a very primitive Spam classifier, like this:

```
let primitiveClassifier (sms:string) =
    if (sms.Contains "FREE")
    then Spam
    else Ham
```

This is a promising start. However, if we want to build anything more serious using this idea, we will need to address two issues. First, we picked "FREE" as a Spam indicator, but didn't really justify why. How do we know if a particular word is, or isn't, a good marker for Spam or Ham? Then, making a decision based on a single word from a whole message seems rather limiting. Can we somehow use multiple words at once and combine their (potentially conflicting) information into a single decision procedure?

Putting a Number on How Certain We Are

It doesn't take an advanced degree in statistics to intuitively see that messages containing "FREE" are very likely Spam. Can we formalize how we reached that conclusion in a manner that doesn't rely on intuition, and quantifies how reliably a specific word indicates whether a message is Ham or Spam?

Personally, I often resort to decision trees as a way to better understand probability problems. In our case, here is what we did: We took our corpus of 5,574 documents, split it into two groups by document type (747 Spam vs. 4,827 Ham), and, for each document group, we counted how many contained the word "FREE." This can be represented as a decision tree, as displayed in Figure 2-2:

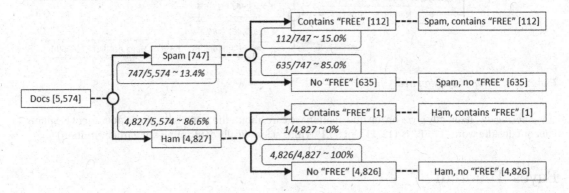

Figure 2-2. *Decision tree*

I like to think of decision trees as a series of tubes (or pipelines, if you will). You start with an initial node, but instead of water you pump in 100% probability. Each node represents an event that could have multiple outcomes; the probability is split between branches, and no probability should disappear.

In this case, we begin with 5,574 documents, which have to be either Ham or Spam. The vast majority of documents are Ham—4,827 out of 5,574, or 86.6%—so without any other information, if I were to pick a random message and ask you "is it Ham or Spam?" your answer should be Ham (and you would be right 86.6% of the time).

The next level of the tree considers how likely it is that a document contains the word "FREE," for each of the groups. For instance, if a message is Spam, we have a 112 in 747 chance that it contains "FREE." Stated in probability terms, we have a 15.0% probability that a document contains "FREE," given that the document is Spam.

This is interesting, but is not useful for our classification purposes. What we really want is the probability that a document is Spam, given that the document contains "FREE." Getting that information is not too difficult, though: We just need to reorganize the tree, beginning with whether the document contains "FREE" or not, instead of starting with Spam versus Ham. Note that regardless of how we structure our tree, we should still end up with the same four leaf groups; for instance, there should still be 112 documents that are Spam and contain "FREE." Out of 5,574 documents, we have 113 that contain "FREE," 112 from the Spam group and 1 from the Ham group. With a bit more reorganization, we should end up with the decision tree shown in Figure 2-3. While entirely equivalent to the previous tree, it provides a different perspective on how the different pieces of information relate to each other.

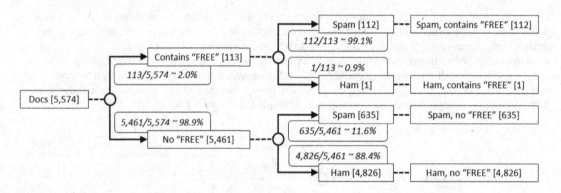

Figure 2-3. *Flipped decision tree*

Specifically, it directly gives us the information we care about: the probability that a document is Spam, if it contains the word "FREE," is 112/113, or 99.1% (thus scientifically confirming our earlier intuition).

Bayes' Theorem

The method we just used has a name: **Bayes' Theorem**. In its driest textbook form, it is usually stated like this:

$$P(A|B) = \frac{P(B|A) \times P(A)}{P(B)}$$

The | symbol should be read as "given that." The example we just went through was about computing the probability that an email is Spam, given that it contains the word "FREE," and, in Bayes' Theorem formulation, would be writ.ke this:

$$P\left(SMS \text{ is Spam} \mid SMS \text{ contains "FREE"}\right)$$
$$= \frac{P(SMS \text{ contains "FREE"} \mid SMS \text{ is Spam}) \times P(SMS \text{ is Spam})}{P(SMS \text{ contains "FREE"})}$$

If you work out the numbers mechanically, you will get the following result, which is precisely what we arrived at with the decision tree:

$$P\left(SMS \text{ is Spam} \mid SMS \text{ contains "FREE"}\right)$$
$$= \frac{\frac{112}{747} \times \frac{747}{5574}}{\frac{113}{5574}} = \frac{112}{113}$$

One way to view Bayes' Theorem is as a balancing act between two pieces of data: our initial knowledge of the world (in our example, how much Spam there is in the first place) and an additional piece of information (how frequently the word "FREE" is found in either Spam or Ham). Bayes' Theorem quantifies how to weigh in that new information: The rarer Spam is, the more our default prediction should lean towards Ham, and the stronger the evidence will have to be before switching predictions.

Another way to look at Bayes' Theorem is in relation to the notion of independence. Two events, A and B, are said to be independent if (and only if!) the following equality holds true:

$$P\left(A \text{ and } B\right) = P(A) \times P(B)$$

... which, if you play a bit with Bayes' Theorem, implies that

$$P\left(A \mid B\right) = P(A)$$

In other words, knowing anything about B doesn't convey any useful information about A (and vice versa). Conversely, if A and B are not independent, Bayes' Theorem would capture how strongly the two pieces of information are related. As a final remark (and word of caution), note how asymmetric the effects can be. If I know an email is Spam, I have a 15% chance of it containing "FREE," and yet, knowing an email contains the word "FREE" gives me a 99% chance of it being Spam!

THE MONTY HALL PROBLEM

If you find the approach confusing, don't worry. It is both simple and complicated—running the calculations is easy, but wrapping your head about what is going on is not. The human brain is notoriously poorly equipped to reason with uncertainty, and very smart people have made embarrassing mistakes on that problem. The most famous such example is the Monty Hall Problem: Once game show contestants have selected one of three doors, one of them hiding a prize, the host indicates a door from the two remaining where there is no prize. The question is, should contestants switch doors at that point? In the 1950s, Marilyn Vos Savant correctly answered the question, but a few famous mathematicians, like Paul Erdos, incorrectly attempted to show her how mistaken she was. My personal lesson from this story is to be very careful when dealing with probabilities, because human intuition doesn't have a good track record there—and of course to think twice before publicly criticizing anyone!

Dealing with Rare Words

Bayes' Theorem gives us a convenient way to decide whether a message is Ham or Spam based on a single word. However, you might have noticed a small issue. If you pick a word that is present in only one of the categories—for instance, "uncle," "honeybee," or "wine," which exist only in Ham—then our formula will assign a 100% probability for one category and 0% for the other. In other words, if we saw a message containing the word "uncle," we would automatically decide, with 100% confidence, that this message cannot be Spam, regardless of the rest of the message.

Clearly, this can't be right; we shouldn't have 100% confidence in anything based on a limited training sample. One way to address this problem is by using **Laplace Smoothing**. Named after the French mathematician Pierre-Simon de Laplace, this very intimidating sounding technique can arguably be described as a "fudge factor." We will eliminate the problem of absent words by augmenting the count of each word by one, and computing P(Spam contains "xyz") = (1 + count of Spam containing "xyz") / (1 + count of Spam). Essentially, we are making up a fictional message containing every token, and as a result, the rarest tokens will have a very low probability, but not zero.

Combining Multiple Words

Using Bayes' Theorem, we figured out how an SMS should be classified depending on whether or not it contained a particular word. This is progress, but we are not done yet. There are many words in a message, each of which pushes toward Ham or Spam with various strength. How can we combine that information, which might be sending conflicting signals, into a single value we can use to make our decision?

Breaking Text into Tokens

As an example, consider the following hypothetical message: "Driving, cant txt." What is the probability it is Spam?

We could try to apply Bayes' Theorem directly and look for the entire message in our dataset. However, I wouldn't expect this approach to work very well. The chances of finding an exact duplicate, let alone many, are slim. On the other hand, what we saw is that the word "FREE" carried some relevant information. What we will do is simply break the message into a set of words, "driving," "cant," and "txt," and use that representation instead of the original text. We can then analyze individual tokens and (hopefully) combine what each of them suggests into a single value that we can rely on to make a decision.

This process of breaking up a block of text into meaningful elements (words, or potentially other symbols), the tokens, is called **tokenization**. Deciding how you will tokenize is an important part of your model, and there is no unique right way to do it—it depends on the problem at hand. For the moment, as always, we will start with the easiest thing we could implement: If one single word, "FREE," is informative, let's extend that idea and break up messages into all their individual words. In effect, we are transforming each message into a collection of features, each feature being the presence or absence of a particular word.

For instance, if we had two strings, "Programming is Fun" and "Functional programming is more fun!," we could decompose them as "programming," "is," "fun," and "functional," "programming," "is," "more," "fun." This representation will allow us to be much more efficient. Instead of having to check whether a message contains a particular substring, we can pre-process every document into a set of tokens and rapidly verify if it contains a particular token we are interested in.

■ **Note**   This general approach is very useful for transforming text into a form a computer can work with. For instance, we could gather the entire set of tokens found in our corpus—["functional"; "programming"; "is"; "more"; "fun"]—and encode each document by counting how many times each token is found. In our example, the first block of text becomes [0; 1; 1; 0; 1], and the second one [1; 1; 1; 1; 1]. Our dataset is now in a form that is completely unreadable by a human, but which looks a whole lot like our digits dataset from Chapter 1: Each row is an observation, each column is a feature, and everything is encoded as numbers—and we could, for instance, use this to determine how similar two documents are. Transforming observations in a set of numeric features that a computer can analyze to find patterns, in a manner no human could, is fairly typical in machine learning.

You might be thinking at this point, "This is a gross over simplification," and you would be right. After all, we are converting full sentences into a raw collection of words, ignoring things like syntax, grammar, or word order. This transformation is clearly losing information; for instance, the two sentences "I like carrots and hate broccoli" and "I like broccoli and hate carrots" will be broken into the same set of tokens [and; broccoli; carrots; hate; i; like], and will therefore be considered identical. At the same time, we are not trying to understand the meaning of sentences here; we merely need to identify which words are connected to a particular behavior.

Another point I want to stress here is that while our tokenization looks fairly straightforward, it contains a lot of implicit decisions already. We decided that "Programming" and "programming" would be treated as the same word, ignoring capitalization. Is that a reasonable assumption? Maybe, maybe not. If you have spent a minimum of time in online discussions, such as forums or YouTube comments, you will probably agree that A HEAVY USAGE OF CAPITAL LETTERS often indicates that the discussion quality is going downhill. So the argument can be made that capitalization matters and could provide relevant information for classifying messages. Another implicit decision here was to drop the "!"; is that reasonable? Punctuation could matter.

The good news is, rather than argue over whether capitalization or punctuation matters, we can settle that question very easily with cross-validation later on. In the immortal words of W. Edwards Deming, "In God we trust—all others must bring data." Create alternate models for each hypothesis, compare their performance, and let the data decide.

Naïvely Combining Scores

Now that we have decided to decompose our message into three tokens—"driving," "cant," and "txt"—we still need to figure out a way to compute the probability that the message is Ham or Spam. "txt" indicates a strong chance of Spam, but "driving" points towards Ham. How should we put all that evidence together?

If we apply Bayes' Theorem to determine the probability that our message is Spam, given that it contains all three tokens, we get:

$$P(SMS\ is\ Spam\,|\,SMS\ contains\ driving\,\&\,cant\,\&\,txt)$$
$$= \frac{P(SMS\ contains\ driving\,\&\,cant\,\&\,txt\,|\,SMS\ is\ Spam) \times P(SMS\ is\ Spam)}{P(SMS\ contains\ driving\,\&\,cant\,\&\,txt)}$$

This is a bit of an intimidating formula. However, if we make one simplifying assumption, things become much nicer. Let's assume for a minute that tokens are independent—that is, seeing one token in a message has no bearing on what other tokens might be present. In that case, we can compute:

$$P(SMS\ contains\ driving\,\&\,cant\,\&\,txt\,|\,SMS\ is\ Spam)$$
$$= P(SMS\ contains\ "driving"\,|\,SMS\ is\ Spam)$$
$$\times P(SMS\ contains\ "cant"\,|\,SMS\ is\ Spam)$$
$$\times P(SMS\ contains\ "txt"\,|\,SMS\ is\ Spam)$$

With a bit of Bayes' Theorem Jiu-Jitsu applied on the formula above, you should end up with the following:

$$P\big(SMS\ is\ Spam\,|\,SMS\ contains\ "driving, cant, txt"\big)$$
$$= P\big(SMS\ contains\ "driving"\,|\,SMS\ is\ Spam\big) \times P\big(SMS\ contains\ "cant"\,|\,SMS\ is\ Spam\big)$$
$$\times P\big(SMS\ contains\ "txt"\,|\,SMS\ is\ Spam\big) \times \frac{P\big(SMS\ is\ Spam\big)}{P\big(SMS\ contains\ "driving, cant, txt"\big)}$$

Fundamentally, here is what we are doing: Instead of trying to model the English language in its full complexity, we are using a much simpler model. Imagine that you have two giant buckets of words, one for Spam, one for Ham, each containing words in different proportion. Messages are generated by pulling random words from one of the buckets and stringing them together. Of course, this is a rather preposterous model of language. At the same time, it has some clear benefits. A more "correct" model would likely be specific to a particular language (taking its grammar and syntax into account, for instance), and presumably would not work on other languages. So, let's start with a model that is pretty bad, but should be similarly bad for any language or type of document, but is easy to work with, and let's see where that leads us!

Simplified Document Score

At this point we are almost ready to dive into code and implement the classifier. We can easily extract P(SMS is Spam), the proportion of Spam messages in the training set, as well as P(SMS contains "X" | SMS is Spam), the proportion of Spam messages that contain the token "X."

Before jumping in, let's make a few final adjustments. First, you might have noticed that for both cases, Spam or Ham, our lengthy Bayes' formula involves a division by the same term, P(SMS contains "driving", "cant", "txt"). In the end, what we are interested in is deciding whether a message is Spam or Ham, and not necessarily the exact probability. In that case, we might as well drop the common term, spare ourselves some unnecessary computations, and simply compute a "score" instead of a probability:

$$Score\Big(SMS\ is\ Spam\Big|SMS\ contains\ driving\ \&\ cant\ \&\ txt\Big)$$
$$= P\big(SMS\ contains\ driving\ |\ SMS\ is\ Spam\big)\times P\big(SMS\ contains\ cant\ |\ SMS\ is\ Spam\big)$$
$$\times P\big(SMS\ contains\ txt\ |\ SMS\ is\ Spam\big)\times P\big(SMS\ is\ Spam\big)$$

If Score(Spam) > Score(Ham), we will classify the message as Spam.

In fact, if the only thing we want is a score, we can go even further and address another issue, one that is related to precision. The probability that we will observe any particular token in a message will be a number less than one, by definition, and typically a number that is close to zero. As our formula involves multiplying together these probabilities, the result will get close to zero, and it could cause rounding problems.

To avoid this issue, it is customary to use an old trick and transform the computation into logarithms. The details are not very important, but here is why it might be a good idea. As log (a * b) = log a + log b, we will be able to turn our formula from a product to a sum, avoiding rounding issues; and because log is an increasing function, transforming the formula through log will preserve the ranking of scores. So, instead of the original formula, we will be scoring messages using:

$$Score\big(SMS\ is\ Spam\ |\ SMS\ contains\ "driving, cant, txt"\big)$$
$$= Log\big(P(SMS\ is\ Spam)\big)+ Log\big(Laplace(SMS\ contains\ "driving"\ |\ Spam)\big)$$
$$+ Log\big(Laplace(SMS\ contains\ "cant"\ |\ Spam)\big)+ Log\big(Laplace(SMS\ contains\ "txt"\ |\ Spam)\big)$$

In a way, this clarifies the algorithm logic. Each token has a Ham score and a Spam score, quantifying how strongly it indicates each case. When trying to decide whether a document is Spam, the algorithm starts with a Spam score, the baseline level of Spam, and each token increases or decreases the document Spam score, independently of other tokens. If the document Spam score ends up being higher than the Ham score, the document is Spam.

Implementing the Classifier

That was a lot of math and modelling discussion, and not much coding. Fortunately, that's all we need: We are now ready to implement a naïve Bayes classifier. Fundamentally, the classifier relies on two elements: a tokenizer to break documents into tokens, and a set of tokens—the words we use to score a document. Given these two components, we need to learn from a sample of examples what score each token gets for both Spam and Ham, as well as the relative weight of each group.

Figure 2-4 outlines the learning phase. Starting from a corpus of labeled messages, we break them into two groups, Spam and Ham, and measure their relative size. Then, for the selected set of tokens (here "free," "txt," and "car"), we measure their frequency and reduce each group of documents to a score corresponding to its overall weight, and come up with a score for each token for that particular group:

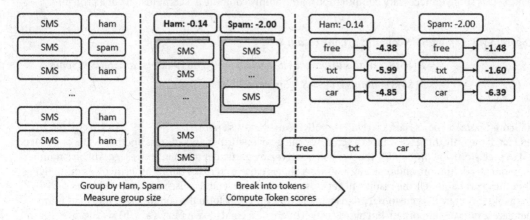

Figure 2-4. *Naïve Bayes learning phase*

Once that information is available, classifying a new document follows the process outlined in Figure 2-5: tokenize the document, compute its score for each of the groups based on the tokens that are present, and predict the highest-scoring group.

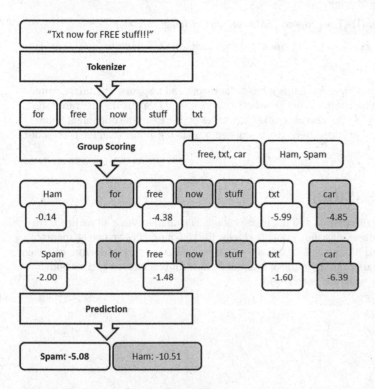

Figure 2-5. *Naïve Bayes classifier outline*

In this particular example, once the document has been tokenized, we look up whether a score is available for each individual token (and ignore it otherwise), compute an overall score for each group, and decide which of the groups is the most likely match.

Extracting Code into Modules

To avoid cluttering the script with too much code, let's extract the classifier itself into a module. In order to do that, simply right click on the solution and pick Add New Item, then choose Source File. Rename that file NaiveBayes.fs, delete any default code that might be there, and replace it with the following:

```
namespace NaiveBayes

module Classifier =

    let Hello name = printfn "Hello, %s" name
```

Finally, right click on the file and select "Move up" (or Alt + Up Arrow) until NaiveBayes.fs appears first in the list of files in the solution (you can also add the file directly at the desired position by selecting a file in the Solution Explorer and using "Add Above" or "Add Below"). You have now created a module in which you can start writing functions and calling them from your script, or consuming them from F# or C# projects. Just for the sake of illustration, here is how you would go about using the Hello function from our current script:

```
#load "NaiveBayes.fs"
open NaiveBayes.Classifier
Hello "World"
```

■ **Note**   You might wonder why you had to move up the file you just created. Unlike in C#, the order of files in an F# solution matters. The main reason for that is the type-inference system. The compiler automatically figures out for you what types you meant, by looking at what you have defined in your code file up to that point. In a similar fashion, if you want to use function f in your code, that function f needs to be defined before the code that uses it. This is a bit of an additional constraint, but in my opinion it is a very reasonable price to pay for the benefits of type inference; and, as an interesting side effect, it provides a natural order in F# solutions, which makes them very easy to interpret: Start from line one and read forward, or from the last line and read backwards!

Scoring and Classifying a Document

Now that we have the module in place, we will write the algorithm itself in the module, then use the script file to explore data using that algorithm. Let's follow a typical F# pattern and build from the bottom up, writing small pieces of code and composing them into larger workflows. The key element of the model is the score computation, which measures how strong the evidence is that a document belongs to a group—for instance, Spam.

.   The score relies on two components: how frequently the group appears in the overall corpus (the training data), and how frequently certain tokens are found in that group. Let's start by defining a couple of types to represent our domain. Rather than representing both documents and tokens as strings, let's call a spade a spade, and define a Token type—a type alias for string. This will give us some clarity in type signatures. For instance, we can now define a Tokenizer as a function that takes in a string (a document) and returns a set of tokens. Similarly, let's provide a name for a document that has been tokenized, using the TokenizedDoc type alias:

```
type Token = string
type Tokenizer = string -> Token Set
type TokenizedDoc = Token Set
```

In order to classify a new document (with an unknown label), we will need to compute its score for each possible group, using the sample of labeled documents we have available. Doing that requires two pieces of information for each group: its proportion (how frequently the group is found in the overall dataset) and a score for each token we selected for our model, which indicates how strongly that token points to the group.

We can model this with a data structure, DocsGroup, which contains a Proportion (how frequently the group is found in the overall data set), and TokenFrequencies, a Map (an F# data structure that serves a role analogous to a Dictionary) that associates each token with its (Laplace-corrected) frequency in the dataset. As an example, in our particular case, we would create two DocsGroup(s)—one for Ham and one for Spam—with the Ham DocsGroup containing the overall proportion of Ham messages in the entire dataset, and, for each token we are interested in, the actual token and the frequency with which it shows up in the Ham messages:

```
type DocsGroup =
    {    Proportion:float;
         TokenFrequencies:Map<Token,float> }
```

Assuming a document has already been broken into a set of tokens, computing its score for a given group is fairly simple. We don't have to worry about how these numbers have been computed. If that part has been done already, all we need to do is sum up the log of the group frequency, as well as the log of every token that is present in both the tokenized document and the list of tokens we are using in our model:

Listing 2-2. Scoring a document

```
let tokenScore (group:DocsGroup) (token:Token) =
    if group.TokenFrequencies.ContainsKey token
    then log group.TokenFrequencies.[token]
    else 0.0

let score (document:TokenizedDoc) (group:DocsGroup) =
    let scoreToken = tokenScore group
    log group.Proportion +
    (document |> Seq.sumBy scoreToken)
```

Classifying a document is then simply a matter of transforming it into tokens using a tokenizer, identifying the group with the highest score in the list of possible docGroups, and returning its label:

Listing 2-3. Predicting the label of a document

```
let classify (groups:(_*DocsGroup)[])
             (tokenizer:Tokenizer)
             (txt:string) =
    let tokenized = tokenizer txt
    groups
    |> Array.maxBy (fun (label,group) ->
        score tokenized group)
    |> fst
```

You might be wondering about the groups:(_*DocsGroup)[] bit in the classify function. Why not use tuples of (DocType*DocsGroup) for each group of documents, and what is this mysterious _ symbol? If you think about it, nothing we have done so far depends on what the labels are, specifically. We have Spam and Ham in mind, but we could equally well apply this to a different corpus of documents, say, predicting whether written movie reviews correspond to a rating of 1, 2, 3, 4, or 5 stars. For that reason, I decided to make the code generic; as long as you have a collection of example documents with a consistent type of labels, it will work. The _ symbol denotes a "type wildcard" (any type will be supported), and if you check the classify function signature, you will see this: groups:('a * DocsGroup) [] -> tokenizer:Tokenizer -> txt:string -> 'a. The wildcard has been replaced by 'a (which denotes a generic type), and the function returns an 'a, which is the (generic) label type.

Introducing Sets and Sequences

Two new types have been introduced here, sequence and set. Let's discuss these briefly, starting with set. As the name implies, a set represents a collection of unique items, and its main purpose is to answer the question "does item X belong to set S?" Given that we want to look for whether specific words (or more generally tokens) are present in an SMS so as to determine whether it is likely to be Spam or Ham, it seems reasonable to use a data structure that can efficiently compare sets of items. By reducing documents to sets of tokens, we will be able to quickly identify documents that contain a token like "txt" without having to incur the cost of using the Contains() string method.

The Set module provides a handful of handy functions revolving around set operations, as illustrated in the snippet below. Type in the following in the F# Interactive window:

```
> let set1 = set [1;2;3]
let set2 = set [1;3;3;5];;

val set1 : Set<int> = set [1; 2; 3]
val set2 : Set<int> = set [1; 3; 5]
```

This created two sets. Note how the duplicate value 3 has been removed from set2. The Set module provides functions with which to compute the union and intersection of sets:

```
> let intersection = Set.intersect set1 set2
let union = Set.union set1 set2;;

val intersection : Set<int> = set [1; 3]
val union : Set<int> = set [1; 2; 3; 5]
```

Set also exposes a useful function, difference, which subtracts a set from another one; that is, it will remove from the first set every element found in the second:

```
> let diff1 = Set.difference set1 set2
let diff2 = Set.difference set2 set1;;

val diff1 : Set<int> = set [2]
val diff2 : Set<int> = set [5]
```

Note that, unlike the intersection and union functions, difference is not commutative; that is, the order of arguments matter, as illustrated in the previous example. Finally, note that sets are immutable: Once a set has been created, it cannot be modified:

```
> let set3 = Set.add 4 set1
set1.Contains 4;;

val set3 : Set<int> = set [1; 2; 3; 4]
val it : bool = false
```

Adding 4 to set1 creates a new set, set3, which does contain 4, but the original set, set1, has not been affected by the operation.

The other type we introduced, sequence, is a lazily evaluated sequence of elements—that is, it is a collection that will be computed only as needed, potentially reducing memory or compute usage. Let's try the following code in the F# Interactive:

```
> let arr1 = [| for x in 1 .. 10 -> x |]
let seq1 = seq { for x in 1 .. 10 -> x };;

val arr1 : int [] = [|1; 2; 3; 4; 5; 6; 7; 8; 9; 10|]
val seq1 : seq<int>
```

The two expressions—arr1 and seq1—are very similar; they both generate integers from 1 to 10. And yet, the array immediately shows its full contents, which have been eagerly evaluated; by contrast, seq1 appears as a sequence of integers, without further detail. The actual contents will be generated only when the code requires it. Let's prove the point further with the following example, which constructs a new sequence by taking seq1 and doubling each of its elements. Note how we added a side effect in the sequence itself: Whenever an element of the sequence is produced, we print out the element being mapped:

```
> let seq2 =
    seq1
    |> Seq.map (fun x ->
        printfn "mapping %i" x
        2 * x) ;;

val seq2 : seq<int>
```

Again, the result is a sequence without actual contents yet, because nothing requires it so far. Let's change that by asking for the sum of the three first elements:

```
> let firstThree =
    seq2
    |> Seq.take 3
    |> Seq.sum;;
mapping 1
mapping 2
mapping 3

val firstThree : int = 12
```

When this code executes, "mapping 1," "mapping 2," and "mapping 3" are printed out, showing that the sequence is pulling out its first three elements, which are required in order to compute the sum. However, the remaining seven elements available, which are still not needed, have been left unevaluated for now.

So, what is the point of sequences when we already have perfectly good collections like arrays available? The first benefit is lazy evaluation. Because a sequence will only be evaluated "as needed," we can use them to generate infinite sequences; for instance, something that would be completely impossible to do with an array. The following snippet provides a somewhat contrived example: We create an infinite sequence, alternating between 1 and -1 forever. Obviously, there is no way we could instantiate such an infinite sequence of numbers in memory, but now that it is defined, we can use it, and, for example, compute its sum for any arbitrary number of elements:

```
> let infinite = Seq.initInfinite (fun i -> if i % 2 = 0 then 1 else -1)
let test = infinite |> Seq.take 1000000 |> Seq.sum;;

val infinite : seq<int>
val test : int = 0
```

The other reason F# sequences are often used is that they are equivalent to the C# IEnumerable; as such, all standard .NET collections can be treated as sequences, and, therefore, functions provided by the Seq module can be used to manipulate them, using functionality that does not appear in the actual collection itself. As an illustration, consider this example:

```
> let arr = [| 1;2;2;3;4;4;4|]
let counts =
    arr
    |> Seq.countBy (fun x -> x)
    |> Seq.toArray;;

val arr : int [] = [|1; 2; 2; 3; 4; 4; 4|]
val counts : (int * int) [] = [|(1, 1); (2, 2); (3, 1); (4, 3)|]
```

We generate an array of integers, and then want to count how many instances of each we have. While arrays do not directly support this functionality (at least, not until F# 4.0 officially ships), sequences do, so we call Seq.countBy on the array and convert back the result to an array in order to trigger the sequence evaluation.

> ■ **Tip** While sequences can have a lot of advantages (who wouldn't want to compute just what is needed, and nothing more?), lazy evaluation also has its drawbacks, including adding some complexity to debugging.

Learning from a Corpus of Documents

In order to use the classify function, we need to have the summary data for each group of documents. What data do we need in order to generate that? The group proportion requires the number of documents in the group, as well as the total number of documents. Then, for each of the tokens we selected to use for our classifier, we need to compute the (Laplace-corrected) proportion of documents that, when tokenized, contain it.

> ■ **Note** Regardless of the language or style you use, approaching the application design in this way works really well: Create small components that have a single responsibility, with a clearly defined task, and don't worry about what is happening in the rest of the program. This helps extract clear models with minimal data structures. You can then wire all these components together, and at that point, if you need to dilute your design, say, for performance reasons, it won't be difficult.

The obvious way to go about collecting summary data is to write a function that has a signature that expects a collection of documents and returns a DocsGroup containing the analysis results for the group of documents that was passed in. Again, we will assume that we obtain the data exactly in the form that would be convenient for the task at hand, and we'll worry later about how to make that happen.

First, let's create a couple of helper functions to spare us some int-to-float conversions when computing proportions and Laplace-smoothed proportions, and to help us count documents where a particular token is present:

```
let proportion count total = float count / float total
let laplace count total = float (count+1) / float (total+1)
let countIn (group:TokenizedDoc seq) (token:Token) =
    group
    |> Seq.filter (Set.contains token)
    |> Seq.length
```

We now have all the building blocks we need in order to analyze a group of documents that have the same label, and then to summarize it into a DocsGroup. All we need to do is

- to compute the relative size of that group, compared to the total number of documents, and

- to find out, for each of the tokens we decided to use to classify the documents, what their Laplace-corrected proportion is within the group.

Listing 2-4. Analyzing a group of documents

```
let analyze (group:TokenizedDoc seq)
            (totalDocs:int)
            (classificationTokens:Token Set)=
    let groupSize = group |> Seq.length
    let score token =
        let count = countIn group token
        laplace count groupSize
    let scoredTokens =
        classificationTokens
        |> Set.map (fun token -> token, score token)
        |> Map.ofSeq
    let groupProportion = proportion groupSize totalDocs

    {
        Proportion = groupProportion
        TokenFrequencies = scoredTokens
    }
```

■ **Note**   Counting tokens. We are determining how frequently words appear by counting in how many documents they show up. This is perfectly appropriate for short messages, but wouldn't work great for longer documents. If you tried to identify whether a book is about, say, computers, counting how many times that word appears is probably a better indication than simply asking "does the word appear at least once in this book?" The approach we are using for SMS is known as "set of words"; another standard approach, "bag of words," relies on overall word frequency, and it might be more suitable for certain document types.

We are almost there. Now that we know how to analyze individual groups of documents, we just need to orchestrate these pieces and fully implement the algorithm we outlined in Figure 2-4. Given a collection of documents and their label, we need to

- break each of them into tokens,
- separate them by label, and
- analyze each group.

Listing 2-5. Learning from documents

```
let learn (docs:(_ * string)[])
          (tokenizer:Tokenizer)
          (classificationTokens:Token Set) =
    let total = docs.Length
    docs
    |> Array.map (fun (label,docs) -> label,tokenizer docs)
    |> Seq.groupBy fst
    |> Seq.map (fun (label,group) -> label,group |> Seq.map snd)
    |> Seq.map (fun (label,group) -> label,analyze group total classificationTokens)
    |> Seq.toArray
```

It's time to wrap that up. What we would really like out of this whole process is a function that takes in a string (the raw SMS message) and gives us the label with the highest score, based on what we learned from the documents training set.

Listing 2-6. Training a naïve Bayes classifier

```
let train (docs:(_ * string)[])
          (tokenizer:Tokenizer)
          (classificationTokens:Token Set) =
    let groups = learn docs tokenizer classificationTokens
    let classifier = classify groups tokenizer
    classifier
```

And that's pretty much it. In roughly 50 lines of code, we have a working naïve Bayes classifier.

Training Our First Classifier

Now that we have a general algorithm implemented, we can finally come back to the problem at hand, namely recognizing which of the messages are Ham and which are Spam. The signature of the train function provides a clear outline of what we are after: To obtain a classifier, we need a training set of examples, a tokenizer, and a selection of tokens to use. The training set is given to us, so our goal now is to identify what combination of tokenizer and tokens works best, using cross-validation to guide our analysis.

Implementing Our First Tokenizer

With that in mind, let's go back to doing the simplest thing that could possibly work, starting with tokenization. What we want to do is to take in a string and break it into words, ignoring casing.

This is a job that screams for regular expressions. The \w+ pattern will match "words" composed of one or more "word" characters (i.e., letters or numbers, but not punctuation). Let's create a regular expression, matchWords, using that pattern, and write a tokens function in script.fsx, following our classic pipeline structure. We convert the input string to lower case and apply the regular expression. matchWords.Matches creates a MatchCollection, a collection of all matches found when applying the expression. We cast this collection to a sequence of Match, retrieve the matched value (each string that matched), and finally convert it to a Set, which contains all the unique words identified by the regex. In your script file, add the following code below the code we already wrote for reading the dataset:

Listing 2-7. Using regular expressions to tokenize a line of text

```
open System.Text.RegularExpressions

let matchWords = Regex(@"\w+")

let tokens (text:string) =
    text.ToLowerInvariant()
    |> matchWords.Matches
    |> Seq.cast<Match>
    |> Seq.map (fun m -> m.Value)
    |> Set.ofSeq
```

This piece of code looks a bit gnarly; truth be told, it would look simpler, were it not for some strange design aspects of .NET regular expressions. In any case, we now have what we need: a function that will decompose a string into all the individual words it contains.

Validating Our Design Interactively

At first sight, the code seems like it might be doing what we want. However, "might be" is not a great place to be; verifying that it actually works would be better. When coding in C#, my habit is to resort to test-driven development, or TDD: Write a test first and then write the code that satisfies the requirements and passes the test. One of the benefits of TDD is that it enables you to run small pieces of code independently of the whole application, quickly making sure that it works as intended, and fleshing out your design ideas as you go. In F#, I tend to have a slightly different workflow. F# Interactive enables a more fluid style of design experimentation. Instead of immediately committing to a design and writing tests for it, potentially requiring later refactoring, you can simply experiment in F# Interactive, and once your design is taking shape, promote the code to unit tests.

In our case, checking that the token function works is trivial. All it takes is typing something like this in FSI and running it:

```
> tokens "42 is the Answer to the question";;
```

You will immediately see the results in the F# Interactive window:

```
val it : Set<string> = set ["42"; "answer"; "is"; "question"; "the"; "to"]
```

Our function looks like it is working. All the words have been isolated, including the number "42," the duplicate "the" appears only once in the results, and the capital "A" in *Answer* is gone. At this point, if I were writing an actual library intended for production, I would simply lift the token function and move it from my exploratory script into an actual proper file in the solution, then convert that little code snippet into an actual unit test. We are "just exploring" for the moment, so I will leave it at that, and won't bother with writing tests right now.

Establishing a Baseline with Cross-validation

Now that we have a model, let's see how well it does. We will be using the same script as before, so we have already loaded all the messages in dataset, an array of (DocType * string). As in the previous chapter, we will use cross-validation, and use one part of the dataset for training, and reserve the rest to validate how well (or how poorly!) each model is doing. In a rather arbitrary fashion, I will reserve 1,000 observations for validation and use all the rest for training. Just to make sure everything is working, let's try out a fairly primitive model, using only the token "txt" to make our decision:

```
#load "NaiveBayes.fs"
open NaiveBayes.Classifier

let txtClassifier = train training wordTokenizer (["txt"] |> set)

validation
|> Seq.averageBy (fun (docType,sms) ->
    if docType = txtClassifier sms then 1.0 else 0.0)
|> printfn "Based on 'txt', correctly classified: %.3f"
```

On my machine, I got 87.7% correct. That is pretty good! Or is it? Without context, a number like 87.7% appears impressive, but you have to look at it in perspective. If I used the dumbest model possible, and always predicted "Ham," regardless of the SMS content, my success rate on the validation set is 84.8%, and scoring 87.7% doesn't seem that impressive anymore.

The important point here is that you should always begin by establishing a baseline: If you used the simplest strategy possible, how good would your predictions be? For a classification problem, predicting the most frequent label all the time, as we did here, will give you a starting point. For time-series models, where you are trying to predict tomorrow based on the past, predicting that tomorrow will be exactly like today is a classic. In some situations, classifying 20% correctly might be great, in some others (like in our Ham versus Spam example), 85% correct would be disappointing. The baseline depends entirely on the data.

The second important point is that you should be very careful with how your datasets are constructed. When splitting my training and validation set, I simply took the first 1,000 for validation. Imagine for a second that my dataset was ordered by label, with all the Spam examples first, followed by all the Ham examples. This would be pretty bad: We would essentially be training our classifier on a sample containing almost exclusively Ham, and testing it on Spam only. At the very least, you would expect the evaluation quality to be pretty poor, because the data the classifier has learned to recognize is pretty different from the data it will actually be handling.

This would be a problem for every model; however, this would be especially bad in our case, because of how the naïve Bayes classifier works. If you recall how the algorithm works, essentially, naïve Bayes weighs in two elements: the relative frequency of tokens in various groups, and the frequency of the groups themselves. The first part would be unaffected by poor sampling; however, the frequency of each group could be totally off, which would greatly impact the predictions. For instance, having way more Ham than Spam in the training set would lead the classifier to completely underestimate the probability that a message is Spam and err on the side of predicting Ham, unless the evidence is absolutely overwhelming.

The point here is that before running potentially lengthy computations to train a model, you need to ask yourself, "Is the sample I am using similar to the real data my model will be dealing with later?" as well as, "Is the composition of my training and validation sets roughly identical?" Having distorted samples can be perfectly fine in some situations—you just want to be aware of it. Specifically for the naïve Bayes classifier, or for Bayes' Theorem–inspired approaches, beware of such distortions, which will have a deep impact on the quality of your model. If you inspect our SMS dataset, you should see that it appears to be roughly balanced: in both the training and the validation samples, the proportion of Ham to Spam is roughly the same.

Improving Our Classifier

We now have a baseline—anything below 84.4% is poor, and the number to beat is 87.7%. It's time to see how much better we can do using the two levers we have at our disposal: the tokenizer and the selection of tokens the classifier will use.

Using Every Single Word

With a single word, we brought our classifier from 84.8% to 87.7% correctly classified. If instead of a single word we used every token available to us, surely our predictions should skyrocket. Let's try the idea out. First, we need to extract every token from the training set. Let's write a vocabulary function that will do just that by applying a tokenizer to each document and merging the tokens into a single set. Retrieving the tokens from our training set is then as simple as taking the second element from each document tuple, using snd, and piping that into our vocabulary function:

```
let vocabulary (tokenizer:Tokenizer) (corpus:string seq) =
    corpus
    |> Seq.map tokenizer
    |> Set.unionMany
```

```
let allTokens =
    training
    |> Seq.map snd
    |> vocabulary wordTokenizer
```

Nice and crisp. Now we can use that big list of tokens to train a new classifier and evaluate its performance:

```
let fullClassifier = train training wordTokenizer allTokens
```

```
validation
|> Seq.averageBy (fun (docType,sms) ->
    if docType = fullClassifier sms then 1.0 else 0.0)
|> printfn "Based on all tokens, correctly classified: %.3f"
```

And instead of the major improvement we were hoping for, what we get is this rather disappointing result: "Based on all tokens, correctly classified: 0.864." Let's face it, this is a failure. All we achieved here is a model that barely beats the naïve predictor, and is worse than our previous model, which relied on a single word, "txt," to make its decision.

The high-level lesson here is that blindly throwing a lot of data into a standard algorithm is only going to lead you so far. In our example, we carefully selected one single feature, and the resulting model was simpler, faster, and better at making predictions. Selecting the right features is a key part of building a good predictor, and that's what we are going to try to do going forward. In this case, there are two things we can do to change the definition of our features without changing the algorithm itself: We can use a different tokenizer to carve out messages differently, and we can select (or ignore) different sets of tokens.

While we are at it, we are starting to repeat some of the code quite a bit; let's wrap the whole "train-and-evaluate" process into one function, which will take in a tokenizer and a set of tokens, run the training, and printout the evaluation results:

Listing 2-8. A generic model-evaluation function

```
let evaluate (tokenizer:Tokenizer) (tokens:Token Set) =
    let classifier = train training tokenizer tokens
    validation
    |> Seq.averageBy (fun (docType,sms) ->
        if docType = classifier sms then 1.0 else 0.0)
    |> printfn "Correctly classified: %.3f"
```

Evaluating a particular model then becomes a one-liner:

```
> evaluate wordTokenizer allTokens;;
Correctly classified: 0.864
```

This gives us a fairly straightforward process moving forward: Select a tokenizer and a set of tokens, and call evaluate to see if this particular combination is any better than whatever we tried before.

Does Capitalization Matter?

Let's start with the tokenizer. If you recall our earlier discussion, the wordTokenizer we are currently using ignores case; from its standpoint, there is no difference between "txt" or "TXT"—both will be considered to be the same token.

This is not an unreasonable thing to do. For instance, consider the two messages "Txt me now" and "txt me now." By ignoring capitalization, we are essentially saying that these two messages are not different in any meaningful way. Capitalization doesn't introduce any relevant information here, and can be treated as noise.

On the other hand, consider these two messages: "are you free now?" and "FREE STUFF TXT NOW!"— arguably, ignoring capitalization is losing information.

So, which one is it? Let's try it out and see if a different tokenizer, one that doesn't reduce everything to lowercase, fares any better than the wordTokenizer:

Listing 2-9. Using regular expressions to tokenize a line of text

```
let casedTokenizer (text:string) =
    text
    |> matchWords.Matches
    |> Seq.cast<Match>
    |> Seq.map (fun m -> m.Value)
    |> Set.ofSeq

let casedTokens =
    training
    |> Seq.map snd
    |> vocabulary casedTokenizer

evaluate casedTokenizer casedTokens
```

Running this in FSI produces 87.5% correct results. On the one hand, we are still below our simplistic classifier that relies on the presence of "txt." On the other hand, we are now pretty close (87.5% versus 87.7%), and this is significantly better than the equivalent approach with the wordTokenizer using every single token (86.4%).

Less Is more

We have what appears to be a better tokenizer; still, the fact remains that by adding a large amount of features, we ended up with a classifier that was both worse and slower. This is obviously not great, and it is also counter-intuitive: How could adding more information possibly make our model worse?

Let's look at the question the other way around and consider why our earlier single-token model was working so well. The reason we picked "txt" as a token is that it is very frequently found in Spam, and rarely found in Ham. In other words, it differentiates well between the two groups, and is pretty specific to Spam.

What we are doing now is using every single token, regardless of how informative it might be. As a result, we are potentially introducing quite a bit of noise into our model. How about being a bit more selective, perhaps by picking only the most frequently found tokens in each document group?

Let's start with a simple function that, given a collection of raw documents (plain strings) and a tokenizer, will return the n most frequently used tokens:

```
let top n (tokenizer:Tokenizer) (docs:string []) =
    let tokenized = docs |> Array.map tokenizer
    let tokens = tokenized |> Set.unionMany
    tokens
    |> Seq.sortBy (fun t -> - countIn tokenized t)
    |> Seq.take n
    |> Set.ofSeq
```

We can now split our training sample into Ham and Spam, dropping the labels in the process:

```
let ham,spam =
    let rawHam,rawSpam =
        training
        |> Array.partition (fun (lbl,_) -> lbl=Ham)
    rawHam |> Array.map snd,
    rawSpam |> Array.map snd
```

We extract and count how many tokens we have in each group, pick the top 10%, and merge them into one token set using Set.union:

```
let hamCount = ham |> vocabulary casedTokenizer |> Set.count
let spamCount = spam |> vocabulary casedTokenizer |> Set.count

let topHam = ham |> top (hamCount / 10) casedTokenizer
let topSpam = spam |> top (spamCount / 10) casedTokenizer

let topTokens = Set.union topHam topSpam
```

We can now integrate these tokens into a new model and evaluate how it performs:

```
> evaluate casedTokenizer topTokens;;
Correctly classified: 0.952
```

We jumped from 87.5% to 95.2%! This is a considerable improvement, which we achieved not by adding more data, but rather, by removing features.

Choosing Our Words Carefully

Can we do better at this point? Let's try! We saw a very significant improvement by selecting a subset of the tokens, trying to keep only tokens that carry meaningful information. Along that line of thought, we could start by inspecting what the most frequently used tokens are in both Ham and Spam, which is fairly easy to accomplish:

```
ham |> top 20 casedTokenizer |> Seq.iter (printfn "%s")
spam |> top 20 casedTokenizer |> Seq.iter (printfn "%s")
```

Running this produces the following results:

Table 2-1. *Most Frequently Used Ham and Spam Tokens*

Group	Tokens
Ham	I, a, and, for, i, in, is, it, m, me, my, not, of, on, s, that, the, to, u, you
Spam	1, 2, 4, Call, FREE, a, and, call, for, from, have, is, mobile, now, on, or, the, to, you, your

Two things immediately jump to our attention. First, the two lists are rather similar; out of 20 tokens, they have 8 in common (a, and, for, is, on, the, to, you). Then again, these words are very generic; regardless of the topic, any sentence is bound to contain a few articles and pronouns. This is not great; these tokens could be described as "filler material," which won't tell us much about whether a message is Ham or Spam, and could even introduce some noise into our analysis. Simply from a performance standpoint, it means that we are spending a lot of CPU cycles analyzing tokens that are conveying limited or no relevant information. For all these reasons, it might be beneficial to remove these tokens from the analysis.

Before doing that, I think another interesting aspect appears in that list. Unlike Ham, the Spam list contains a couple of rather specific words, like "call," "free," "mobile," and "now"—and doesn't contain "I" or "me." If you think about it, that makes sense: While regular text messages have a multitude of purposes, a Spam message is usually a "phishing" attempt, trying to lure you into doing something. In that context, it isn't a surprise to see words like "now" and "free," which reek of advertising; and because flattery is rarely a wrong way to get people to do what you want, it is no surprise either than Spam messages would be less about "I" and more about "you."

■ **Note**   What is Phishing? Phishing is the act of using email, SMS, or the phone to steal money from someone. Phishing typically uses a bit of social engineering (impersonating respectable institutions, threat, or seduction) to get the target to take some action the scammer cannot perform by himself, like clicking a link that will install malicious software on your machine.

We will come back to that point soon. In the meantime, let's see if we can remove the "filler material." A common approach is to rely on a predefined list of such words, which are usually called "stop words." You can find an example of such a list here: `http://norm.al/2009/04/14/list-of-english-stop-words/`. Unfortunately, there is no universally correct way to go about this; obviously this depends on the language your documents are written in, and even the context could matter. For instance, in our sample, "u," a common way to shorten "you" in text messages, would make a great stop word. Yet, most standard lists would not contain it because that usage is extremely specific to SMS, and is highly unlikely to be found in any other document type.

Instead of relying on a list of stop words, we will do something simpler. Our topHam and topSpam sets contain the most frequently used tokens in Ham and in Spam. If a token appears in both lists, it is likely simply a word that is frequently found in English text messages, and is not particularly specific to either Ham or Spam. Let's identify all these common tokens, which correspond to the intersection of both lists, remove them from our tokens selection, and run the analysis again:

```
let commonTokens = Set.intersect topHam topSpam
let specificTokens = Set.difference topTokens commonTokens
evaluate casedTokenizer specificTokens
```

With this simple change, the percentage of correctly classified SMS messages jumps from 95.2% to 97.9%! This is starting to be pretty good, and as we get closer to 100.0%, improvements will become harder to achieve.

Creating New Features

One approach I often find useful when trying to come up with new ideas is to flip a problem on its head in order to look at it from a different angle. As an example, when I write code, I typically begin by imagining the "happy path," the minimum steps needed for the program to do something useful, and then I simply implement them. This is a great approach until you want to test your code; your mind has become so focused on the success path that it is difficult to think about failure. So I like to approach testing by reversing the question, asking, "What is the fastest possible way I could get this program to crash?" I found this very effective, and it makes testing fun, too!

Let's try out this method for improving our classifier. Looking at the most frequent words in each class ended up with a very significant improvement, because the Bayes classifier relies on frequent words in a category to recognize it. How about looking at the least frequently found words in each document category? With a slight modification of the code we wrote previously, we can extract the least frequently used tokens in a group:

Listing 2-10. Extracting least frequently used tokens

```
let rareTokens n (tokenizer:Tokenizer) (docs:string []) =
    let tokenized = docs |> Array.map tokenizer
    let tokens = tokenized |> Set.unionMany
    tokens
    |> Seq.sortBy (fun t -> countIn tokenized t)
    |> Seq.take n
    |> Set.ofSeq

let rareHam = ham |> rareTokens 50 casedTokenizer |> Seq.iter (printfn "%s")
let rareSpam = spam |> rareTokens 50 casedTokenizer |> Seq.iter (printfn "%s")
```

The table below summarizes the results:

Table 2-2. *Least Frequently Used Ham and Spam Tokens*

Group	Tokens
Ham	000pes, 0quit, 100, 1120, 116, 1205, 128, 130, 140, 15pm, 16, 180, 1Apple, 1Cup, 1IM, 1Lemon, 1Tulsi, 1mega, 1stone, 1thing, 2000, 21, 21st, 24th, 255, 26, 2B, 2DOCD, 2GETHA, 2GEVA, 2Hook, 2I, 2MOROW, 2MORRO, 2MWEN, 2WATERSHD, 2bold, 2geva, 2hrs, 2morow, 2morrowxxxx, 2mro, 2mrw, 2nhite, 2nite, 2u, 2u2, 2years, 2yrs, 30ish
Spam	0089, 0121, 01223585236, 0207, 02072069400, 02085076972, 021, 0430, 050703, 0578, 07, 07008009200, 07090201529, 07090298926, 07099833605, 07123456789, 07742676969, 07781482378, 077xxx, 078, 07801543489, 07808247860, 07808726822, 07821230901, 078498, 0789xxxxxxx, 0796XXXXXX, 07973788240, 07XXXXXXXXX, 08, 08000407165, 08000938767, 08002888812, 08002986030, 08081263000, 0825, 083, 0844, 08448350055, 08448714184, 0845, 08450542832, 08452810075over18, 08700435505150p, 08700469649, 08700621170150p, 08701213186, 08701237397, 0870141701216, 087016248

Do you notice a pattern here? The Spam list is full of what appears to be phone numbers or text codes. Again, this makes sense: If I am targeted by a phishing attempt, someone wants me to do something—and on a phone, that means calling or texting a number.

This also highlights a problem: While we as humans immediately see this list as "a lot of phone numbers," each one is treated as an individual token in our model, which will appear very rarely. Yet, the presence of a phone number in an SMS message seems to be a likely flag for Spam. One way we can address the issue is by creating a new feature that captures whether or not a message contains a phone number, regardless of what specific number it is. This will let us compute how frequently phone numbers are found in Spam, and (potentially) use that as a token in our naïve Bayes classifier.

If you examine the rare tokens list closely, you might see more-specific patterns emerge. First, the phone numbers listed have a similar structure: They begin with 07, 08, or 09, followed by nine other digits. Then, there are other numbers in the list, mainly five-digit numbers, which are likely txt numbers.

Let's create a feature for each case. Whenever we see something that looks like 07 followed by nine digits, we will convert it to the token __PHONE__, and whenever we encounter a five-digit number, we'll transform it into __TXT__:

Listing 2-11. Recognizing phone numbers

```
let phoneWords = Regex(@"0[7-9]\d{9}")
let phone (text:string) =
    match (phoneWords.IsMatch text) with
    | true -> "__PHONE__"
    | false -> text

let txtCode = Regex(@"\b\d{5}\b")
let txt (text:string) =
    match (txtCode.IsMatch text) with
    | true -> "__TXT__"
    | false -> text

let smartTokenizer = casedTokenizer >> Set.map phone >> Set.map txt
```

The smartTokenizer simply chains three functions together. The casedTokenizer function takes a string and returns a set of strings, with the individual tokens identified. Because it returns a set of strings, we can apply Set.map, running the phone function on each of the tokens and transforming each token that looks like a phone number into the "__PHONE__" token—and then performing the same with the txt function.

Let's make sure it works by running the following code in F# Interactive:

```
> smartTokenizer "hello World, call 08123456789 or txt 12345";;
val it : Set<string> =
  set ["World"; "__PHONE__"; "__TXT__"; "call"; "hello"; "or"; "txt"]
```

This is what we expected—we seem to be in business. Let's try out our tweaked tokenizer, manually adding the two tokens we just created to the list (if we didn't, the token list would still contain individual numbers, which wouldn't match with the __PHONE__ token produced by the "smart tokenizer"):

```
let smartTokens =
    specificTokens
    |> Set.add "__TXT__"
    |> Set.add "__PHONE__"

evaluate smartTokenizer smartTokens
```

Drumroll, please ... another jump up, from 96.7% to 98.3% correct! Given our current level of performance, that is a very nice boost. It's worth taking a bit of time to discuss what we did here. We transformed our dataset, creating a new feature by aggregating existing features. This process is a key part of what developing a good machine learning model entails. Starting from an original dataset, perhaps one containing low-quality data, and as you begin to understand the domain well and find relationships between variables, you will progressively reshape the data into a new representation that better fits the problem at hand. This cycle of conducting experiments and refining raw data into good features is at the core of machine learning.

Dealing with Numeric Values

Let's finish this section on feature extraction with a quick discussion. In this chapter, we have been considering discrete features only; that is, features that can only take a discrete set of values. What about continuous features, or simply numeric features? For instance, imagine you have an intuition that message length matters. Can you use any ideas from what we have seen so far?

One possibility is to reduce the problem to a known problem and make the message length (which can take any value between 0 and 140 characters) into a binary feature, separating them into two categories, short messages and long messages. The question then becomes, "What is a good value at which to split between long and short messages?"

This we can address directly using Bayes' Theorem: For a given threshold, we can compute the probability that a message is Spam, if its length is greater than the threshold. Identifying a "good" threshold is then simply a matter of testing various values and picking the most informative one. The code below does just that, and shouldn't be too hard to follow:

Listing 2-12. Spam probability based on message length

```
let lengthAnalysis len =

    let long (msg:string) = msg.Length > len

    let ham,spam =
        dataset
        |> Array.partition (fun (docType,_) -> docType = Ham)
    let spamAndLongCount =
        spam
        |> Array.filter (fun (_,sms) -> long sms)
        |> Array.length
    let longCount =
        dataset
        |> Array.filter (fun (_,sms) -> long sms)
        |> Array.length

    let pSpam = (float spam.Length) / (float dataset.Length)
    let pLongIfSpam =
        float spamAndLongCount / float spam.Length
    let pLong =
        float longCount /
        float (dataset.Length)

    let pSpamIfLong = pLongIfSpam * pSpam / pLong
    pSpamIfLong

for l in 10 .. 10 .. 130 do
    printfn "P(Spam if Length > %i) = %.4f" l (lengthAnalysis l)
```

If you run that code, you will see that the probability that a message is Spam goes up significantly with length, which is not a surprise. Spammers send a lot of messages and want to get the most bang for their buck, so they will pack as much as possible into a single SMS. I will leave it at that for now; we will revisit this topic in Chapter 6, from a slightly different angle, but I wanted to show how Bayes' Theorem can come in handy in a variety of situations, without much effort.

Understanding Errors

Remember how 87.7% correctly classified sounded great, until we put it in perspective and compared it to a naïve baseline? We managed to bring that number up to 98.3%, which is clearly much better. However, whenever you are reducing an entire dataset to a single number, by definition you are leaving something out. People love single-number summaries, because they are easy to compare. My advice to you is the following: Whenever you are presented with a statistic, it pays to think twice about what that number could be leaving out or hiding.

In our case, what we know is that out of 1,000 messages, we will misclassify about 17 on average. One thing we don't know is where the model is making its errors. Widely different situations could lead to that same number of 98.3%: These 17 could be mainly Spam, mainly Ham, or anything in between. Depending on the context, this can be a crucial distinction. For instance, I suspect most people would prefer a classifier that misses a couple of Spam messages and leaves them in their inbox, over an overly aggressive one that sends perfectly good messages automatically to a Spam folder because it was incorrectly labeled as Spam.

So, how is our classifier doing? Let's find out and measure how well it recognizes Spam and Ham. We just need to separate out Ham and Spam in our validation set, and then compute the percentage correctly classified in each group. This is easily done—we just add a couple of lines to our script and run them in F# Interactive:

Listing 2-13. Error by class

```
let bestClassifier = train training smartTokenizer smartTokens
validation
|> Seq.filter (fun (docType,_) -> docType = Ham)
|> Seq.averageBy (fun (docType,sms) ->
    if docType = bestClassifier sms
    then 1.0
    else 0.0)
|> printfn "Properly classified Ham: %.5f"
validation
|> Seq.filter (fun (docType,_) -> docType = Spam)
|> Seq.averageBy (fun (docType,sms) ->
    if docType = bestClassifier sms
    then 1.0
    else 0.0)
|> printfn "Properly classified Spam: %.5f"
```

... which produces the following output:

```
Properly classified Ham: 0.98821
Properly classified Spam: 0.95395
```

This is pretty good. Our classifier works fairly well on both categories, and performs its best on the Ham group, with 1.2% messages misclassified. This number is known as the false-positive rate, the proportion of cases where we detect a situation that is actually not present. Similarly, the false-negative rate is the proportion of cases where we missed a problem; in our case, in about 4.6% cases we fail to detect Spam.

So, why is this piece of information useful? There are at least two reasons.

First, looking deeper into classification errors and understanding whether they are false positives or false negatives is hugely important in assessing the business value of a classifier. That value is entirely context dependent, and depends essentially on which type of error is more costly. Missing a meeting with your boss because one message was misclassified as Spam is a much bigger problem than having to manually delete one Spam message from your inbox. In that case, false positives are much more costly than false negatives are, and shouldn't be weighted the same way.

This is also helpful in that it allows us to focus our efforts in the right direction and avoid wasting time on pointless work. If our classifier had already reached 100% correct Ham recognition, the only direction left for improvement would be in the other category. Perhaps a starting point would be to inspect the messages that our current model doesn't recognize as Spam, and see if a pattern emerges?

Here, ideally, what we want is to recognize Ham as reliably as possible, even at the expense of missing some Spam. One way to achieve this would be, for instance, to "tone down" the sensitivity to Spam, and to try harder on Ham. As a quick and dirty approach, we could reduce the number of tokens we retain from the Spam side, while expanding the number of tokens from the Ham side. In other words, we keep only highly specific Spam tokens, which are strong indicators, and widen the net for Ham tokens. Instead of retaining 10% of the most frequent tokens for each class, as we do in our current best model, how about keeping 20% on the Ham side, and 5% on the Spam side? Let's try that out, keeping our code identical but modifying topHam and topSpam like this:

```
let topHam = ham |> top (hamCount / 5) casedTokenizer
let topSpam = spam |> top (spamCount / 20) casedTokenizer
```

Using this code gives me the following results: 97.4% correct overall, down from 98.3%, but 99.0% correct Ham instead of 98.8%, and 92.8% correct Spam, down from 95.4%. In other words, we get a small improvement on Ham, at the expense of the other category. A 0.2% improvement might not seem like much, but what we really achieved here is a reduction of the error rate from 12 misclassified out of 1,000, to 10, or a 16.7% improvement on the most important category.

So What Have We Learned?

I am sure there is more we could do with this model; after all, we are still 1.7% away from perfection! However, I will leave that to you as an interesting exercise, and will review instead some of the key points of this chapter.

First, we discussed Bayes' Theorem, and the notion of independence. I find this result particularly interesting, for at least a couple of reasons. First, its general formulation is fairly simple. Then, it is very powerful: Bayes' Theorem provides a general framework for describing and quantifying the relationship between different pieces of imperfect information. As such, it is a key result in statistics and machine learning, as both disciplines try to draw conclusions from incomplete samples and to find patterns between data. that is, to identify where data is not independent and take advantage of it.

Arguably, the naïve Bayes classifier itself is a pretty trivial application of the Bayes' Theorem: We made a few simplifying hypotheses on how text works in order to make the math workable, and simply unfolded the consequences of applying Bayes' Theorem. Perhaps more interesting than the classifier itself was the process of text tokenization. Machine learning algorithms typically require a collection of features to operate, and a raw block of text doesn't fit that pattern well. By breaking the text into tokens, thus identifying and counting words that are present in a document, we managed to transform text into a more convenient structure.

Finally, we spent a lot of time refining a basic model and improving it by extracting new features. The key point here is that we used one fairly simple algorithm all the way through, but improved the predictive power of our model from mediocre to quite good just by taking the time to understand the data, then using that knowledge to reorganize it a bit. Deciding what algorithms to use is certainly an important part of machine learning, but building a good model is usually less about finding the one and only algorithm that will magically solve the problem, and more about gaining a better understanding of the problem domain and using that knowledge to extract better features.

In this particular case, a few patterns emerged. First, more data is not always better. Some features contain a lot of information, and some don't. Finding highly informative features and eliminating the rest will help models by giving them information that carries more signal and less noise, and is easier to exploit. Then, we saw two opposite phenomena at play. We ended up using a tokenizer that kept word casing. What happened is that we realized that our original feature was too coarse, so we split it into multiple, more-specific features (for instance, "FREE" and "free"). Conversely, we noticed that we had a lot of phone numbers and aggregated them into a single over-arching feature that didn't exist before in order to see its impact. Again, knowing your domain and data is absolutely crucial: A good algorithm looking at features the wrong way won't go very far, and small changes in features are often how you can go from having a decent model to having an excellent one.

USEFUL LINKS

- The University of California–Irvine maintains a wonderful repository of machine learning datasets: http://archive.ics.uci.edu/ml/

- The following web page contains a useful basic list of common English stop words: http://norm.al/2009/04/14/list-of-english-stop-words/

- If you want to explore further ways to work with text, the Stanford NLP page has a wealth of resources: http://nlp.stanford.edu/

CHAPTER 3

■ ■ ■

The Joy of Type Providers

Finding and Preparing Data, from Anywhere

Let me let you in on the dirty little secret of machine learning: If you were to look solely at the topics publicly discussed, you would think that most of the work revolves around crafting fancy algorithms, the remaining time being spent on designing ways to run these algorithms in a distributed fashion, or some other similarly interesting engineering challenge. The sad truth is that this is a rather marginal part of the job; most of your time will likely be spent on a much more prosaic activity: data janitorial tasks. If you want the machine to learn anything, you need to feed it data, and data has a way of coming from all sorts of different sources, in shapes and formats that are impractical for what you want to do with it. It usually has missing information, and is rarely properly documented. In short, finding and preparing data is both hugely important for machine learning and potentially a source of great pain.

Besides the data itself being in a sorry state, there is another reason why mastering data is a challenge. This reason is technical: If you think about it, what you are trying to do is to pull information—which knows nothing about your programming language—into your programming language type system so that you can actually manipulate it using that programming language. Two broad directions are possible here. If your language of choice is on the dynamic side, like Python, for instance, hacking at data is rather easy. You can write code in an optimistic manner without worrying too much about language types; if it works, great! On the downside, you are getting no assistance from the compiler. The only way to know whether your code works is to run it. If you observe no runtime error, you have to assume that it probably works. Conversely, if you are using a language like C#, which has a much stricter type system, getting data into your world will be significantly more painful and time consuming. It will probably require heavy machinery, like an object-relational mapping system (ORM), for instance. On the plus side, though, it will save you from dumb mistakes like misspellings or obvious type-cast errors.

This is an unpleasant trade-off: Either you can get your data quickly, but you are not quite sure about what you have, or you can get solid data, at the expense of agility. Fortunately, F# provides a really interesting option by which to get all the goodness of static types while sacrificing nothing, using the mechanism known as type providers. At the time of writing, type providers exist in no other mainstream language. A type provider (or TP, in short) is a component designed to target a specific type of resource or data format, such as SQL, XML, or JSON. You can then simply point the appropriate type provider at the data source you are interested in, and it will do the heavy lifting for you by inspecting its schema and creating on the fly a statically typed representation that you can safely work with.

While the topic of type providers is arguably only tangentially related to machine learning, data access and manipulation is such a central part of the data science activity that I want to spend a bit of time on the general question of data exploration. In this chapter, we will illustrate how to use type providers to consume data from widely different sources. We will introduce Deedle, a .NET Data Frame library that greatly simplifies manipulating and reshaping datasets. Finally, we will also demonstrate a usage of type providers that is directly relevant to machine learning, namely using the open-source statistical language R right from within F#.

Exploring StackOverflow data

I suspect that for most people who have written any code, StackOverflow doesn't really need an introduction. However, in the unlikely case that you have not heard about it, StackOverflow is the brainchild of Jeff Atwood and Joel Spolsky, and has quickly become the de facto go-to place for any programming question. Over time, a few similar sites have sprouted that focus on different specialty areas ranging from mathematics to English usage or home brewing, and these are unified under the StackExchange umbrella (incidentally, the Cross-Validated site, at `http://stats.stackexchange.com`, is a great resource for statistics and machine learning). StackOverflow has had a very open, wiki-like philosophy from the beginning, and so it is no surprise that they provide an open API to StackOverflow and their sister sites, allowing you to programmatically dig into all that data. In this section, we will see how we can take advantage of F# type providers to explore the data made available through that API.

The StackExchange API

The StackExchange API is documented at `http://api.stackexchange.com/docs`. It is a REST API, which returns JSON responses. Some methods require authentication, and the usage is throttled. In case you wanted to use the API to build an actual application, you can get a key, but for lightweight exploration, the usage limits are not a problem. Every method available can be tried out directly in a web page, which helps you to understand how the arguments work. For instance, going to `http://api.stackexchange.com/docs/questions` lets you search StackOverflow questions, querying by various criteria such as dates or tags.

Figure 3-1 illustrates how you would go about searching for C# questions asked between January 1 and 2, 2014. The query is broken down by pages of 20, and we are asking for the second page of results; that is, question numbers 21 to 40. If you hit the "Run" button, the current query will be executed, and its result will be displayed right below, in the same window.

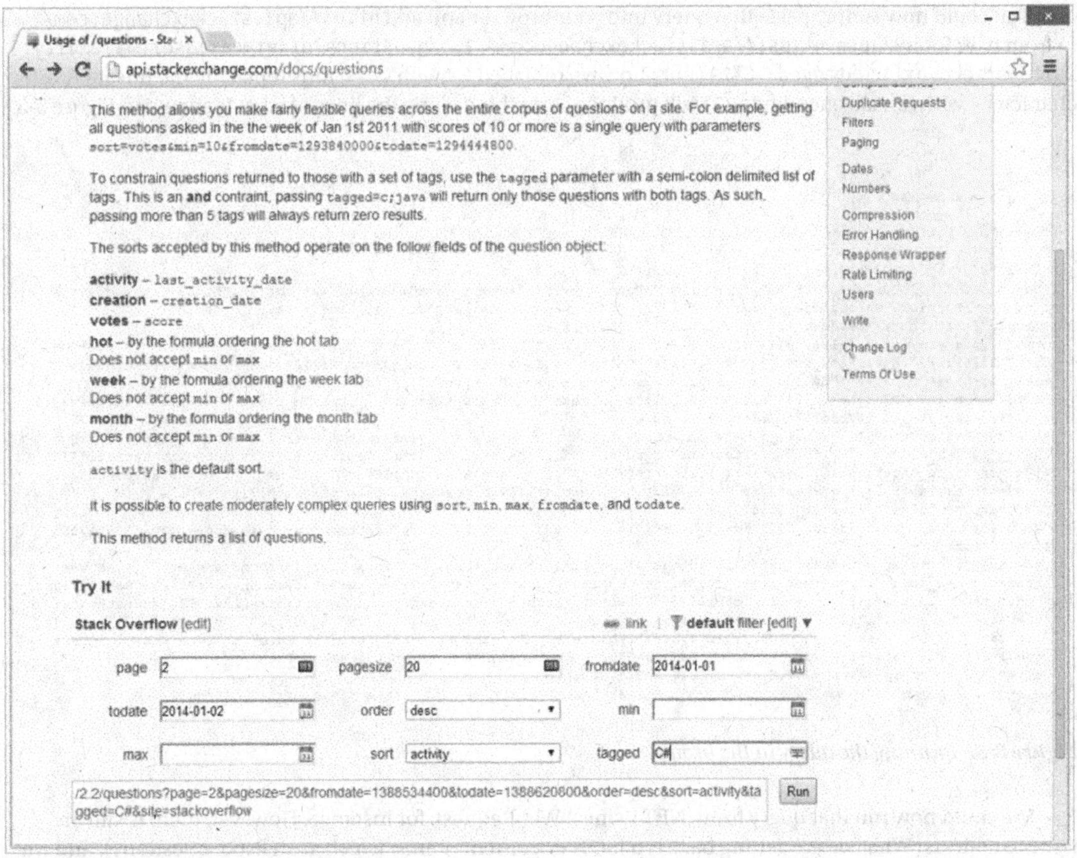

This method allows you make fairly flexible queries across the entire corpus of questions on a site. For example, getting all questions asked in the the week of Jan 1st 2011 with scores of 10 or more is a single query with parameters `sort=votes&min=10&fromdate=1293840000&todate=1294444800`.

To constrain questions returned to those with a set of tags, use the `tagged` parameter with a semi-colon delimited list of tags. This is an **and** contraint, passing `tagged=c;java` will return only those questions with both tags. As such, passing more than 5 tags will always return zero results.

The sorts accepted by this method operate on the follow fields of the question object:

activity – `last_activity_date`
creation – `creation_date`
votes – `score`
hot – by the formula ordering the hot tab
Does not accept `min` or `max`
week – by the formula ordering the week tab
Does not accept `min` or `max`
month – by the formula ordering the month tab
Does not accept `min` or `max`

`activity` is the default sort.

It is possible to create moderately complex queries using `sort`, `min`, `max`, `fromdate`, and `todate`.

This method returns a list of questions.

Try It

Stack Overflow [edit]   ⇔ link ▼ **default** filter [edit] ▼

page	2	pagesize	20	fromdate	2014-01-01
todate	2014-01-02	order	desc	min	
max		sort	activity	tagged	C#

`/2.2/questions?page=2&pagesize=20&fromdate=1388534400&todate=1388620800&order=desc&sort=activity&tagged=C#&site=stackoverflow`   `Run`

Figure 3-1. *The StackExchange API "Try It" feature*

Note also how as you edit your query, the section to the left of the "Run" button changes, reflecting your edits. What shows up is the actual query, which you can use to obtain data. As an example, if you were looking for questions tagged C#, the screen shown in Figure 3-2 would appear on the page:

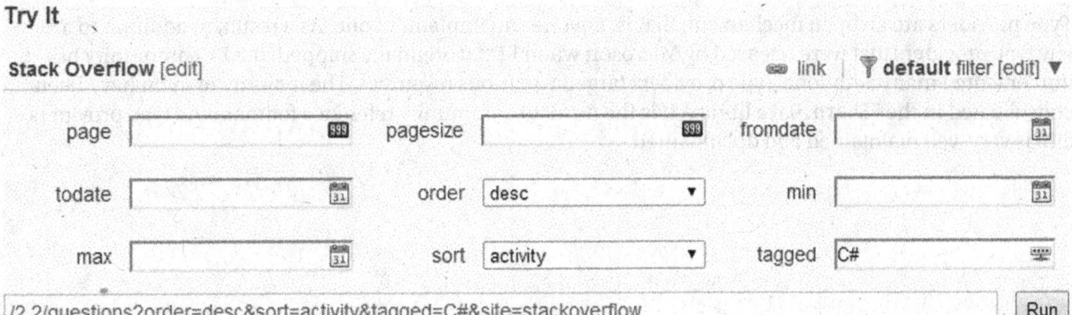

Try It

Stack Overflow [edit]   ⇔ link ▼ **default** filter [edit] ▼

page		pagesize		fromdate	
todate		order	desc	min	
max		sort	activity	tagged	C#

`/2.2/questions?order=desc&sort=activity&tagged=C#&site=stackoverflow`   `Run`

Figure 3-2. *A simple query*

You could now simply paste that query into your browser and add `http://api.stackexchange.com/` in front of it; for instance, `https://api.stackexchange.com/2.2/questions?order=desc&sort=activity` `&site=stackoverflow&tagged=` C%23 (note how we replaced C# with C%23, thus replacing the unsafe ASCII character # with its safe encoding %23) will produce something along the lines of what is shown in Figure 3-3.

Figure 3-3. *Running the query in the browser*

We could now run that query from .NET using a WebRequest, for instance. However, there is still an issue to address: What we are getting back is a JSON document (items, which are a list of questions), and we would still need to create a .NET class to represent these, and then deserialize each item into it. While this is not a particularly complex task, it is tedious. It would be nice if we had a mechanism available to us that would "just" look at that schema, do the grunt work of creating an adequate type for it, and load the response into it. The good news is that this is exactly what a type provider does.

Using the JSON Type Provider

Type providers are an open mechanism; that is, anyone can implement one. As a result, in addition to a few type providers that were released by Microsoft when F# 3.0 originally shipped, the F# community has implemented many additional type providers targeting various resources. The majority of them have been consolidated in the `FSharp.Data` library; it is the de facto community reference for mainline type providers, and is very well maintained and documented.

NUGET PACKAGES AND F# SCRIPTS

To use a library in an F# script, you need to reference it by using the `#r` directive. As an example, to use the library MyLibrary, which is part of the dll `libraryAssembly.dll`, you would run the following two lines in your script:

```
#r "path-to-the-dll/libraryAssembly.dll"
open MyLibrary
```

A quick-and-dirty way to use a NuGet package is to install the package, look it up in the Solution Explorer, inside the References folder, and copy/paste its full path from the Properties window into the script, as shown in Figure 3-4.

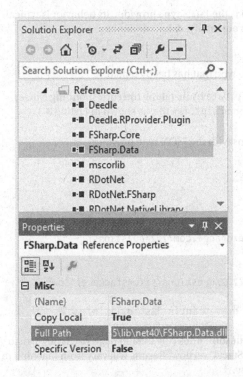

Figure 3-4. *Retrieving the full path to an assembly*

There are some issues with this approach, though. By default, NuGet packages are downloaded into a Packages folder in the solution, where each package is stored in a folder that contains its name and specific version number. As a result, using the default Visual Studio project structure, your script will look like this:

```
#r @"\Mathias\Documents\Visual Studio 2013\Projects\ProjectName\packages\
PackageName.1.2.3\lib\net40-full\Assembly.dll"
```

This is obviously not awesome: The path depends on the local machine and on the version number, which could both change. You can address the first issue by using relative paths and the #l directive, which adds a path where assemblies should be searched:

```
#I "..\packages"
#r @"PackageName.1.2.3\lib\net40-full\Assembly.dll"
```

The version number problem is trickier; every time you update to a newer version of a library, your script will break until you fix the path manually. Paket (http://fsprojects.github.io/Paket/), a dependency-management library for .NET, offers an elegant solution to that issue. We will be using version-specific paths in the rest of this book, because in this case it has the benefit of clarifying which version was used.

Among the type providers you can find in FSharp.Data is the JSON type provider. Its behavior is typical of how a canonical type provider works. The following steps are involved:

- First, create types by looking at sample data,

- then load data from actual data sources into the type that has been created.

Let's create a new F# solution, add a reference to FSharp.Data by installing the corresponding NuGet package, and reference the FSharp.Data library in the default Script.fsx file, as shown in Listing 3-1.

Listing 3-1. Retrieving the latest StackOverflow C# questions with the JSON type provider

```
#I @"..\packages\"
#r @"FSharp.Data.2.2.0\lib\net40\FSharp.Data.dll"

open FSharp.Data

type Questions = JsonProvider<"""https://api.stackexchange.com/2.2/questions?
site=stackoverflow""">

let csQuestions = """https://api.stackexchange.com/2.2/questions?site=stackoverflow&
tagged=C%23"""
Questions.Load(csQuestions).Items |> Seq.iter (fun q -> printfn "%s" q.Title)
```

Running this sample code should produce a list of 30 question titles (the default page size is 30), which are the most active questions tagged C# that were asked on StackOverflow. Results will vary from machine to machine, because of the time-dependent nature of the query.

■ **Tip** F# supports two mechanisms to handle strings that contain special characters. Verbatim strings will ignore escape characters, like \, and allow you to embed quotes inside a string by using a double quote, like this: `printfn @"He said ""hello""!"`. Triple-quotes also ignore escape characters, but directly allow the usage of quotes inside, like this: `printfn """He said "hello"!"""`.

So what's going on here? The first piece, `type Questions = JsonProvider<...>`, creates a type, Questions, based on sample data. The sample data is accessed over the wire from the URL we supplied, which, as we saw previously, calls the StackExchange API and returns 30 recent questions as a JSON document. The type provider scans that sample and creates the appropriate Properties and Types as needed.

For instance, if you type `Questions.` inside your script file in Visual Studio and wait for IntelliSense to provide you with hints, you will see two things. First, `Questions` contains a couple of classes that have been automatically created based on what the sample contained: `Item`, `Owner`, and `Root`. Try clicking on `Item` in the drop-down menu that shows up once IntelliSense kicks in; you should see that it exposes a bunch of Properties, such as `member  AcceptedAnswerId:Option<int>`. Based on the sample, the TP has generated a class with appropriate types (the accepted answer ID should be an integer when it exists, but could also not exist, if no satisfactory answer was supplied).

`Questions` also exposes a `Load` method. This method can be used to retrieve data from a specific source, and it is expected to return something that will fit the Questions type. This is what is taking place in the second part of the script: We pass in a query that requests the most recent questions tagged C# (encoded as C%23), and the type provider goes over the wire, makes the request, receives a JSON document, and automatically converts it to a full-blown type.

You can use the JSON type provider in a slightly different manner, which might help clarify the mechanics at work here. Instead of calling the StackExchange API to generate the Questions type, you could also directly supply it with a sample, either as a file or as an in-line string. Listing 3-2 illustrates this process: We provide a valid sample of the JSON output we expect from the API as a plain string (marked with the [`<Literal>`] attribute, which compiles it as a constant literal), and pass that sample to the type provider, which will create a new F# type based on how the data is structured in the sample.

Listing 3-2. Creating a type from a local JSON sample

```
[<Literal>]
let sample = """{"items":[
{"tags":["java","arrays"],"owner": // SNIPPED FOR BREVITY"},
{"tags":["javascript","jquery","html"],"owner": // SNIPPED FOR BREVITY"},],
"has_more":true,"quota_max":300,"quota_remaining":299}"""

type HardCodedQuestions = JsonProvider<sample>
```

At this point, the compiler has created a type based on the sample string, and you can use it to access data from the StackExchange API by passing in a query that is expected to return a JSON response that follows the same structure; for instance, pulling Java-related questions:

```
[<Literal>]
let javaQuery = "https://api.stackexchange.com/2.2/questions?site=stackoverflow&tagged=java"

let javaQuestions = HardCodedQuestions.Load(javaQuery)
```

In other words, the sample is used by the compiler to generate a type; whether the JSON comes from a local file or over the wire doesn't matter. Once the type is created, it can be used to load data that has the appropriate shape. If, for instance, we were to call a different API endpoint using this type, we would get a runtime exception.

One interesting difference between the two methods is that they have different implications if the schema changes over time. Imagine that, for instance, the Title property was renamed to something else. In the first case, we would get a compile-time error, because the type is created every time we build by accessing the API, and the compiler would catch that we are using a property that doesn't exist anymore. By contrast, when using a "local sample," we would get a runtime error: Our type is based on a stale sample, which would still have the old property, and the mismatch would be only caught when we try to access live data.

Building a Minimal DSL to Query Questions

The StackExchange API is pretty straightforward, and it would not be very difficult to simply write queries by hand as we go. However, this would introduce a lot of repetition in our code, which creates potential for both typos and bugs. Let's avoid that and create a minimal domain-specific language, or, as they are commonly called, a DSL.

You probably noticed that the StackExchange API requests follow a pattern: From a base URL (`https://api.stackexchange.com/2.2/`) we append a string encoding what entity we are interested in getting (questions), followed by a question mark and optional parameters specifying the query further (`?site=stackoverflow&tagged=C%23;F%23`). One way to simplify our query construction is to take advantage of that pattern, creating small functions that describe how we are modifying the base query to fit our needs, in such a way that we can compose these operations in a nice and readable pipeline. See Listing 3-3.

Listing 3-3. Building a minimal query DSL

```
let questionQuery = """https://api.stackexchange.com/2.2/questions?site=stackoverflow"""

let tagged tags query =
    // join the tags in a ; separated string
    let joinedTags = tags |> String.concat ";"
    sprintf "%s&tagged=%s" query joinedTags

let page p query = sprintf "%s&page=%i" query p

let pageSize s query = sprintf "%s&pagesize=%i" query s

let extractQuestions (query:string) = Questions.Load(query).Items
```

In essence, questionQuery defines the base query from which we are starting. The three functions that follow are appending optional query details to that query, and the last function, extractQuestions, attempts to load data using whatever query string has been constructed, and then retrieves the corresponding items. Note how we didn't have to provide type annotations, because sprintf contains enough hints for the compiler to infer the correct types.

Let me draw your attention to one pattern here: Every function features query as its final argument. Coming from C#, this is fairly unusual. Typically, the arguments in a C# method are ordered by importance, starting from the indispensable ones and moving toward those that are less important. You will see this "inverted" pattern very often in F# code, as it enables the composition of functions into workflows using the pipe-forward operator |>. The pipe-forward operator allows you to substitute the last argument of a function with whatever the previous function evaluated to, so that, for instance, add 42 1 is equivalent to 1 |> add 42. In our example, we can retrieve 100 questions tagged C#, and 100 tagged F#, using very human readable code. See Listing 3-4.

Listing 3-4. Using our DSL to extract questions tagged C# and F#

```
let ``C#`` = "C%23"
let ``F#`` = "F%23"

let fsSample =
    questionQuery
    |> tagged [``F#``]
    |> pageSize 100
    |> extractQuestions
```

```
let csSample =
    questionQuery
    |> tagged [``C#``]
    |> pageSize 100
    |> extractQuestions
```

■ **Tip**   Any string surrounded by double backticks, like "C#", is a valid identifier. This can be very helpful for making code more human-readable; in this situation, for example, the meaning of "C#" is much more obvious than the "C%23" form. A common usage of this feature is in the context of testing: Instead of naming a test method The_Price:Should_Be_Positive(), you can simply write "The price should be positive"().

It took us seven lines of code to reference the JSON type provider and write a minimal DSL; at this point, we are fully ready to hack at the data itself and explore. For instance, comparing what tags or topics are most frequently associated with either group is a matter of lines, as seen in Listing 3-5.

Listing 3-5. Comparing tags by language

```
let analyzeTags (qs:Questions.Item seq) =
    qs
    |> Seq.collect (fun question -> question.Tags)
    |> Seq.countBy id
    |> Seq.filter (fun (_,count) -> count > 2)
    |> Seq.sortBy (fun (_,count) -> -count)
    |> Seq.iter (fun (tag,count) -> printfn "%s,%i" tag count)

analyzeTags fsSample
analyzeTags csSample
```

Taking as an input a sequence of Item, we collect the tags to flatten the sequence of sequences into a single sequence, count each tag, filter out tags that show up less than twice, sort by descending count, and finally print out the tags and their count.

■ **Tip**   Underscores are used as a wildcard character when "unpacking" a tuple. This spares you the hassle of creating a name for unused variables, and can also help signal what elements of the tuple you are actively using.

You will probably observe slightly different results if you run this, because the query is time dependent. However, I suspect the gist of it would remain along what I observed (see Table 3-1).

Table 3-1. *Most frequent tags attached to C# and F# questions*

C# Tags	F# Tags
c#,100	f#,100
wpf,13	f#-data,10
.net,13	type-providers,7
asp.net,11	functional-programming,6
entity-framework,5	f#-3.0,6
asynchronous,5	c#,5
asp.net-mvc-4,5	.net,5
sql,5	f#-interactive,5
linq,4	
xaml,4	
windows-store-apps,4	

A large portion of the C# topics of interest revolve around client-side technology and web, whereas F# looks more data focused (which at this point should not surprise you much). Amusingly, a large part of the C# questions are related to technologies that F# type providers greatly simplify (sql and data access, xaml, and so on).

Our goal in this chapter is not to produce a full analysis of StackOverflow (we will investigate that question later on in chapter 5), but rather to illustrate how type providers and F# make working with data of various origins ridiculously easy. While we focused on a JSON example here, most data-oriented type providers (CSV, XML, and so forth) follow a similar pattern of first acquiring a data sample to infer what types to create, and then using the type that was created to load data. We will leave our exploration of StackOverflow at that for this section—feel free to explore more on your own!

All the Data in the World

Now that we have seen what type providers are and how they make programming against data incredibly easy, I want to focus on two related topics that are specifically relevant to data scientists. The first one is Deedle, a .NET data-frame library, which simplifies considerably the manipulation and analysis of datasets. The second is the R type provider, which makes the R statistical language available from within F# and opens up its huge ecosystem of statistical and visualization packages.

The World Bank Type Provider

The World Bank is a United Nations international financial institution that provides loans to developing countries for capital programs. It is also famous for maintaining and making available to the public a very rich dataset of socioeconomic information. You can get a sense for what the dataset contains at http://data.worldbank.org/; for every one of over 200 countries in the world, you can download decades of yearly data for over 1,400 indicators covering topics ranging from Economy & Growth to Gender or Infrastructure, and more.

So, everything is all ponies and unicorns, then? Well, not quite. The issue is that while the data is there, getting to it is a bit tedious. If I wanted to, say, grab the population in 2000 and 2010, and the current land surface for every country in the world, I would have to do a lot of navigating around to select the appropriate countries, indicators, and years; what I would get is a file (either Excel, CSV, or XML), which I would probably still have to massage a bit to put in a shape and form that suits my needs. Furthermore, finding the series (or countries) I care about might not always be obvious, if I don't know what it is called.

Note that this is by no means a criticism of the World Bank website, which is actually excellent. The problem is that it is difficult to create a user interface to freely select what the user wants, while navigating hierarchically in a large corpus of data. What would be awfully convenient here is a different mechanism that enables me to query and discover the data on the fly—and this is exactly what the FSharp.Data World Bank type provider offers. It follows a slightly different pattern from what we have seen so far. Instead of creating types for a generic data format using schema information, it is written exclusively for that data source, with the single purpose of making the data discoverable and available with minimal effort.

Using the World Bank type provider simply requires installing the FSharp.Data NuGet package, adding a reference to it in a script, and creating a data context, which will establish the connection to the World Bank, as seen in Listing 3-6.

Listing 3-6. Using the World Bank type provider

```
#I @"..\packages\"
#r @" FSharp.Data.2.2.0\lib\net40\FSharp.Data.dll"

open FSharp.Data

let wb = WorldBankData.GetDataContext ()
wb.Countries.Japan.CapitalCity
```

Once the data context is created, it can be used to directly access the World Bank and discover what data is available using IntelliSense (see Figure 3-5).

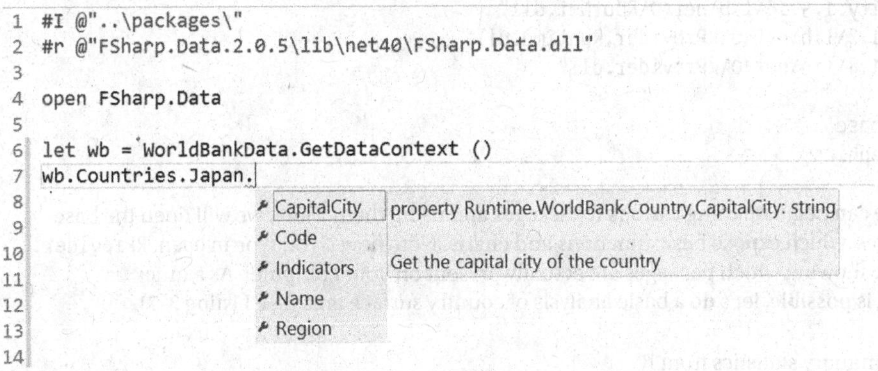

Figure 3-5. *Navigating World Bank data with IntelliSense*

What we will do here is simply retrieve the population for every country in the world, in both 2000 and 2010, which is fairly straightforward:

```
let countries = wb.Countries

let pop2000 = [ for c in countries -> c.Indicators.``Population, total``.[2000]]
let pop2010 = [ for c in countries -> c.Indicators.``Population, total``.[2010]]
```

The World Bank type provider gives us immediate access to a treasure trove of data; that being said, now we have a new problem on our hands, namely, how can we extract some interesting information from it? Poking around data points for hundreds of countries hoping to notice patterns is not the most effective way to approach mining the data for interesting facts. It would be nice to have some statistical tools at our disposal—and, fortunately, we have that, thanks to the R type provider.

The R Type Provider

R is "a free software environment for statistical computing and graphics.", in its own words (www.r-project.org) It is a programming language designed and implemented by statisticians for statisticians. It is open source and entirely free, and comes with an amazing ecosystem of packages created by the R community that cover virtually every area of statistics.

The R type provider is an interesting creature. So far we have seen examples where the focus was on making data discoverable. The R provider does something similar, but for a completely different type of external resource: a programming language. Assuming you have R installed on your machine, it will discover what packages are already installed and then let you to open them in your F# environment, just as if they were normal .NET libraries. It will also make it possible to discover what R functions are available to you, and to directly call them from F#.

■ **Installing R**   Using the R type provider requires having R installed on your machine. R is entirely free and open source, and runs on all platforms. You can find instructions and documentation about R at http://www.r-project.org/. Note that while R runs fine on all platforms, at the time of writing, the R type provider is only partly supported on mono.

Let's see what the R provider can do for us. First, let's install the NuGet package, RProvider, and add the required references to it in our script:

```
#r @"R.NET.Community.1.5.16\lib\net40\RDotNet.dll"
#r @"RProvider.1.1.8\lib\net40\RProvider.Runtime.dll"
#r @"RProvider.1.1.8\lib\net40\RProvider.dll"
open RProvider
open RProvider.``base``
open RProvider.graphics
```

At this point, we can begin opening various R packages and using them. Here, we will open the base and graphics packages, which expose basic functions and charts. Note how if you type in open RProvider., IntelliSense will start showing which packages are actually present on your computer. As a quick introduction to what is possible, let's do a basic analysis of country surface area (see Listing 3-7).

Listing 3-7. Basic summary statistics from R

```
// Retrieve an (F#) list of country surfaces
let surface = [ for c in countries -> c.Indicators.``Surface area (sq. km)``.[2010]]
// Produce summary statistics
R.summary(surface) |> R.print
```

We retrieve the surface area of every country using the World Bank type provider and store the values in an F# list. Using R will show, via IntelliSense again, which functions are currently available in our environment. First, let's produce a summary of the surface area variable by calling R.summary, and then R.print, which generates the following "pretty print:"

Min.	1st Qu.	Median	Mean	3rd Qu.	Max.	NA's
2	11300	99900	630200	450300	17100000	1

■ **Note** If you run only R.summary, you might notice that it returns an RDotNet.SymbolicExpression. In order to avoid unnecessary and costly conversions between R and .NET types, the R type provider typically sends information to R via R Symbolic Expressions, the R representation of data and/or operations, and keeps as much as possible in that form, converting back to .NET types only when requested.

There's nothing earth shattering here, but it is very convenient. The summary returns the minimum and maximum values, as well as the average, the three quartiles (the values that are greater than 25%, 50%, and 75% of the sample), and the number of missing values (NA). At a glance, we see that surface areas are wildly different, ranging from 2 square kilometers for the smallest one to 17 million for the largest—and one country where we found no data. That is useful, but given how dispersed the values seem to be, a chart would help us understand better how the data "looks." This is pretty easy to do with the R.hist(surface) function, which produces the chart seen in Figure 3-6.

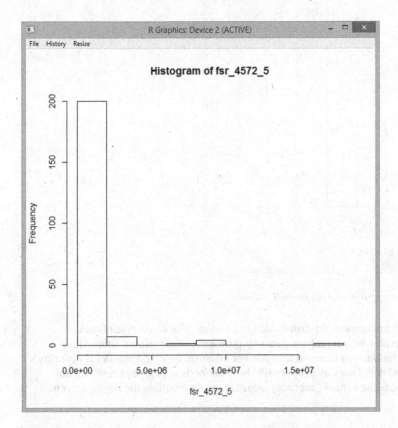

Figure 3-6. *Basic histogram of country surfaces using R graphics*

I will give it to you—this is not a pretty chart. Instead of surface area, the X axis shows a variable with the very unevocative name of fsr_4572_5. We will see later how we could create nicer charts, but remember, it just took us one call to R.hist to generate this chart, which is perfectly fine for exploration, and shows us quickly all we need to know, namely that the surface area distribution is highly uneven, with a vast majority of relatively small countries, and a few gigantic ones.

If we wanted to see a bit better what is going on in the middle of the pack, we could plot the logarithm of the country surface area. What is nice here is that we can use whichever tool we think is best for the job: F# code or R functions. In this case, we could, for instance, use F# code like R.hist(surface |> List.map log); however, the R.log function is even shorter, so we'll go for R.hist(surface |> R.log), which produces the chart seen in Figure 3-7.

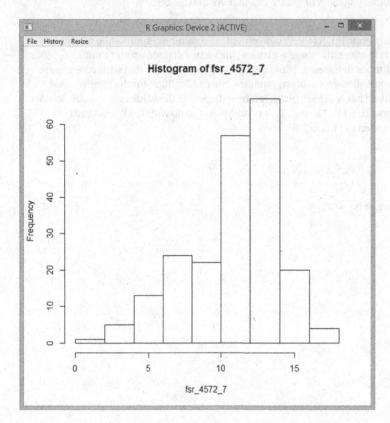

Figure 3-7. *Log-transformed country surface areas using R graphics*

Histograms are a good way to understand the distribution of a feature. The workhorse of data visualization, though, is the scatterplot, which projects data points on a two-dimensional chart. This is a very convenient way to explore relationships between features. For instance, we might wonder if a country's surface area and population are related. One way to approach the question is to plot Population on one axis and Surface Area on the other, using R.plot(surface, pop2010) and eyeballing the result, as seen in Figure 3-8.

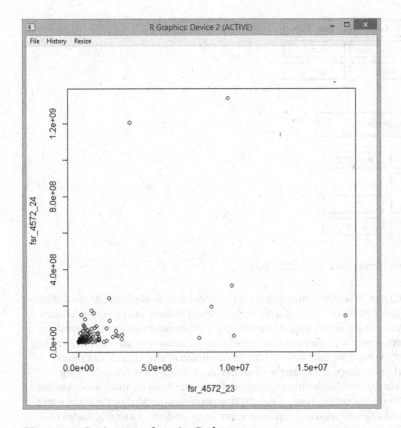

Figure 3-8. *Basic scatterplot using R.plot*

From the looks of it, Surface and Population seem to have at best a limited relationship; the scatterplot shows no obvious pattern.

This simple scenario illustrates how R can help us understand individual features better by producing simple statistics and charts. However, working one feature at a time will quickly end up being a nightmare if your dataset is non-trivial. When digging through data, you will typically have a lot of features, and you will need to be able to explore their relationships quickly and to rearrange them into new features by combining existing ones. This is why data frames, the topic we will explore next, are such a popular tool among data scientists.

Analyzing Data Together with R Data Frames

In a nutshell, a data frame is a data structure geared toward the manipulation of a collection of observations. Each observation corresponds to an individual row in the data frame, but individual features can also be accessed as columns. In that sense, data frames are similar to database tables, but are geared toward in-memory manipulation. By itself, this is already very convenient: This retains type information on individual rows, but greatly simplifies operations such as "compute the average Order Quantity feature for Customers which had a Revenue greater than 1 million," which are not difficult, but require repeating similar code over and over again. See Figure 3-9.

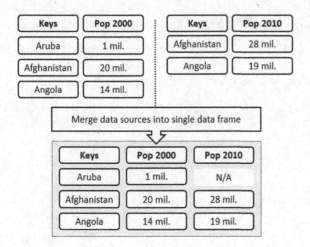

Figure 3-9. *Merging various data sources into a single data frame*

The other main purpose of data frames is to help in merging data sources into a single frame. As such, data frames usually rely on keys to uniquely identify each row of data, so that various features can be associated with the correct rows and then joined. Another important related functionality is the management of missing values: If I am attempting to join two features—say, the surface area and population for countries—and have incomplete data for some of them, I would want the resulting data frame to contain the union of all countries, but signal which ones have missing data, and handle that missing data without too much hassle when computing, for instance, the average surface area. Finally, data frames usually support dynamic column creation. In our previous example, I might want to look into a new feature like country density (the population divided by the surface area); data frames typically allow you to add a new column and express column combinations in a simple manner.

Data frames are one of the core types of R; today, most programming languages used by data scientists have a data-frame library. They are usually inspired by the R data frame, but come in different flavors, depending on the language characteristics. .NET is no exception; there are a couple of good commercial products, and a great open-source library, Deedle, which we will briefly demonstrate here.

But before looking into Deedle, let's see for a second how we would use the native R data frame. The R type provider comes with a couple of utility functions that make creating R data frames from F# easier. As an example, try out the code in Listing 3-8.

Listing 3-8. Creating and plotting an R data frame

```
let pollution = [ for c in countries -> c.Indicators.``CO2 emissions (kt)``.[2000]]
let education = [ for c in countries -> c.Indicators.``School enrollment, secondary
(% gross)``.[2000]]

let rdf =
    [ "Pop2000", box pop2000
      "Pop2010", box pop2010
      "Surface", box surface
      "Pollution", box pollution
      "Education", box education ]
    |> namedParams
    |> R.data_frame
```

```
// Scatterplot of all features
rdf |> R.plot

// Summary of all features
rdf |> R.summary |> R.print
```

We retrieve a couple of additional features (pollution measured as CO2 emissions, and education measured as secondary school enrollment percentage) and create a data frame containing five columns, each of which is associated with a name. Once the data frame is created, we can generate a summary, which produces the following output:

```
>
     Pop2000              Pop2010             Surface           Pollution
 Min.   :9.419e+03   Min.   :9.827e+03   Min.   :       2   Min.   :     15
 1st Qu.:6.255e+05   1st Qu.:7.981e+05   1st Qu.:   11300   1st Qu.:   1050
 Median :5.139e+06   Median :5.931e+06   Median :   99900   Median :   6659
 Mean   :2.841e+07   Mean   :3.207e+07   Mean   :  630216   Mean   : 122608
 3rd Qu.:1.631e+07   3rd Qu.:2.097e+07   3rd Qu.:  450300   3rd Qu.:  53601
 Max.   :1.263e+09   Max.   :1.338e+09   Max.   :17098240   Max.   :5713560
                                         NA's   :1          NA's   :20

    Education
 Min.   :  6.051
 1st Qu.: 41.699
 Median : 78.588
 Mean   : 70.782
 3rd Qu.: 93.882
 Max.   :160.619
 NA's   :70
```

We can even visualize all features together by passing the entire data frame directly to R.plot, as seen in Figure 3-10.

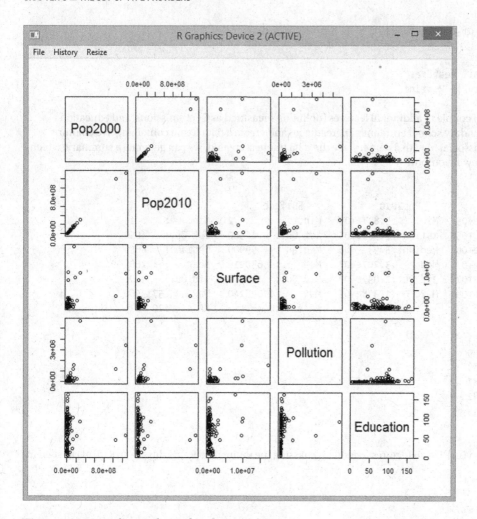

Figure 3-10. *Visualizing relationships between features*

Such charts are very useful. At a glance, it is immediately obvious that Pop2000 and Pop2010 are related: Their scatterplot forms a nearly perfect line. Education appears to be independent from all four other features (no clear visual pattern emerges), and Surface Area and Pollution seem somewhat related to Population (larger populations tend to go with higher values). Note also that while we had a significant number of missing values, R didn't blink, and handled that issue gracefully.

The specifics here are not particularly important; the point I hope I got across here is that a data frame comes in handy for dealing with multiple features. However, beyond simple cases like this one, manipulating data from F# using the R data frame itself is rather unpleasant. This is where Deedle comes in: It is native to .NET, with a syntax designed to be .NET friendly (for both C# and F#), but can be fed directly to R using the Deedle RProvider plugin.

Deedle, a .NET Data Frame

The two core building blocks of Deedle are series and frames. A *series* is a key-value pairs collection; series can be merged into a data frame and matched on keys, automatically managing missing values. Let's start with a toy example first to illustrate how Deedle works, and then use it on a more interesting scenario (see Listing 3-9).

Listing 3-9. Creating series and data frames with Deedle

```
#r @"Deedle.1.0.7\lib\net40\Deedle.dll"
open Deedle

let series1 = series [ "Alpha", 1.; "Bravo", 2.; "Delta", 4. ]
let series2 = series [ "Bravo", 20.; "Charlie", 30.; "Delta", 40. ]
let toyFrame = frame [ "First", series1; "Second", series2 ]

series1 |> Stats.sum
toyFrame |> Stats.mean
toyFrame?Second |> Stats.mean

toyFrame?New <- toyFrame?First + toyFrame?Second
toyFrame |> Stats.mean
```

We create two Series, associating a key ("Alpha", "Bravo", …) with a value, and create a Frame from it, giving each series a name ("First", "Second"). We can now perform operations on each Series (for instance, get its sum), or on the entire data frame—or access each series from the data frame, in a dynamic fashion, using the syntax DataframeName?ColumnName, as in toyFrame?Second. Note how the data frame gracefully handles computing the mean, in spite of both series having missing values.

The most interesting part in this example is the last two lines, where we create and name a new column on the fly and define it based on the other columns. At this point, our data frame contains three columns instead of the two originally seen, and we can start working with the new column just as if it had been there from the beginning.

■ **Tip** The ? operator is used to access dynamic properties. Its usage is rather rare in F#, because it means abandoning the safety of static types. However, it makes sense for a library like Deedle. If we need to freely add data to an existing frame, we cannot create a single type with known properties ahead of time. For that reason, a frame behaves along the lines of an Expando Object, with new properties being created when new series are added to it.

There is much more to Deedle than what we saw here; I encourage you to go to the documentation page (http://bluemountaincapital.github.io/Deedle/) and see for yourself what you can do with it. This example was intended to give you a sense for what data frames are about, and help you get started by presenting some of the key ideas behind Deedle. Now let's take a look at an example integrating R and Deedle.

Data of the World, Unite!

In the previous section, we started looking into the world population, grabbing data from the World Bank type provider. Beyond a certain point, it is difficult to distinguish any patterns in large datasets, and with a list of over 200 countries, we need something else. What would really work well is a map. Fortunately, one of the many existing R packages, rworldmap, does just what its name suggests: creates world maps. One way to do this is simply to attach data to countries, and then let the package work its magic.

Let's start with plotting the population by country in 2000 and 2010. First, we will create a Deedle data frame and fill it in with data from the World Bank. To do this, we need to build a series, which, if you recall, are constructed as collections of key-value pairs. We also want that information to be usable by rworldmap so that it can connect the right data points to the right countries. As it turns out, both rworldmap and the World Bank support ISO3 codes, three-letter codes that uniquely identify countries—this is what we will use for our keys.

For the sake of clarity, let's create a new script file, WorldMap.fsx, and build our data frame, as shown in Listing 3-10.

Listing 3-10. Constructing a Deedle data frame with World Bank data

```
#I @"..\packages\"
#r @"FSharp.Data.2.2.0\lib\net40\FSharp.Data.dll"
#r @"Deedle.1.0.7\lib\net40\Deedle.dll"

open FSharp.Data
open Deedle

let wb = WorldBankData.GetDataContext ()
let countries = wb.Countries

let population2000 =
    series [ for c in countries -> c.Code, c.Indicators.``Population, total``.[2000]]
let population2010 =
    series [ for c in countries -> c.Code, c.Indicators.``Population, total``.[2010]]
let surface =
    series [ for c in countries -> c.Code, c.Indicators.``Surface area (sq. km)``.[2010]]

let ddf =
    frame [
        "Pop2000", population2000
        "Pop2010", population2010
        "Surface", surface ]
ddf?Code <- ddf.RowKeys

#r @"R.NET.Community.1.5.16\lib\net40\RDotNet.dll"
#r @"RProvider.1.1.8\lib\net40\RProvider.Runtime.dll"
#r @"RProvider.1.1.8\lib\net40\RProvider.dll"
#r @"Deedle.RPlugin.1.0.7\lib\net40\Deedle.RProvider.Plugin.dll"let dataframe =
    frame [
        "Pop2000", population2000
        "Pop2010", population2010
        "Surface", surface ]
dataframe?Code <- dataframe.RowKeys
```

We simply retrieve the populations in 2000 and 2010, as well as the country surface areas, and create three series, keying each country on its country code. We then create a Deedle data frame, giving each series an individual name, and finally add another series, "Code," which directly exposes the country code (we will need that in order to tie in the map to country data).

Now that we have data in the data frame, we need to create a map and define how to join each country with data. This is fairly straightforward and is shown in Listing 3-11.

Listing 3-11. Creating a map with rworldmap

```
#r @"R.NET.Community.1.5.16\lib\net40\RDotNet.dll"
#r @"RProvider.1.1.8\lib\net40\RProvider.Runtime.dll"
#r @"RProvider.1.1.8\lib\net40\RProvider.dll"
#r @"Deedle.RPlugin.1.0.7\lib\net40\Deedle.RProvider.Plugin.dll"

open RProvider
open RProvider.``base``
open Deedle.RPlugin
open RProvider.rworldmap

let map = R.joinCountryData2Map(dataframe,"ISO3","Code")
R.mapCountryData(map,"Pop2000")
```

We open the Deedle R plugin (which makes Deedle data frames directly consumable by R) and the rworldbank package, and then we create a map, defining where the data is coming from (the dataframe ddf) and how to join each country on the map to data in the data frame by using the column "Code" (which maps to the World Bank country code) as an ISO3 code (one of the built-in options in rworldbank). And we are good to go: Running R.mapCountryData(map,"Pop2000") will now retrieve all values in the Pop2000 column from the data frame and attach it to countries by matching the Code column to the Country ISO3 code, producing a map like the one in Figure 3-11. Not too bad for a dozen lines of code!

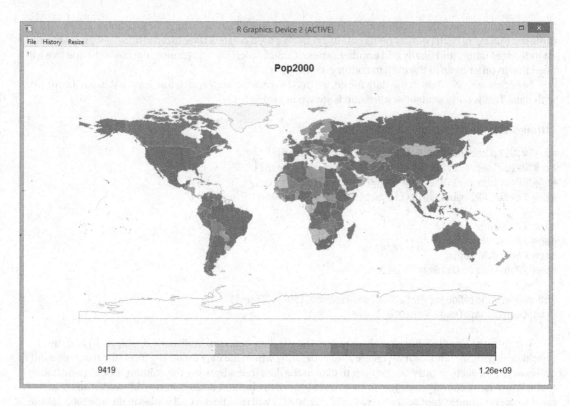

Figure 3-11. Map of 2000 world population

■ **Note** Installing R packages. When you install R on your machine, it installs a minimal set of packages, which provide basic functionality. However, one of the key benefits of R is its huge ecosystem of packages, which offer solutions to virtually any visualization or statistics scenario. R comes with a built-in package manager, which allows you to easily download and install packages on your local machine. For instance, the package rworldmap we are using here is not standard. To install it, you can either call `install.packages("rworldmap")` from the R environment itself, or use the R type provider from F# Interactive using `open RProvider.utils` and `R.install_packages(["rworldmap"])`. This will prompt you for a download site, and then will install the package and its dependencies on your machine, which will then be available to you.

This is a nice map, and a much better way to quickly figure out patterns in our dataset. However, this isn't hugely instructive: What we see here is that there are very few people in Greenland, the Himalayas, and the Sahara Desert. Let's see if we can produce some more-interesting maps. One of the benefits of using a data frame like Deedle, rather than manipulating raw data, is that it makes creating new features pretty easy. As an example, let's consider country population density; that is, how many persons there are living per square kilometer (or mile). With Deedle, this is a breeze, as seen in Listing 3-12 and Figure 3-12.

Listing 3-12. Producing a population density map

```
dataframe?Density <- dataframe?Pop2010 / dataframe?Surface
let map = R.joinCountryData2Map(dataframe,"ISO3","Code")
R.mapCountryData(map,"Density")
```

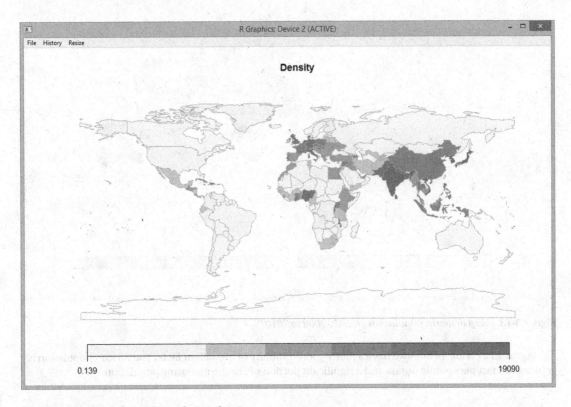

Figure 3-12. *Map of world population density*

We create a new column on the fly called `Density`, defined as a function of two other columns, and simply rebind the map to the updated data frame. This is a much more interesting map, highlighting a few very high-density areas in the world, located in Western Europe, Southeast Asia, and Africa.

Similarly, we can visualize where the world population is growing in a couple of lines, seen in Listing 3-13 and Figure 3-13.

Listing 3-13. Producing a population growth map

```
dataframe?Growth  <- (dataframe?Pop2010 - dataframe?Pop2000) / dataframe?Pop2000
let map = R.joinCountryData2Map(dataframe,"ISO3","Code")
R.mapCountryData(map,"Growth")
```

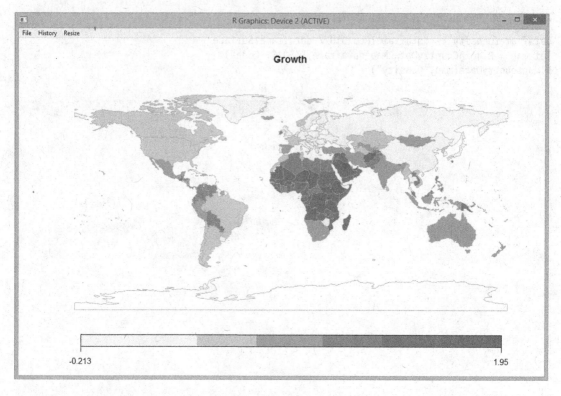

Figure 3-13. *Map of world population growth, 2000 to 2010*

Again, in a couple of lines we have a pretty good summary of the salient facts: The African population is growing at a fast pace, while Russia and a significant portion of Europe are losing population.

So, What Have We Learned?

In this chapter, we saw how type providers, a feature unique to F#, make it possible to seamlessly bring external data or resources into the .NET type system. This is an obvious productivity boost for any data-exploration scenario. Type providers manage a remarkable feat: Getting to the data itself is every bit as easy as with a dynamic language, but working with statically typed data gives the user additional help from the compiler and tools, and prevents silly mistakes (such as property typos or incorrect type casts) that would otherwise be caught only at runtime.

What is perhaps more interesting is that having typed data also provides huge benefits in terms of data discoverability. Data is typically stored in formats that are primarily meant to address computer I/O concerns, not human readability. As a result, coming to grips with a dataset is often an unnecessarily unpleasant experience, at least for humans. Type providers offer a very interesting mechanism, using tools that have been used for decades to help developers navigate and understand the internal organization of large code bases (which are arguably complex data sets), and applying them to "normal" data via IntelliSense. This is a surprisingly powerful mechanism. Being able to discover how pieces of data are connected to each other by typing ",", or having the computer automatically find items that partially match something I typed, is, in my experience, an extremely effective way to dive into a dataset and understand how it is organized.

The other main point in this chapter illustrated how the same mechanism can be used to make all of the resources of R available from within the F# environment. R has its fans and haters, but one aspect that is hard to argue with is the depth of its ecosystem. If you have a statistics problem, chances are that "there's a package for that." R has packages for virtually every statistical problem there is, and is also known for producing beautiful, publication-grade charts and visualizations, and every single one of them is available to you in F#.

The R type provider is a great example of F# as an effective glue language. Using R-specific tools like RStudio may provide a slightly better experience using R than calling it from F# via the type provider. However, picking R as the primary development environment has large implications. R was never built with integration in mind, and running it in production, or talking to other systems, is not something that it is particularly good at. On top of that, R has nothing close to type providers; gone is the ability to explore and load data from everywhere.

By contrast, F# is a language that was built to run critical code in production; it just happens to have pretty decent scripting abilities, too. In that frame, using F# as a primary environment makes a lot of sense. A data scientist can use it to write scripts, using whatever combination of tools they please to prototype a model, along with all the might of the .NET framework; that same script can then very easily be converted to a class or module, which will run with no problem at all in production, at scale.

Finally, we also saw how function composition with the pipe-forward operator made it very easy to create miniature, domain-specific languages. By creating small functions and thinking carefully about how to organize their arguments, we were able to write a couple of lines code that could then be chained together in a flexible manner, while at the same time being very human-readable. There is much more to the topic of DSLs in F# than the simplified examples found here, but this should at least give you an inkling for why the language is a great fit for that!

Going Further

We saw a small sample of type providers in this chapter, but there is one available for virtually any data format that exposes some form of schema. Type providers for XML, Soap, CSV, SQL, JSON, and so forth are an open mechanism: Anyone can write one to target a specific type of data, and the F# community has been busy creating a wide array of type providers. At this point in time, fsharp.data is the largest and best-documented collection of type providers. A few other ones are worth mentioning, in particular the SQL Command type provider (http://fsprojects.github.io/FSharp.Data.SqlClient/) for statically typed access to input parameters and result sets of T-SQL command and the SQL type provider (https://github.com/fsprojects/SQLProvider), which enables the exploration and querying of various SQL implementations.

Beyond data, type providers targeting different languages, in a fashion similar to R, are also being developed; most interesting from a machine-learning perspective, there are ongoing efforts to create Matlab and Python type providers. However, at the time of writing, these haven't reached the same level of maturity as the R type provider.

USEFUL LINKS

- *FSharp.Data* is a well-maintained and -documented collection of open-source F# type providers: `http://fsharp.github.io/FSharp.Data/`

- The World Bank Data website: `http://data.worldbank.org/`

- The R statistical environment: `http://www.r-project.org/`

- The F# R Provider: `http://bluemountaincapital.github.io/FSharpRProvider/`

- Deedle, a .NET dataframe library: `http://bluemountaincapital.github.io/Deedle/`

- Nice tutorial on getting started with the rworldmap package: `http://cran.r-project.org/web/packages/rworldmap/vignettes/rworldmap.pdf`

- Paket, a dependency manager for .NET: `http://fsprojects.github.io/Paket/`

- Fsharp.Data.SqlClient, at `http://fsprojects.github.io/FSharp.Data.SqlClient`, and the SQLProvider, at `http://fsprojects.github.io/SQLProvider`, are two complementary type providers dedicated to working with SQL databases.

CHAPTER 4

■ ■ ■

Of Bikes and Men

Fitting a Regression Model to Data with Gradient Descent

So far, the problems we have tackled have involved classifying items between a limited set of possible categories. While classification has applications in many practical situations, an arguably more common problem is to predict a number. Consider, for instance, the following task: Given the characteristics of a used car (age, miles, engine size, and so forth), how would you go about predicting how much it is going to sell for? This problem doesn't really fit the pattern of classification. What we need here is a model that differs from classification models in at least two aspects:

- What the model predicts are actual numbers, which can take a wide range of values, and can be meaningfully compared.

- We are interested in the functional relationship between features and their predicted values; that is, how a change in the feature impacts the prediction.

In our car example, what we are looking for is a model along these lines:

$$price = \theta_0 + \theta_1 \times age + \theta_2 \times miles$$

Unlike the classification models we saw earlier, the predicted prices are not limited to a fixed set of possible choices; they can take a wide range of values. Furthermore, if you were to plug different values for miles in the model, you could directly observe how a change in the feature impacts the predicted value, and possibly compare that to changes in the age value, to understand how sensitive price is to various features.

This type of model is called a **regression model**, and it has a relatively young history, with significant developments beginning in the nineteenth century. Its origins stem from physics and the need to validate physical models against experimental observations, which lead to the foundation of modern statistics. The methods spread to biology, economics, and other fields, evolving and adapting along the way so as to handle questions specific to each discipline, and are an important part of machine learning today.

In this chapter, our goal is to predict the number of people using a bicycle-sharing service for a given day, given information such as weather conditions or day of the week. We will start with a fairly simple model and progressively build up refinements in order to improve accuracy, introducing important machine-learning techniques along the way. As we advance, we will

- explain how finding a straight line that fits the data well can be stated as finding the line with the lowest overall error;

- introduce gradient descent, a very powerful and general technique to find the minimum of a function, and then put it into action to create our first prediction model;

- explore how linear algebra can help write much shorter models and algorithms, and potentially speed up calculations;

- present a simple approach to easily creating and modifying models, using functions to define features that select what part of the data we want to use to make predictions; and

- refine our predictions further, illustrating how to use more of the data by handling different data types and creating more-complex, nonlinear features.

Getting to Know the Data

In this chapter, we will use another dataset from the University of California–Irvine Machine Learning Repository, the "bike-sharing dataset," which you can find here: `https://archive.ics.uci.edu/ml/datasets/Bike+Sharing+Dataset`.

The dataset is based off the Capital Bikeshare program. In its own words,

> *Capital Bikeshare puts over 2500 bicycles at your fingertips. You can choose any of the over 300 stations across Washington, D.C., Arlington and Alexandria, VA and Montgomery County, MD and return it to any station near your destination. Check out a bike for your trip to work, Metro, run errands, go shopping, or visit friends and family.*

Source: `http://www.capitalbikeshare.com`

The full dataset combines data made publicly available by Capital Bikeshare with other public data sources, like weather and public holidays.

What's in the Dataset?

Before diving into the model-building part, let's take a quick look at what we are dealing with. The dataset itself can be found at `https://archive.ics.uci.edu/ml/machine-learning-databases/00275/`; the zip file Bike-Sharing-Dataset.zip contains three files: day.csv, hour.csv, and readme.txt. The file we will be working on is day.csv, which contains data aggregated by day; hour.csv is the same data, but aggregated on an hour-by-hour level. I will let you take a wild guess at what readme.txt contains!

As usual, let's start by creating an F# library project with a script file, and then add our data file, day.csv, to the project. If you click on the file in Visual Studio, you will see the contents of our data, as in Figure 4-1.

```
1  instant,dteday,season,yr,mnth,holiday,weekday,workingday,weathersit,temp,atemp,hum,windspeed,casual,registered,cnt
2  1,2011-01-01,1,0,1,0,6,0,2,0.344167,0.363625,0.805833,0.160446,331,654,985
3  2,2011-01-02,1,0,1,0,0,0,2,0.363478,0.353739,0.696087,0.248539,131,670,801
4  3,2011-01-03,1,0,1,0,1,1,1,0.196364,0.189405,0.437273,0.248309,120,1229,1349
5  4,2011-01-04,1,0,1,0,2,1,1,0.2,0.212122,0.590435,0.160296,108,1454,1562
6  5,2011-01-05,1,0,1,0,3,1,1,0.226957,0.22927,0.436957,0.1869,82,1518,1600
7  6,2011-01-06,1,0,1,0,4,1,1,0.204348,0.233209,0.518261,0.0895652,88,1518,1606
8  7,2011-01-07,1,0,1,0,5,1,2,0.196522,0.208839,0.498696,0.168726,148,1362,1510
9  8,2011-01-08,1,0,1,0,6,0,2,0.165,0.162254,0.535833,0.266804,68,891,959
10 9,2011-01-09,1,0,1,0,0,0,1,0.138333,0.116175,0.434167,0.36195,54,768,822
```

Figure 4-1. *Contents of the day.csv file*

The file follows the usual .csv format, with a first row containing headers describing column names, followed by 731 rows of observations, one for each day. So what do we have in here? If you dig into the readme.txt file, you will find the following definitions for each column:

- instant: record index *(indicates the number of days elapsed since the first observation of the dataset)*

- dteday: date

- season: season (1:spring, 2:summer, 3:fall, 4:winter)

- yr: year (0: 2011, 1:2012)

- mnth: month (1 to 12)

- holiday: whether day is holiday or not (extracted from `http://dchr.dc.gov/page/holiday-schedule`)

- weekday: day of the week

- workingday: if day is neither weekend nor holiday is 1, otherwise is 0.

- weathersit:

  - 1: Clear, Few clouds, Partly cloudy, Partly cloudy

  - 2: Mist + Cloudy, Mist + Broken clouds, Mist + Few clouds, Mist

  - 3: Light Snow, Light Rain + Thunderstorm + Scattered clouds, Light Rain + Scattered clouds

  - 4: Heavy Rain + Ice Pellets + Thunderstorm + Mist, Snow + Fog

- temp: Normalized temperature in Celsius. The values are divided to 41 (max)

- atemp: Normalized feeling temperature in Celsius. The values are divided to 50 (max)

- hum: Normalized humidity. The values are divided to 100 (max)

- windspeed: Normalized wind speed. The values are divided to 67 (max)

- casual: count of casual users

- registered: count of registered users

- cnt: count of total rental bikes including both casual and registered

We have a couple of different features available to us: time/calendar information, whether it was a regular workday or a "special" one, multiple measurements pertaining to the weather, and finally the count of people who rented a bicycle that day, broken down into registered and casual users.

Our focus here will be on creating a model to predict cnt, the count of people who rented a bicycle on a particular day, using the measurements we have available for that day (excluding, of course, casual and registered, because there wouldn't be much fun in that, as by definition casual + register = cnt). Note that our data is not homogeneous: While some of the features are numeric— that is, actual numbers (for instance, temp, the temperature)—quite a few of them are categorical—that is, each number encodes a state (for instance, weathersit or workingday).

Inspecting the Data with FSharp.Charting

As usual, let's start by working in the script file and take a closer look at the data, loading it in memory using the CSV type provider from fsharp.Data, which we first install from NuGet:

```
#I @"packages\"
#r @"FSharp.Data.2.2.1\lib\net40\FSharp.Data.dll"

open FSharp.Data

type Data = CsvProvider<"day.csv">
let dataset = Data.Load("day.csv")
let data = dataset.Rows
```

Unlike some of the problems we looked at previously, this dataset has a fairly obvious set of features to start with. In this case, it might be worth simply inspecting the data manually to see if we can spot any patterns. Let's start by plotting bicycle usage over time. To do this, we'll use another F# library, fsharp. Charting, which offers a collection of classic charts. Let's install the library with Nuget and create our first chart, plotting the total usage as a line:

```
#load @"FSharp.Charting.0.90.10\FSharp.Charting.fsx"
open FSharp.Charting

let all = Chart.Line [ for obs in data -> obs.Cnt ]
```

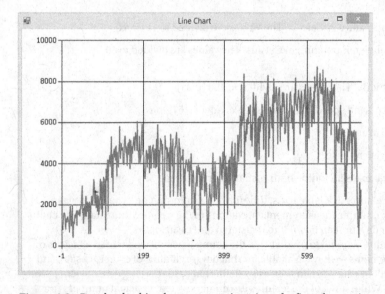

Figure 4-2. *Day-by-day bicycle usage over time since the first observation*

■ **Tip**   FSharp.Charting can be used as a regular library, but also comes with utilities that make it friendly to use from the interactive scripting environment. In particular, creating a chart, as in Chart.Line [...], will automatically display it as well, without having to call .ShowChart(). To use the "interactive mode," simply load fsharp.Charting.fsx instead of opening the dll fsharp.Charting.

A few things immediately stand out. First, the data is pretty irregular—there are large fluctuations on a day-to-day basis. For that matter, there are also fluctuations on a larger scale: Usage seems to go through high and low phases over time. Finally, it also seems like, overall, there is a trend upward.

Spotting Trends with Moving Averages

Can we confirm our intuition that there is a bit of a trend going on? One way to do this is by using what is called a moving average. In order to reduce the day-to-day noise in the data, we can average out observations over windows of a certain length, and then plot the resulting curve so as to isolate deeper trends from short-term fluctuations. The F# Seq module contains a handy function, Seq.windowed, that will take a sequence and transform it into a new sequence that contains chunks of consecutive observations:

```
let windowedExample =
    [ 1 .. 10 ]
    |> Seq.windowed 3
    |> Seq.toList
```

This chunks the series 1 .. 10 into blocks of three consecutive values: [[|1; 2; 3|]; [|2; 3; 4|]; [|3; 4; 5|]; [|4; 5; 6|]; [|5; 6; 7|]; [|6; 7; 8|]; [|7; 8; 9|]; [|8; 9; 10|]]. From there, generating the moving average is only a matter of computing the average of each of the chunks:

```
let ma n (series:float seq) =
    series
    |> Seq.windowed n
    |> Seq.map (fun xs -> xs |> Seq.average)
    |> Seq.toList
```

Let's plot the original series overlaid with the moving averages over seven days and thirty days:

```
Chart.Combine [
    Chart.Line count
    Chart.Line (ma 7 count)
    Chart.Line (ma 30 count) ]
```

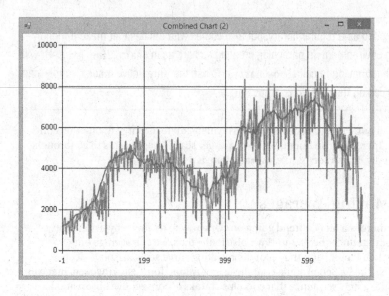

Figure 4-3. *Seven- and thirty-days moving averages*

While not conclusive by itself, the moving averages do hint at a longer trend, and clearly show a certain regularity in the fluctuations over the year, including seasonal spikes.

Fitting a Model to the Data

Our objective going forward will be to build a model that predicts bicycle usage based on the information we have available in the dataset. Before diving in further, let's quantify this a bit and establish a baseline for our task. How can we define what constitutes a good or bad result? The most naïve model we could create is to always predict the same number, the average. In that case, what would our typical error be?

```
let baseline =
    let avg = data |> Seq.averageBy (fun x -> float x.Cnt)
    data |> Seq.averageBy (fun x -> abs (float x.Cnt - avg))
```

Using this naïve approach, on average our prediction would be off by 1581.79 from the correct value—this is the number to beat. Let's see if we can do better.

Defining a Basic Straight-Line Model

What's the simplest model that could possibly work? The average usage over time seems to be increasing, so we could start by trying to improve our naïve model by incorporating a trend, along these lines:

$$usage(t) = constant + t \times increaseRate$$

In other words, we are representing usage as a straight line, starting with an initial value and increasing linearly over time. It's probably not the best we can do—for instance, this will not account for the seasonal effects we spotted—but it should hopefully perform better than our naïve "predict the average" model.

Any timescale for t would do, but as it happens, the dataset observations all contain a field instant, the number of days elapsed since the first observation, which serves as the epoch. In a slightly more formal way, we can specify a prediction model in the following fashion:

$$f_\theta(obs) = \theta_0 + \theta_1 \times obs.Instant$$

In other words, we can define a whole class of prediction models, called **linear regression models**, that all follow the same general pattern. We are trying to predict a value using one or more input variables (in this case, obs.Instant). Each input variable gets its own "generic" multiplier, Theta, identified by index—the **regression coefficient**. Predictions are computed by multiplying each variable by its coefficient and adding them together, forming what is called a **linear combination**.

Later on, we will look into using more than one input variable. For the moment, we'll stick to our single variable, obs.Instant. If we set the values of Theta0 and Theta1 (or, in short, Theta, to denote the combination of values Theta0 and Theta1), we get a specific prediction model. This directly translates into F#:

```
type Obs = Data.Row

let model (theta0, theta1) (obs:Obs) =
    theta0 + theta1 * (float obs.Instant)
```

Let's illustrate on two arbitrary cases, with a model, model0, where Theta0 is set to the average of the series, and another model, model1, where we arbitrarily set Theta0 to 6000.0, and Theta1 to -4.5. We can now plot the predictions of these two models against the actual data:

```
let model0 = model (4504., 0.)
let model1 = model (6000., -4.5)

Chart.Combine [
    Chart.Line count
    Chart.Line [ for obs in data -> model0 obs ]
    Chart.Line [ for obs in data -> model1 obs ] ]
```

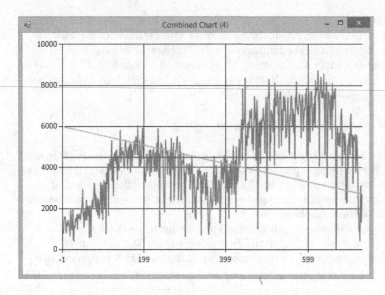

Figure 4-4. Visualizing two demo linear regression models

Obviously, neither of these models is a great fit for the data. On the bright side, we have a general structure with which to define a wide range of prediction models. However, we have a new problem on our hands: How can we go about picking "good" values for Theta?

Finding the Lowest-Cost Model

The first problem here is to define more clearly what our goal is. In an informal way, what we are looking for is the line that fits the data best. Stated a bit differently, what we want is a curve of predicted values that gives us the smallest possible error when compared to the actual observed values—or, equivalently, the curve that has the smallest distance to the real data. We have seen a similar approach in Chapter 1! We can simply adapt the distance function; instead of computing the distance between two images pixel by pixel, we will compute the Euclidean distance between our predicted curve and the actual one, comparing the true value and the forecasted one for each data point.

You might ask why I chose to pick the Euclidean distance, rather than something else. After all, we started with the Manhattan distance in Chapter 1 because it was easy to compute. There are a couple of reasons for this choice. The first one is driven by modelling considerations. The Euclidean distance penalizes errors by squaring differences; as a result, larger errors will be penalized much more heavily than smaller ones, which is a good thing. When trying to minimize the distance, we will then focus primarily on avoiding large errors, and not so much on small ones. The second reason is technical: It makes the math considerably simpler.

As an example, let's compute the costs of our two models:

```
type Model = Obs -> float

let cost (data:Obs seq) (m:Model) =
    data
    |> Seq.sumBy (fun x -> pown (float x.Cnt - m x) 2)
    |> sqrt
```

```
let overallCost = cost data
overallCost model0 |> printfn "Cost model0: %.0f"
overallCost model1 |> printfn "Cost model1: %.0f"
```

First, we create a type Model, which captures what all our models do— namely, convert an observation Obs into a float, the predicted value for Cnt, the number of users. Computing the cost over a particular dataset is then as simple as summing up the square difference between each Obs and the corresponding predicted value, and taking the square root. We can then use partial application to create an overallCost function that will compute the cost over the entire dataset, and then test it out on our two models, which produces the following result:

```
>
Cost model0: 52341
Cost model1: 71453
```

In this case, model0 has a much lower cost that model1, which indicates that it fits the data better, and is consistent with Figure 4-4. At this point, we can restate our problem: What we are trying to achieve is to find a value for Theta such that the cost function is minimized. Great! Now that we know what we want to do, let's do it!

Finding the Minimum of a Function with Gradient Descent

The approach we will be using is called **gradient descent**. The idea is to start with a value of Theta, observe the prediction error, and gradually adjust Theta to progressively reduce the error. In order to do that, what we need is a way to take our current model and move Theta0 and Theta1 in a direction that will decrease the error.

Before diving into our actual problem, we'll start with a small calculus refresher. Our goal here is to explain a bit of the mechanics of gradient descent. If you are not very comfortable (or interested) in calculus, don't worry about it—you'll still be able to apply gradient descent. However, it's interesting to understand how it works. It's a fairly general technique that is applicable in situations where you want to find the maximum value for a function. In particular, it is widely used in machine learning to identify the best parameters that fit a dataset, which is what we will do here.

Let's begin with a simple example:

$$y = f(x), \text{with } f(x) = 3 \times x - 7$$

The function f describes a straight line, and its derivative is:

$$f'(x) = 3$$

What does this number represent? The derivative corresponds to the slope of f around a value x, or, stated differently, how much increase in y we should expect if we increased x "a little" from its current value. This particular example is not extremely interesting: Regardless of where we are on the straight line, the slope is constant. This also implies that f doesn't have a minimum value: For any value x, we can decrease f(x) by decreasing x. However, let's consider a more interesting example:

$$y = g(x), \text{with } g(x) = 2 \times x^2 - 8 \times x + 1$$

The function g is a polynomial of degree 2, and its derivative is:

$$g'(x) = 4 \times x - 8 = 4 \times (x - 2)$$

This is much more interesting. In this case, the slope changes for every value of x. Furthermore, it changes sign: It is negative for x < 2, positive for x > 2, and zero at x = 2. What this means is that for x > 2, the slope is oriented upward: If we decrease x "a bit," we will go down the slope, and g(x) should decrease. Conversely, for values of x below 2, the derivative is negative, and small increases of x will follow the slope downward and decrease g.

As an illustration, Figure 4-5 illustrates g and its derivative at x = 3. g'(3) = 4: In the neighborhood of x = 3, increasing x a bit would result in a four-fold increase in y.

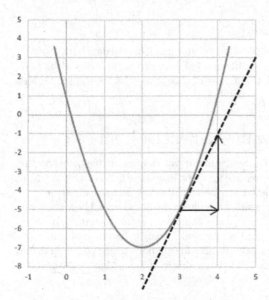

Figure 4-5. *Using the derivative to find the slope of a curve*

How about x = 2? For that value, the slope is 0, which means we reached a flat area, so to speak: There is nowhere obvious to go. A point where the derivative is 0 is known as an **extremum**, and can be one of two things: a minimum or a maximum.

So, why is this interesting? Because we can use this to devise a general strategy to find the minimum value of a function. Starting from an arbitrary value x, we can measure the derivative (or gradient) and take small steps toward the direction of descent:

$$x_{k+1} = x_k - \alpha \times g'(x_k)$$

The value alpha is known as the **learning rate**. The slope is only correct close to x, and alpha allows us to tune how large of a step we want to take when updating x. Note also how the change depends on g'. When the slope is steep, we'll make larger changes in x; when g' is small, and we are presumably close to a mimimum, we will make smaller adjustments. Using that approach, if everything works according to plan, we can generate a series of values x0, x1, and so forth, each of which produces a lower value for g. This is the gradient-descent algorithm.

Using Gradient Descent to Fit a Curve

Let's apply this idea to the problem at hand. We are going to twist our problem a bit here: Instead of focusing on the value our model predicts, we will consider the error, or cost function, which is the value we are trying to reduce. And, in another twist, instead of considering x, our observation, as the input parameter, we will now turn the tables and consider Theta as our parameter. In that frame, the cost function, which measures the cost of a model using parameters Theta, is:

$$cost(\theta_0, \theta_1) = (obs.Cnt - (\theta_0 + \theta_1 \times obs.Instant))^2$$

In other words, this function measures the error we would get for an observation obs, if we were to use parameters Theta0 and Theta1 for our model. By how much would the error change if we were to increase Theta1 by a little? This is what the derivative of the cost, with respect to Theta1, will give us, so let's compute that. First, let's make things explicit and rewrite the cost as a function of Theta1, expanding it somewhat and reorganizing the terms to look like a * Theta12 + b * Theta1 + c:

$$cost(\theta_1) = \theta_1^2 \times obs.Instant^2 - \theta_1 \times (2 \times obs.Instant \times (obs.Cnt - \theta_0)) + (obs.Cnt - \theta_0)^2$$

This is a simple polynomial, and, remembering that the derivative of a * x2 is 2 * a * x, and that of b * x is b, we get the derivative of the cost, which is:

$$\frac{\partial cost}{\partial \theta_1} = 2 \times obs.Instant^2 \times \theta_1 - 2 \times obs.Instant \times (obs.Cnt - \theta_0)$$

Great! This was a lot of work, so let's see if this works. Moving Theta1 by "a little bit" following the derivative should reduce the prediction error. Let's make "a little bit" a parameter alpha, and now we have an update procedure to iteratively modify Theta1, reducing the error on the observation at each step:

$$\theta_1 \leftarrow \theta_1 - 2\alpha \times obs.Instant \times (\theta_0 + \theta_1 \times obs.Instant - obs.Cnt)$$

Note that this formula has a relatively straightforward interpretation, helping us clarify what the algorithm does. The last term in the equation is exactly the error term. Assuming obs.inst is positive, if the forecasted value is lower than obs.cnt—the actual value we are trying to predict—the model is undershooting, and the algorithm will increase the value of Theta1 by a bit, which will move us in the correct direction. Conversely, if the opposite is true, the value of Theta1 will be reduced. Note also that the correction will be more important for larger values of obs.inst.

Finally, note also that while this approach will move Theta1 in the correct direction, depending on the value of alpha we might end up overcompensating. As we will see shortly, alpha is a parameter that needs to be manually tuned. If alpha is small enough, the algorithm will progress nicely towards the optimal value of Theta1. However, smaller values also mean a slower correction, which could mean waiting for a long time for the procedure to produce a good value for Theta1.

A More General Model Formulation

Before applying this method to the problem at hand, and while the math is still fresh in our minds, let's make two remarks that will allow us to make our algorithm more general. Imagine for a minute that instead of trying to fit a simple line like we have been, we had N features X1, X2, ... XN, and were trying to fit a prediction model of the form

$$Y = \theta_0 + \theta_1 X_1 + \theta_2 X_2 + \ldots + \theta_N X_N$$

This is exactly the same type of model as the one we are dealing with, just with more features. Our simple straight-line model simply happens to have N = 1. A first convenient trick is to introduce a "dummy" feature into our model, X0, and set X0 = 1 for every single observation. The reason this is convenient is that it now allows us to write the prediction model in a consistent fashion for all Thetas, with no special treatment for the constant term Theta0:

$$Y = \theta_0 X_0 + \theta_1 X_1 + \theta_2 X_2 + \ldots + \theta_N X_N$$

As a result, you could now rewrite the cost function, and for any values of Theta, it will look like this:

$$cost(\theta_k) = \left(Y - \left(\theta_0 X_0 + \theta_1 X_1 + \theta_2 X_2 + \ldots + \theta_N X_N\right)\right)^2$$

The beauty here is that if you now tried to figure out how to update Thetak, for any of the ks between 0 and N, you would end up with the following formula after performing the derivation and replicating the steps we did above:

$$\theta_k \leftarrow \theta_k - 2\alpha \times X_k \times \left(\theta_0 X_0 + \theta_1 X_1 + \theta_2 X_2 + \ldots + \theta_N X_N\right)$$

This is pretty awesome. Using this approach, we now have an algorithm that we can use to simultaneously update all the parameters Theta (including Theta0, which applies to the constant term), for any number of features.

Let's illustrate how we could use this idea on our model—a real example might help make this less abstract. We could, for instance, try to predict the number of users, using instant and temperature, which would play the role of X1 and X2. In that case, the regression model would look like this:

$$obs.Cnt = \theta_0 \times 1 + \theta_1 \times obs.Instant + \theta_2 \times obs.Temp$$

If we were trying to update the value Theta2 to reduce the prediction error (the cost), applying our procedure would yield the following update rule:

$$\theta_2 \leftarrow \theta_2 - 2\alpha \times obs.Temp \times \left(\theta_0 \times 1 + \theta_1 \times obs.Instant + \theta_2 \times obs.Temp\right)$$

Furthermore, the same rule can now be applied to updating Theta0 and Theta1; the only modification required is to substitute the right Thetak and Xk in the formula.

Implementing Gradient Descent

Now that we have a big hammer with gradient descent, let's go back to our bicycle problem and use our algorithm to finally fit that straight line through our dataset. We will start with a direct application of our update method and then analyze the results to see how we can improve the approach.

Stochastic Gradient Descent

The first approach we could take is to simply iterate over the observations and perform a small adjustment at each step. Let's try that. First, we need a function that, given an observation and a value for Theta, will update Theta, at a learning-rate alpha:

```
let update alpha (theta0, theta1) (obs:Obs) =
    let y = float obs.Cnt
    let x = float obs.Instant
    let theta0' = theta0 - 2. * alpha * 1. * (theta0 + theta1 * x - y)
    let theta1' = theta1 - 2. * alpha * x * (theta0 + theta1 * x - y)
    theta0', theta1'
```

This is a straightforward implementation of the formula we derived earlier. We compute the updated values for Theta and return it as a tuple. Let's confirm with an example that this approach works, using, for instance, the hundredth observation, and starting with an initial value of (0.0, 0.0) for Theta:

```
let obs100 = data |> Seq.nth 100
let testUpdate = update 0.00001 (0.,0.) obs100
cost [obs100] (model (0.,0.))
cost [obs100] (model testUpdate)
```

It looks like everything is working: After we apply the update, the new prediction for that specific observation is improved, with a smaller error. All we need to do at this point is to apply this to the entire dataset, progressively updating Theta on each observation, starting from the value of Theta we got from the previous step:

```
let stochastic rate (theta0,theta1) =
    data
    |> Seq.fold (fun (t0,t1) obs ->
        printfn "%.4f,%.4f" t0 t1
        update rate (t0,t1) obs) (theta0,theta1)
```

We are using Seq.fold here, which is equivalent to the C# Enumerable.Aggregate method in LINQ. A fold simply takes an initial value and a sequence of values and updates an accumulator by applying the same function to every element of the sequence. A simple example might help illustrate the idea better:

```
let data = [0;1;2;3;4]
let sum = data |> Seq.fold (fun total x -> total + x) 0
```

The fold keeps track of a total value, which is initially 0, and adds each value x to the total until there is nothing left in the sequence—at which point, the total value is returned.

In our case, we follow the same pattern: We initialize our accumulator with two values—theta0 and theta1—and update them for every observation in our dataset until there are no observations left, and then return the final value of Theta.

We are nearly done. The only remaining problem is to calibrate the learning-rate alpha, taking a value that is sufficiently small to avoid over adjusting, and large enough that our algorithm doesn't progress too slowly. That's easy enough to do, as we can just test out various values of Alpha (0.1, 0.01, 0.001...) and compare the quality of the results after one pass of updates over the dataset, starting with Theta = (0.0, 0.0):

```
let tune_rate =
    [ for r in 1 .. 20 ->
        (pown 0.1 r), stochastic (pown 0.1 r) (0.,0.) |> model |> overallCost ]
```

If you print out the cost for each value of the learning-rate alpha, this is what you will get:

```
Alpha                       Cost
0.1                       : NaN
0.01                      : NaN
0.001                     : NaN
0.000,1                   : NaN
0.000,01                  : Infinity
0.000,001                 : 94,007
0.000,000,1               : 93,189
0.000,000,01              : 59,367
0.000,000,001             : 107,780
0.000,000,000,1           : 129,677
0.000,000,000,01          : 132,263
0.000,000,000,001         : 132,526
0.000,000,000,000,1       : 132,552
0.000,000,000,000,01      : 132,555
0.000,000,000,000,001     : 132,555
```

The results are fairly typical. For larger values of alpha, the adjustments are overly aggressive, to such an extent that the values of Theta vary wildly and never settle on anything stable. Conversely, for smaller values, adjustments are so small that they barely make a dent in improving the fit. The most effective value of alpha looks to be 1e-8, or 0.000,000,01, and gives us a cost of around 59,367, for a value of Theta of about (0.03, 8.21); if we plot the resulting line, this is what we get:

```
let rate = pown 0.1 8
let model2 = model (stochastic rate (0.0,0.0))

Chart.Combine [
    Chart.Line count
    Chart.Line [ for obs in data -> model2 obs ] ]
```

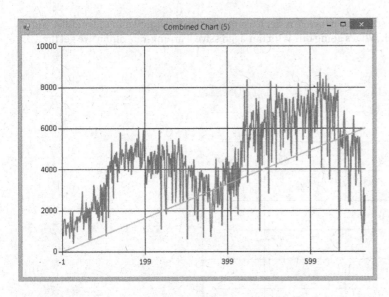

Figure 4-6. Best-fit curve using stochastic gradient descent

■ **Note**   We found a reasonably effective value for alpha, but there is another subtle issue here. The slope for our curve looks pretty good, but its starting value, Theta0, looks too low. The problem is that our variables are on very different scales: The constant is 1, but instant ranges from 0 to about 700. As a result, adjustments are driven mainly by the feature with larger amplitude, Theta1. In order to get a faster adjustment for Theta0, we would need to prepare the dataset so that all inputs are on a comparable scale, a process known as rescaling. We will ignore that issue for now, but will discuss feature scaling in more detail in Chapter 5.

Analyzing Model Improvements

Now what? The next step would be to keep repeating the procedure, making multiple passes over the dataset, until we observe no significant improvement. However, rather than doing this, let's look a bit at the behavior of the algorithm and, specifically, at how the prediction error evolves as we go. The details of the code are not overly important—what we are doing here is taking a highly aggressive value of alpha (10 times higher than the "sweet spot" value we identified earlier), and plotting the overall error after each adjustment is performed:

```
let hiRate = 10.0 * rate
let error_eval =
    data
    |> Seq.scan (fun (t0,t1) obs -> update hiRate (t0,t1) obs) (0.0,0.0)
    |> Seq.map (model >> overallCost)
    |> Chart.Line
```

This is intriguing. After a slow start, the error starts decreasing steadily, slows down in the middle, and begins climbing back up in the end. What's going on? With our aggressive learning-rate alpha, we get the chart in Figure 4-7.

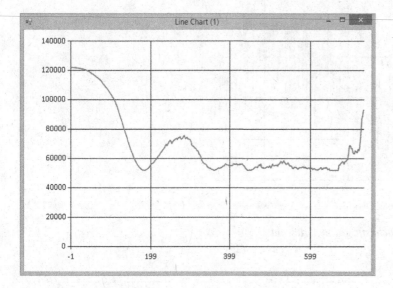

Figure 4-7. *Step-by-step error using stochastic gradient descent*

What is happening is that, because we have a seasonal effect at play in our dataset (presumably, using a bicycle to go to work in the middle of the winter is a much less appealing proposition than during spring), multiple consecutive observations display the same tendency, either above or below the ideal line. As a result, the update procedure, which looks at only one observation at a time, makes a series of corrections that are all tilted toward the same direction (because the errors are all leaning the same direction) and begins drifting away, temporarily increasing the error on the overall model.

This has a couple of implications. First, beyond gradient descent, we need to be very careful if we use cross-validation to evaluate the quality of our work. If we were to, say, set the last 200 observations as our validation sample, we would get a very biased estimate of our prediction error, because over that specific time span, the curve follows a downward trend that is (presumably) only temporary, and certainly is not representative of the overall shape of the data.

This indicates a potential limitation in our stochastic-descent approach. In a very informal way, what we are trying to achieve is a consensus estimate, but our process essentially probes every observation one after the other and follows the direction indicated by the latest observation. This might cause some unnecessary fluctuations when, for instance, we encounter a highly atypical observation, or a succession of them. To be fair, this can be mitigated to an extent—by picking observations in a random order instead of sequentially (which will limit the risk of successive observations presenting a similar bias), and by progressively reducing the rate alpha (which will reduce the weight given to any individual observation and slow down the update process)—but even then, the fact remains that this approach will potentially fluctuate.

One way to address this issue is to avoid relying on individual observations, and instead perform an update based on the entire dataset. This is the basis for batch gradient descent, which we will see in action next. At the same time, stochastic gradient descent should not be discarded altogether. It is reasonably easy to implement and is applicable to a wide range of situations. More interesting, it allows what is known as "online learning." The algorithm doesn't require the entire dataset upfront to learn; if you were to obtain new data over time, your model could simply be updated using only your current model and the latest observation that arrived.

Batch Gradient Descent

So how could we go about adapting our model to perform updates based on the entire dataset, instead of based on individual observations? As it turns out, this is reasonably straightforward to do. In the stochastic descent approach, our goal was to minimize the error on a single observation, defined by the cost function:

$$cost\left(\theta_0,\theta_1\right)=\left(obs.Cnt-\left(\theta_0+\theta_1\times obs.Instant\right)\right)^2$$

Instead of a single observation, we might as well focus on the average error over the entire dataset, which is simply the average of all individual errors. The resulting cost function looks like this, with every observation indexed from 1 to N:

$$cost\left(\theta_0,\theta_1\right)=\frac{1}{N}\left[\left(obs_1.Cnt-\left(\theta_0+\theta_1\times obs_1.Instant\right)\right)^2+...+\left(obs_N.Cnt-\left(\theta_0+\theta_1\times obs_N.Instant\right)\right)^2\right]$$

Following the same idea as before, we need to compute the derivative of the cost with respect to its arguments Theta0 and Theta1. This is actually pretty easy, if you remember that the derivative of f(x) + g(x) is the sum of their individual derivatives; the derivative of the aggregate error is the sum of the derivatives on each of the individual observations. The update of Theta1 simply becomes the following:

$$\theta_1 \leftarrow \theta_1 - 2\alpha \times \frac{1}{N} \times \left[\begin{array}{l} obs_1.Instant \times \left(\theta_0+\theta_1\times obs_1.Instant-obs_1.Cnt\right) \\ +...+obs_N.Instant \times \left(\theta_0+\theta_1\times obs_N.Instant-obs_N.Cnt\right)\end{array}\right]$$

One way to interpret this function is that instead of updating based on individual observation errors, the algorithm will now compute the adjustment that would be performed on every one of them, and then take the average correction. This can easily be extended to all Thetas in a fashion similar to what we did for stochastic descent. Because we like to save trees, we won't go through every step this time, and invoke the classic "we'll leave it as an exercise for the reader to work out the details," skipping directly to one possible implementation of the update algorithm:

```
let batchUpdate rate (theta0, theta1) (data:Obs seq) =
    let updates =
        data
        |> Seq.map (update rate (theta0, theta1))
    let theta0' = updates |> Seq.averageBy fst
    let theta1' = updates |> Seq.averageBy snd
    theta0', theta1'
```

What we are doing here is taking each observation, computing the adjustment we would make for Theta based on that observation alone, and then taking the average of all adjustments. We can then repeat the update procedure, progressively refining our estimation for Theta, stopping after a certain number of iterations, or possibly when the search has stabilized and the values for Theta don't change much from one iteration to the next:

```
let batch rate iters =
    let rec search (t0,t1) i =
        if i = 0 then (t0,t1)
        else
            search (batchUpdate rate (t0,t1) data) (i-1)
    search (0.0,0.0) iters
```

We just have to find a suitable value for the learning-rate alpha, following the same steps as before. For a value of Alpha = 0.000,001, if we plot the error as a function of iterations, we get a nice and smooth curve, which shows a regular decrease of the error without any bumps. See the following:

```
let batched_error rate =
    Seq.unfold (fun (t0,t1) ->
        let (t0',t1') = batchUpdate rate (t0,t1) data
        let err = model (t0,t1) |> overallCost
        Some(err, (t0',t1'))) (0.0,0.0)
    |> Seq.take 100
    |> Seq.toList
    |> Chart.Line

batched_error 0.000001
```

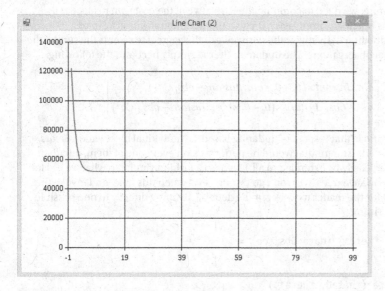

Figure 4-8. *Step-by-step error using batch gradient descent*

This is much better. On one hand, we are now using the entire dataset at once, which in our case is not an issue, but could be problematic if it were much larger. On the other hand, our procedure now converges steadily toward the optimal value without any bump along the way: The longer you wait, the better the estimate. The nice thing here is that the same approach is applicable to situations that extend beyond fitting a straight line through data. Essentially, as long as your cost function can be differentiated and is convex, the same general approach can be taken.

However, there are still minor drawbacks to our approach. First, there is the annoyance of having to manually tune the learning-rate alpha—it would be nice if that wasn't required. Then, if you run the algorithm for a large number of iterations, you will notice that the cost keeps decreasing, and the parameter Theta0 increasing, and it ends up stabilizing only after a very long time. This is due to the issue we mentioned earlier: Theta0 and Theta1 are on very different scales, and given the slow learning rate, it takes a fairly large number of iterations for the algorithm to reach the "correct" value. In the next section, we will see how, for the specific problem at hand (linear regression without any regularization penalty terms), we can use a bit of linear algebra to make our lives simpler, and our algorithm much, much faster.

Linear Algebra to the Rescue

So far, the direction we have followed has been to stick to our domain, representing the dataset as a collection of observations with named properties, applying transformations using maps and folds that were specific to the domain at hand. However, if you think about it, once we start applying our update procedure, the specifics of the domain do not matter anymore. It wouldn't make a difference if we were trying to predict the price of a car as a function of its engine size and mileage (for instance), instead of bicycle usage as a function of wind speed. In the end, in both cases we'll end up reducing observations into rows of doubles and using them to try to predict another double.

In that frame, rather than focusing on the specifics of the domain, which do not matter at that point, it would make sense to focus on the structure of the data, transform the domain into a common structure, and apply the same general algorithm to solve problems that share the same structure. This is where algebra comes in handy: It provides us with a well-established language with which to describe rows of numbers, and methods by which to perform various operations on them.

LINEAR ALGEBRA REFRESHER

The two base elements of linear algebra are vectors and matrices. A vector of size n is simply a collection of n elements, indexed from 1 to n, such as:

$$x = \begin{bmatrix} 1.0 & 5.0 & -2.0 \end{bmatrix} = \begin{bmatrix} x_1 & x_2 & x_3 \end{bmatrix}$$

A matrix is described by its dimension (or size), m x n, where m refers to its rows and n to its columns. As an example, M is a 3 × 2 matrix:

$$M = \begin{bmatrix} x_{1,1} & x_{2,1} \\ x_{2,1} & x_{2,2} \\ x_{3,1} & x_{3,2} \end{bmatrix}$$

As a loose analogy, we could describe vectors and matrices as the mathematical equivalent of arrays and 2D arrays.

Vectors can be represented as row vectors or column vectors; this distinction is primarily important when working with matrices. A matrix can be seen as a collection of either row vectors or column vectors, and most operations on vectors can be seen as special cases of matrix operations.

The four core operations we need are addition, scalar multiplication, transposition, and multiplication. Adding matrices (or vectors) simply requires adding elements by index, and it requires the two matrices to be of identical sizes:

$$\begin{bmatrix} 1 & 2 \\ 3 & 4 \end{bmatrix} + \begin{bmatrix} 5 & 6 \\ 7 & 8 \end{bmatrix} = \begin{bmatrix} 6 & 8 \\ 10 & 12 \end{bmatrix}$$

Scalar multiplication describes multiplying a matrix (or vector) by a single number, the scalar; each element is multiplied by the scalar:

$$2 \times \begin{bmatrix} 1 & 2 \\ 3 & 4 \end{bmatrix} = \begin{bmatrix} 2 & 4 \\ 6 & 8 \end{bmatrix}$$

Matrix transposition, denoted by a T, consists of reorienting a matrix so that rows become columns, and vice-versa:

$$\begin{bmatrix} 1 & 2 \\ 3 & 4 \\ 5 & 6 \end{bmatrix}^{T} = \begin{bmatrix} 1 & 3 & 5 \\ 2 & 4 & 6 \end{bmatrix}$$

Finally, matrix multiplication is computed as the dot product (or inner product) of every row vector of the first matrix by every column vector of the second one. The dot product of two vectors is a single number, computed as the sum of the product of each of their entries:

$$\begin{bmatrix} 1 & 3 & -5 \end{bmatrix} \cdot \begin{bmatrix} 4 & -2 & -1 \end{bmatrix} = 1 \times 4 + 3 \times (-2) + (-5) \times (-1) = 3$$

When applied to multiplying matrices, this is what we get:

$$\begin{bmatrix} row_1 \\ \dots \\ row_m \end{bmatrix} \times \begin{bmatrix} col_1 & \dots & col_n \end{bmatrix} = \begin{bmatrix} row_1 \cdot col_1 & & row_1 \cdot col_n \\ \dots & \dots & \dots \\ row_m \cdot col_1 & & row_m \cdot col_n \end{bmatrix}$$

Note that in order to be properly defined, this method requires the first matrix to have the same number of columns as the number of rows in the second one.

Honey, I Shrunk the Formula!

Let's see how we could rephrase our problem in terms of algebra. Earlier on, we defined our prediction model like this:

$$Y = \theta_0 X_0 + \theta_1 X_1 + \theta_2 X_2 + \dots + \theta_N X_N$$

If we define Y as obs.cnt, and Theta and X as two vectors, with

$$\theta = \begin{bmatrix} \theta_0; \theta_1; \theta_2; \dots \theta_N \end{bmatrix}$$

$$X = \begin{bmatrix} X_0; X_1; X_2; \dots X_N \end{bmatrix}$$

...then our prediction model can be restated, in a much more compact form, as the product of the two vectors:

$$Y = \theta \times X$$

Similarly, the cost function we were trying to minimize in the batch gradient-descent algorithm is the sum of the squared errors on each observation, averaged out over N observations:

$$cost(\theta_0, \theta_1) = \frac{1}{N} \times \left[\left(obs_1.Cnt - (\theta_0 + \theta_1 \times obs_1.Instant) \right)^2 + \ldots + \left(obs_N.Cnt - (\theta_0 + \theta_1 \times obs_N.Instant) \right)^2 \right]$$

Again, this can be restated much more compactly by denoting with Yn the output value for the nth observation (that is, the nth element of the Y vector), and with Xn the row of data that describes the nth observation:

$$cost(\theta) = \frac{1}{N} \times \left[(Y_1 - \theta \times X_1)^2 + \ldots + (Y_N - \theta \times X_N)^2 \right]$$

Or, even better, if we stack together all the observations, we get a matrix X, where Xn, the nth row of the matrix, contains the nth observation:

$$cost(\theta) = \frac{1}{N} \times \left[Y - \theta \times X^T \right] \times \left[Y - \theta \times X^T \right]$$

We could keep going like this and rewrite the entire batch gradient-descent algorithm as a series of vector and matrix operations. Before getting into that, let's first make sure that this actually works, and that when we use linear algebra, our results are indeed identical to the original formulation.

Linear Algebra with Math.NET

While other options exist, the best starting point for "doing algebra" on .NET is Math.NET. Math.NET is an open-source library that is well maintained and has been battle tested quite a bit over its years of existence. Rather than cramming more code in the same script we have been using so far, let's start a new one and import Math.NET and its F# extensions via NuGet, together with the other packages we have been using so far. First, let's see how to perform basic algebra with Math.NET:

```
#I @"packages\"
#r @"FSharp.Data.2.2.1\lib\net40\FSharp.Data.dll"
#load @"FSharp.Charting.0.90.10\FSharp.Charting.fsx"
#r @"MathNet.Numerics.Signed.3.6.0\lib\net40\MathNet.Numerics.dll"
#r @"MathNet.Numerics.FSharp.Signed.3.6.0\lib\net40\MathNet.Numerics.FSharp.dll"

open FSharp.Charting
open FSharp.Data
open MathNet
open MathNet.Numerics.LinearAlgebra
open MathNet.Numerics.LinearAlgebra.Double
```

Let's create a vector A and a matrix B for illustrative purposes, and perform some operations on them:

```
let A = vector [ 1.; 2.; 3. ]
let B = matrix [ [ 1.; 2. ]
                 [ 3.; 4. ]
                 [ 5.; 6. ] ]
```

```
let C = A * A
let D = A * B
let E = A * B.Column(1)
```

Everything appears to be working as we would expect, and, as a nice bonus, the code looks very similar to the mathematical formulation you would see if you opened a math book. Now, let's rewrite our prediction and cost functions, "algebra-style":

```
type Data = CsvProvider<"day.csv">
let dataset = Data.Load("day.csv")
let data = dataset.Rows

type Vec = Vector<float>
type Mat = Matrix<float>

let cost (theta:Vec) (Y:Vec) (X:Mat) =
    let ps = Y - (theta * X.Transpose())
    ps * ps |> sqrt

let predict (theta:Vec) (v:Vec) = theta * v

let X = matrix [ for obs in data -> [ 1.; float obs.Instant ]]
let Y = vector [ for obs in data -> float obs.Cnt ]
```

▓ **Tip**   For convenience, we create two types, `Vec` and `Mat`, which correspond to `Vector<float>` and `Matrix<float>`. This turns out to be very convenient for simplifying our code: Math.NET supports algebra on numeric types other than float/double, which can be very useful, but can also clutter the code and require some additional type annotations to clarify what specific type is intended. Given that we are going to operate exclusively on floats, keeping everything generic doesn't add anything, and would create some noise, hence the simplification.

We can now compare the predictions and costs we obtained previously with the results of our new formulation, using the same value for Theta:

```
let theta = vector [6000.; -4.5]
```

```
predict theta (X.Row(0))
cost theta Y X
```

Everything matches. We are on safe ground, so let's proceed and estimate Theta.

Normal Form

We could rewrite our batch gradient descent "algebra style." However, we will take a different route here that highlights some of the benefits of using algebra. As it happens, the problem we are trying to solve (finding a value for Theta that minimizes the cost) has what math people call a closed-form solution; that is, an explicit, exact solution that can be computed directly from the inputs without requiring any numeric approximation.

Explaining how to derive the result would go a bit beyond the scope of this book, and wouldn't add much value to understanding the machine-learning part, so I will simply state the result "as is"; if you are curious about it, look in your favorite search engine for "normal form regression." With no justification whatsoever, the problem

$$\min cost(\theta) = \frac{1}{N} \times \left[Y - \theta \times X^T \right] \times \left[Y - \theta \times X^T \right]$$

has a solution Theta, which is

$$\theta = \left(X^T \times X \right)^{-1} \times X^T \times Y$$

This is one case where having a linear algebra library available pays off big time. Matrix transposition and inversion is implemented for us, and our algorithm now becomes a one-liner. Better yet, we don't have to go through the lengthy process of tuning a learning rate or running thousands of expensive iteration while hoping that we are getting close to the correct value—we get the correct solution in one shot. See the following:

```
let estimate (Y:Vec) (X:Mat) =
    (X.Transpose() * X).Inverse() * X.Transpose() * Y
```

Does this make our entire earlier work on gradient descent a waste of time? Most certainly not! Besides the pedagogical value of the exercise, which hopefully clarified the general process, gradient descent is a more general algorithm that applies to situations where, for instance, we decide to use a different, non-linear cost function, provided the appropriate modifications are done to the derivatives. By contrast, the normal form is a solution to a very specific equation, and doesn't generalize out of the box. That being said, the class of problems it solves is pretty broad.

Pedal to the Metal with MKL

So far, the main advantage we highlighted for using an algebra-centric approach was that, for suitable problems, it enables a much more compact formulation. There is another, completely different reason why algebra is such an important topic in machine learning, and that is performance.

Were it used for machine learning alone, algebra would probably not be a big deal in software. Thankfully, there is another area where developers care about algebra in a big way, and that is the gaming industry. 3D graphics are all about moving polygons around, which is fundamentally an algebra problem. As a result, thanks to the relentless push for ever faster and more-detailed game universes, significant efforts have gone into making high-performance algebra work, including at the hardware level. The most visible example in that area is GPGPU (general-purpose computing on graphics processing units), which, by using hardware that was originally designed with vector graphics in mind, can achieve huge speedups for certain types of computations.

Using GPGPUs is powerful, but also takes some work. However, Math.NET offers you the option of leveraging something similar, with virtually no work involved. The library supports a MKL provider, a mechanism that essentially allows you to send your computations to **MKL**, the **Math Kernel Library**, a set of highly-optimized math libraries that are built within Intel processors.

Using MKL with Math.NET is fairly straightforward. Once you add the corresponding NuGet package to the project, two libraries will appear: MathNet.Numerics.MKL.dll and libiomp5md.dll. Right-click the MKL dll, and in Properties, set Copy to Output Directory to "Copy Always."

115

■ **Tip** MKL comes in multiple flavors: 32 bits versus 64 bits, and Windows versus Linux. Make sure you select the package that is appropriate for your machine when installing the NuGet package.

At this point, sending the computation to MKL is as simple as this:

```
System.Environment.CurrentDirectory <- __SOURCE_DIRECTORY__

open MathNet.Numerics
open MathNet.Numerics.Providers.LinearAlgebra.Mkl
Control.LinearAlgebraProvider <- MklLinearAlgebraProvider()
```

The purpose of the somewhat ugly first line is to set the current directory to the directory where our source code is located; this is required in order for the script to pick up the MKL dll, which is located in that directory. Once that is done, it is simply a matter of replacing the default LinearAlgebraProvider by its MKL equivalent, and we are good to go.

So, what does this gain us, exactly? Mileage will vary, based on the computer you are using and the problem size you are tackling. Typically, on smaller matrices (like the one we are dealing with right now), the benefits will be negligible, if visible at all. However, if running computations on larger datasets, it would not be unusual to see a ten-fold speedup.

Evolving and Validating Models Rapidly

We went from a small hammer with gradient descent to a pretty mighty one with the normal form. Fitting a model to our dataset suddenly became rather simple and generic: As long as we can transform observations into a vector of doubles, we are golden. In this section, we will rework our code to benefit from our generic algorithm. Our goal will be to make it as easy as possible to change the way we use data to make predictions, and to experiment with different models by adding or removing features. However, if we are to create multiple models, the first thing we'll need is a process by which to compare their quality. Let's start by putting that in place, and once we are on safe ground we will explore how to rapidly evolve and refine models.

Cross-Validation and Over-Fitting, Again

It shouldn't come as a surprise that we'll use cross-validation as a basis for model comparison. We will set aside a proportion of our dataset for validation and train our models on only 70% of the data, holding 30% out for validation purposes.

Note that this is particularly important in our case. Consider for a second the following situation: Suppose you were considering using a set of features [Theta0; Theta1; ... ThetaN], and an alternate model [Theta0; Theta1; ... ThetaN; ThetaM]—that is, the same model but with one extra feature added. Could the error resulting from the second selection ever be worse than that resulting from the first one?

The answer is, the second feature set, which contains all the features from the first, and an additional one, will always have a lower error than the first. As an informal proof, think about this: In the worst possible case, ThetaM could have a value of 0, in which case the two models would be equivalent, and obviously have the same error. So, at the very least, the algorithm searching for the lowest possible cost can achieve the same level in both cases. However, in the second case, once that value is reached, the option exists to change ThetaM from 0 to another value, potentially changing the other Thetas, to attain an even lower cost.

Another way to say this, is that the more features we add, the lower the cost will be, regardless of how good or bad these extra features are. If I were to add a completely random feature, say, the daily price of a pound of turnips in Tokyo, mechanically, I would get a better fit—or at the very least, an equally good fit.

The conclusion is simple: A good fit on our training data is not always a good thing. Again, what we are after is not a model that perfectly fits the data we fed it, but rather a model that produces robust predictions on new data it has never seen before.

One extra twist we have to deal with here is that if we simply cut the dataset and used the first 70% of observations for training, and used the last 30% for validation, our validation set would not be "representative" of arbitrary new observations we might get in the future. Because of the clear seasonal patterns, the last chunk groups together similar observations, and ignores completely certain cases. To avoid that, we will simply shuffle the sample first to get rid of the seasonal effects, doing so using the classic Fisher-Yates random shuffle algorithm, as follows:

```
let seed = 314159
let rng = System.Random(seed)

// Fisher-Yates shuffle
let shuffle (arr:'a []) =
    let arr = Array.copy arr
    let l = arr.Length
    for i in (l-1) .. -1 .. 1 do
        let temp = arr.[i]
        let j = rng.Next(0,i+1)
        arr.[i] <- arr.[j]
        arr.[j] <- temp
    arr
```

The shuffle algorithm simply takes a generic array and returns a new array, with the same elements rearranged in random order:

```
let myArray = [| 1 .. 5 |]
myArray |> shuffle
>

val myArray : int [] = [|1; 2; 3; 4; 5|]
val it : int [] = [|4; 1; 5; 2; 3|]
```

■ **Tip** When using a random number generator, like System.Random, it is often a good idea to specify the seed. That way, you can replicate results from one session to another, which helps in making sure your computations are behaving the way you expect to—something difficult to do when results change every time you run your code!

We can now create a training and validation set by simply shuffling the dataset and returning two slices, the first 70% as training, the remaining 30% as validation:

```
let training,validation =
    let shuffled =
        data
        |> Seq.toArray
        |> shuffle
    let size =
        0.7 * float (Array.length shuffled) |> int
    shuffled.[..size],
    shuffled.[size+1..]
```

Simplifying the Creation of Models

We are all set, with an evaluation harness in place. At this point, what we want is to easily create various models by including or removing features, and then to run the numbers to see what works.

What we need for that is a way to convert an observation into a list of features, each of which extracts a float from an observation, so that we can convert our observations to a matrix of features and estimate the corresponding Theta via normal form. To achieve this, we'll create a new type, Featurizer, which will take an Obs and turn it into a list of floats:

```
type Obs = Data.Row
type Model = Obs -> float
type Featurizer = Obs -> float list
```

Using this approach, we will be able to simplify the way we define a model by listing how we want to extract data from an observation with a "featurizer." As an illustration, here is how we could recreate our simple straight-line model, with a constant dummy variable that always takes a value of 1.0, and extract the Instant from an observation:

```
let exampleFeaturizer (obs:Obs) =
  [   1.0;
      float obs.Instant; ]
```

For convenience, let's also create a predictor function, which will take in a Featurizer and a vector Theta and return a function that converts an individual observation into a predicted value:

```
let predictor (f:Featurizer) (theta:Vec) =
    f >> vector >> (*) theta
```

While we are at it, let's also create a function that will evaluate the quality of a particular model on a given dataset. That way, we will be able to compare models to each other, on both the training and the validation sets. We could definitely use the cost function for that, but, instead, we will use another classic metric, the mean absolute error (a.k.a. MAE), the average absolute prediction error, because it is somewhat easier to grasp. The MAE indicates by how much our prediction is off, on average, as follows:

```
let evaluate (model:Model) (data:Obs seq) =
    data
    |> Seq.averageBy (fun obs ->
        abs (model obs - float obs.Cnt))
```

Let's now put this together:

```
let model (f:Featurizer) (data:Obs seq) =
    let Yt, Xt =
        data
        |> Seq.toList
        |> List.map (fun obs -> float obs.Cnt, f obs)
        |> List.unzip
    let theta = estimate (vector Yt) (matrix Xt)
    let predict = predictor f theta
    theta,predict
```

The model function takes in a featurizer f, describing what features we want to extract from an observation, and a dataset that we will use to train the model. First, we extract out from the dataset the output Yt and the matrix Xt. Then, we estimate Theta using Yt and Xt and return the vector Theta, bundled together with the corresponding predictor function, which is now ready to use.

Adding Continuous Features to the Model

Let's test this on our simple straight-line model, which we will call model0:

```
let featurizer0 (obs:Obs) =
    [   1.;
        float obs.Instant; ]

let (theta0,model0) = model featurizer0 training
```

Nice and easy! We can now evaluate the quality of our model, model0, on the training and validation sets:

```
evaluate model0 training |> printfn "Training: %.0f"
evaluate model0 validation |> printfn "Validation: %.0f"
>
Training: 1258
Validation: 1167
```

Visualizing the result of our model against the real data (see Figure 4-9) shows a nice, straight line, which does indeed look like a pretty reasonable fit:

```
Chart.Combine [
    Chart.Line [ for obs in data -> float obs.Cnt ]
    Chart.Line [ for obs in data -> model0 obs ] ]
```

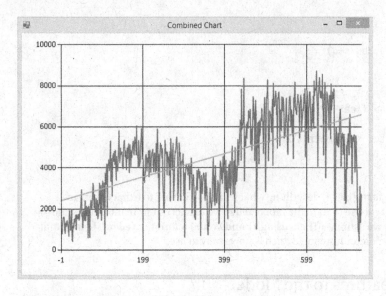

Figure 4-9. *Visualization of the straight-line regression*

Now we can start adding features to our model, selecting from the available continuous variables—that is, variables that have a numerical meaning, like temperature or windspeed—and adding them to a new featurizer:

```
let featurizer1 (obs:Obs) =
    [   1.
        obs.Instant |> float
        obs.Atemp |> float
        obs.Hum |> float
        obs.Temp |> float
        obs.Windspeed |> float
    ]

let (theta1,model1) = model featurizer1 training

evaluate model1 training |> printfn "Training: %.0f"
evaluate model1 validation |> printfn "Validation: %.0f"
>
Training: 732
Validation: 697
```

Obviously, we are doing something right: The MAE dropped significantly, both on the training set (which is expected) and on the validation set (which is what matters). Before, we were off by about 1,200 units on average, and we are now down to around 750. Not perfect, but a clear improvement! This is readily visible if we plot the new predicted curve—the new predicted curve is beginning to stick to the target much more closely (see Figure 4-10).

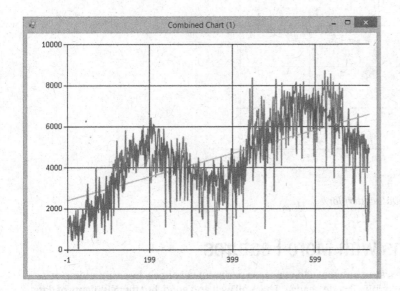

Figure 4-10. *Including more-continuous features*

Let's take a slightly different look at the data and plot the actual value against the predicted one:

```
Chart.Point [ for obs in data -> float obs.Cnt, model1 obs ]
```

Figure 4-11 confirms that our model is starting to look like the real thing. The scatterplot, while not perfect, follows roughly a 45-degree straight line, with some noise sprinkled on top.

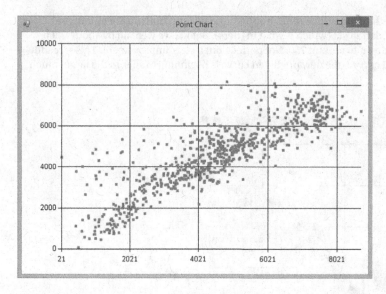

Figure 4-11. Predicted versus actual scatterplot

Refining Predictions with More Features

At this point, we have put in place a structure that allows us to experiment very freely by easily adding or removing data from a model, with minimal code change. That's all well and good, but there is plenty of data in the dataset that we are not tapping into yet. In this section, we will explore how we can go even further and include even more features in our model so as to improve our results.

Handling Categorical Features

We have included a large part of the data we have at our disposal in the dataset, but we have also left out some of it. How about holidays, for instance? It wouldn't be unreasonable to assume that weekends have an impact on bicycle usage. What about the day of the week—there is no reason that people wouldn't behave differently, say, on Mondays and Fridays.

We have one issue here, though: These variables are **categorical**. While weekdays are encoded as 0, 1, … 6 for Sunday to Monday, these numbers have no numerical significance. A Wednesday is not worth three times a Monday, and it wouldn't make sense to model bicycle usage as a multiple of the weekday code.

What we could do, however, is use the same trick that worked for us to represent the constant term in the equation. If we created a feature for each day of the week—for instance, a feature for Mondays marking an observation with value 1.0 for Mondays, and 0.0 otherwise—the estimate for Theta should capture the impact of Mondays. Let's try this out:

```
let featurizer2 (obs:Obs) =
    [   1.
        obs.Instant |> float
        obs.Hum |> float
        obs.Temp |> float
        obs.Windspeed |> float
        (if obs.Weekday = 0 then 1.0 else 0.0)
        (if obs.Weekday = 1 then 1.0 else 0.0)
```

```
        (if obs.Weekday = 2 then 1.0 else 0.0)
        (if obs.Weekday = 3 then 1.0 else 0.0)
        (if obs.Weekday = 4 then 1.0 else 0.0)
        (if obs.Weekday = 5 then 1.0 else 0.0)
        (if obs.Weekday = 6 then 1.0 else 0.0)
    ]
```

```
let (theta2,model2) = model featurizer2 training
```

And ... uh? Our estimate of Theta comes back as seq [nan; nan; nan; nan; ...]. What's going on here? The technical term for the problem we are facing is **collinearity**. Before going into why we are hitting the problem here, let's look at a simpler case that illustrates the root of the issue. Remember our first model, where we defined features as the following:

$$Y = \theta_0 + \theta_1 \times obs.Instant$$

Imagine for a minute now that we modified the features and opted instead for the following specification:

$$Y = \theta_0 + \theta_1 \times obs.Instant + \theta_2 \times obs.Instant$$

This would, of course, be a silly specification, but let's roll with it for a minute. In this case, what would happen? We would have a bit of a problem, is what would happen. There are an infinite number of possible combinations for Theta1 and Theta2 that would work. If our original optimal value of Theta1 (in the initial model) was, say, 10.0, then any combination of Theta1 and Theta2 that sums up to 10.0 would also be optimal for the modified model. 10.0 and 0.0, 5.0 and 5.0, 1000.0 and -990.0 would work equally well, and we don't have a way to decide between any of these. This is essentially the same problem the algorithm is facing: It cannot find a unique, optimal value for Theta, and therefore fails miserably.

So, why do we have a collinearity issue here? If you think about it, if any of our features can be expressed as a linear combination of the other features, we will encounter this problem. Well, any given day has to be one of the seven existing weekdays, so Monday + Tuesday + ... + Sunday = 1.0. But 1.0 is also the value for our constant term, the one that maps to Theta0. What can we do about this?

There are two things we could do. First, we could remove one of the weekdays from the list. In that case, in effect what we would be doing is setting that day as "day of reference," and the Thetas assigned to each of the six remaining days would be capturing the differential gain or loss when compared to that day. The other approach would be to remove the constant term from our equation; in that case, we would end up with a direct estimate for each of the seven days of the week.

Let's go ahead and remove Sundays, which will be our point of reference. The estimation now runs like a champ, and we even get a small quality improvement:

```
let featurizer2 (obs:Obs) =
    [   1.
        obs.Instant |> float
        obs.Hum |> float
        obs.Temp |> float
        obs.Windspeed |> float
        (if obs.Weekday = 1 then 1.0 else 0.0)
        (if obs.Weekday = 2 then 1.0 else 0.0)
        (if obs.Weekday = 3 then 1.0 else 0.0)
        (if obs.Weekday = 4 then 1.0 else 0.0)
        (if obs.Weekday = 5 then 1.0 else 0.0)
        (if obs.Weekday = 6 then 1.0 else 0.0)
    ]
```

```
let (theta2,model2) = model featurizer2 training

evaluate model2 training |> printfn "Training: %.0f"
evaluate model2 validation |> printfn "Validation: %.0f"

>
Training: 721
Validation: 737
```

If we inspect Theta a bit, matching the last six coefficients to the corresponding days, it seems that Saturdays are the most popular days for bicycling, whereas Sundays are better spent doing something else.

We won't go further into potentially including more categorical features into our model, but feel free to play with it and see how much improvement you can squeeze in there! The two main points we wanted to make here are that first, with a minimum of effort, it is possible to use categorical variables in a regression model by splitting categories into individual features and using indicator variables (1 it's there, 0 it's not) to denote their activation. Then, we discussed collinearity and how it can wreak havoc in a model, as well as ways to handle the problem when it arises.

Non-linear Features

We have included pretty much everything and the kitchen sink. Is there nothing else with which we can try to improve our predictions?

To address that question, let's first take another look at the data and plot bicycle usage versus temperature (see Figure 4-12):

```
Chart.Point [ for obs in data -> obs.Temp, obs.Cnt ]
```

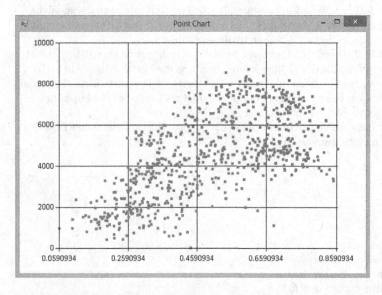

Figure 4-12. Bicycle usage against temperature scatterplot

The data is pretty messy, but it seems that, overall, usage goes up with temperature only to a certain point, and starts to decrease afterward. This is not unreasonable: Biking loses some of its appeal when it's freezing cold or scorching hot. Unfortunately, our current model is not well suited to capturing that. All the effects are represented as linear functions; that is, they are of the form `Theta x Feature value`. If Theta is positive, all things being left equal, higher values of the feature will always result in higher predicted values; conversely, if Theta is negative, higher values of the feature will always produce lower predicted values.

This is not going to cut it for what we want to capture with temperature; we expect usage to go down both when temperature is getting very low or getting very high. So, what can we do?

If a linear relationship is not sufficient, we could use something else, for instance, higher-order polynomials. The simplest thing that could possibly work would be to add a square term to the mix. Instead of modelling the effect of temperature as

$$obs.Cnt = \theta_0 + \theta_1 \times obs.Temp$$

we could go for

$$obs.Cnt = \theta_0 + \theta_1 \times obs.Temp + \theta_2 \times obs.Temp^2$$

Let's try out the idea, ignoring all other features for a moment, to demonstrate what curve comes out of this equation:

```
let squareTempFeaturizer (obs:Obs) =
    [   1.
        obs.Temp |> float
        obs.Temp * obs.Temp |> float ]

let (_,squareTempModel) = model squareTempFeaturizer data

Chart.Combine [
    Chart.Point [ for obs in data -> obs.Temp, obs.Cnt ]
    Chart.Point [ for obs in data -> obs.Temp, squareTempModel obs ] ]
```

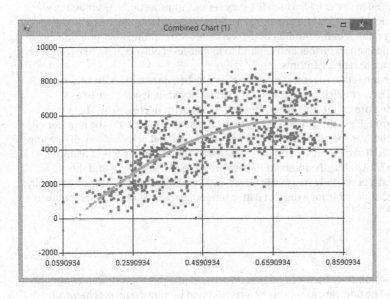

Figure 4-13. *Fitting square temperature*

Instead of a straight line, we get a curve with a slight bend,. The curve increases to reach a maximum value and then decreases again. The class of curves generated by this equation is known as a parabola, and it always follows the same general shape (symmetrical around a minimum or maximum value), which makes it a natural candidate for capturing effects in a model where one of the features reaches peak impact for a certain value.

Let's now incorporate this new feature into our model and see if this improves anything:

```
let featurizer3 (obs:Obs) =
    [   1.
        obs.Instant |> float
        obs.Hum |> float
        obs.Temp |> float
        obs.Windspeed |> float
        obs.Temp * obs.Temp |> float
        (if obs.Weekday = 1 then 1.0 else 0.0)
        (if obs.Weekday = 2 then 1.0 else 0.0)
        (if obs.Weekday = 3 then 1.0 else 0.0)
        (if obs.Weekday = 4 then 1.0 else 0.0)
        (if obs.Weekday = 5 then 1.0 else 0.0)
        (if obs.Weekday = 6 then 1.0 else 0.0)
    ]

let (theta3,model3) = model featurizer3 training

evaluate model3 training |> printfn "Training: %.0f"
evaluate model3 validation |> printfn "Validation: %.0f"
    >
Training: 668
Validation: 645
```

Nice! Our error dropped from 750 to under 670, which is a very serious improvement. Even better, we now have a general direction in which to try to refine the model further. We could introduce new features—for instance, the squares of other variables, or the product of two variables—to capture other potential non-linear effects in our model. We could even go further and expand to higher-level polynomials, like cubes, or other functional forms—say, exponentials or logarithms.

A small drawback of this approach is that the interpretation of results becomes trickier. In a linear model, understanding what each Theta coefficient means is fairly straightforward. It can be read as a multiplier: Increase the value of a feature by 1.0, and the output will increase (or decrease) by Theta.

This creates a bit of a conundrum. First, this introduces a practical issue. As we expand the number of potential features to consider, manually inspecting what features should be left out or included will become quite a hassle. For instance, if we had N variables available, a linear model would contain N + 1 features (each variable and a constant term). Including the interaction between each of the features and their squares adds N x (N + 1) / 2, and a potentially staggering number of combinations to consider. Manually inspecting each combination remains possible for a dataset with a moderate number of variables, but won't work as the dataset width increases.

Regularization

The larger problem is, of course, the point we discussed before. If we could just throw every feature and the kitchen sink at the model, we would be fine. But, as we saw before, doing so blindly would mechanically improve the quality on the training set without necessarily resulting in a robust prediction model. This problem is known as **over-fitting**: The search algorithm uses all the features it can use to fit the dataset, and in the process ends up doing too good of a job at that task, potentially capturing artifacts in the training dataset that will not generalize beyond it.

So, how could we avoid this issue? One method commonly used is known as **regularization**. The idea is the following: One of the symptoms of over-fitting is that, in its attempt to fit the training set with features, the algorithm will begin to produce "wild" values for some of the Theta coefficients, whereas in a "reasonable" model, coefficients would be expected to remain within a certain range, enforcing that changes in the inputs won't cause crazy fluctuations.

We won't go through the whole example of regularization, and will instead simply sketch out how you would go about it in general.

If the goal is to prevent each parameter Theta from fluctuating too wildly, one possibility is to introduce a penalty so that high individual values will be more costly than smaller ones. For instance, we could introduce the following penalty to our cost function:

$$Penalty(\theta) = l \times \left[\theta_1^2 + \ldots + \theta_N^2 \right]$$

Why would this be a good candidate? As we discussed before in the context of the original cost function, because the square function increases faster as values are further away from zero, larger values for each individual Theta will be penalized more heavily. As a result, by default, this penalty will tend to favor more-balanced values over highly differentiated ones. For instance, a Theta of [1.0; 1.0] would have a cost of 2.0, whereas [0.0; 2.0] would incur a cost of 4.0.

Putting this all together, we could now replace our original cost function with the following:

$$cost(\theta) = \frac{1}{N} \times \left[(Y_1 - \theta \times X_1)^2 + \ldots + (Y_N - \theta \times X_N)^2 \right] + l \times \left[\theta_1^2 + \ldots + \theta_N^2 \right]$$

This formulation has a fairly straightforward interpretation. The cost of a model combines two elements: how large the error is on the fit and how small the parameters are. In other words, there is now a cost to improving the fit by increasing a parameter Theta, and the algorithm will "prefer" fit improvements that use more-balanced parameters.

Before looking into how we could go about using this in an actual algorithm, there are a couple of important technical considerations to take into account.

The first one is that in order for this to work, each of the features needs to be on a comparable scale. This matters because the penalty term we introduced assumes that similar changes in the coefficients Theta can be compared with each other. One way of stating what we are trying to achieve with this penalty is "when you can improve fit quality by increasing the coefficient of features, prefer increasing the feature that has the smallest coefficient." This is a great criterion, as long as the features themselves are comparable. For instance, in our case, obs.Instant goes from 1 to 731, whereas obs.Windspeed goes from roughly 0 to 0.5. Increasing the coefficient on Instant by 1.0 would cause a change between 1 and 731 on the output, whereas the same change on Windspeed would at best have an impact of 0.5.

The approach used to address this issue is called **normalization**. Normalization simply takes all the features in a model and rescales them to make them comparable. There are a few ways this can be done; the easiest is to put every feature on a 0 to 1 scale by applying the following transformation: normalized = (x - xmin) / (xmax - xmin).

The second point worth noting is the omission of Theta0 from the regularization penalty term. This is not a typo. First, we would be hard pressed to find a way to normalize it, because every single observation for that feature has value 1.0. Then, Theta0 plays the role of an offset: For every other feature being normalized, Theta0 sets the baseline of the model, which could be any value.

The third and final note is the parameter lambda in front of the penalty term. This parameter can be interpreted as a weight; it drives how much the regularization penalty will count for in the cost function. That parameter needs to be tuned manually so as to determine what level of regularization works best. The process is a habitual one: Try out various levels and pick the value of lambda that works best on the validation set; that is, the value that has the lowest 'error.

Assuming the dataset has been prealably normalized, we can easily update our original gradient-descent algorithm using this new formulation, with the following update rule:

$$\theta_1 \leftarrow \theta_1 - 2a \times \frac{1}{N}$$

$$\times \begin{bmatrix} obs_1.Instant \times (\theta_0 + \theta_1 \times obs_1.Instant - obs_1.Cnt) + \ldots + obs_N.Instant \\ \times (\theta_0 + \theta_1 \times obs_N.Instant - obs_N.Cnt) \end{bmatrix} - l \times \theta_1$$

So, What Have We Learned?

Let's face it, this was a dense chapter. We discussed a lot of ideas and spent a fair amount of time discussing problems in a rather abstract, mathematical way. Let's see if we can regroup and summarize the key learnings from this chapter.

Minimizing Cost with Gradient Descent

The most important technique we discussed in this chapter applies to multiple areas in machine learning, and not simply to regression. We presented the gradient-descent algorithm, a general approach for identifying parameters that minimize the value of a function, by iteratively adjusting the parameters following the gradient—the direction of steepest descent from the current state.

Gradient descent might appear a bit intimidating at first, thanks to the heavy serving of calculus that comes with it, but once the initial hurdle is passed, it is a rather simple algorithm. More interesting, it is applicable to a broad range of situations; essentially, if there is a minimum value and the function is differentiable (we do need a derivative!) and not too pathological, you are in good shape. As it turns out, that makes it a great go-to tool for most machine-learning problems: If you are trying to find a model that best fits a dataset, you are minimizing some form of distance or cost function, and gradient descent will likely help you find it.

We also saw two variants of the algorithm, stochastic and batch gradient descent, each having their own advantages and limitations. Stochastic gradient descent updates parameters one observation at a time. It doesn't require operating on the entire dataset at once, which makes it convenient for online learning. If your dataset is expanding over time, and you are receiving new observations as time goes by, you can simply update your estimates using just the latest data points that arrived, and keep learning gradually. The downside, as we saw in our example, is that it's comparatively slow and potentially less stable: While the algorithm keeps going the right direction overall, each individual step is not guaranteed to produce an improvement. By contrast, batch gradient descent operates on the entire dataset at once, producing an improved model at each step. The downside is that each step is computationally more intensive; also, using the entire dataset might be impractical, in particular if the dataset is large.

Predicting a Number with Regression

The main goal we were after in this chapter was to predict the number of users for a bike-sharing service on a particular day using whatever data we have available for that day. This is known as a regression model. Unlike classification models, where the objective is to predict what category an observation belongs to, here we are trying to predict a numeric value by finding a function that combines the features and fits the data as closely as possible.

Starting from the simplest possible model, fitting a straight line through the data, we progressively built up a more-complex model by including more features, illustrating a few simple techniques along the way. In particular, we demonstrated how one can go beyond continuous features and include categorical features in a model by breaking them into multiple features, each indicating with a 1 or a 0 which of the states is active. We also saw how including non-linear terms, such as squares or higher-degree polynomials, can be used to model more-complex relationships between inputs and outputs that cannot be properly captured by a linear model.

Adding more-complex features to a model is a double-edged sword, and the potential for better predictions comes at a price. First, it creates an explosion in the number of features, and managing which ones to include or not can become a problem in and of itself. Then, it introduces a deeper issue: Adding any feature will mechanically improve how well the model fits the training set, regardless of whether it has anything to do with the problem at hand. That issue is known as over-fitting: More features give the algorithm more "freedom" to use them in creative, contorted ways, and a better fit doesn't necessarily translate into better predictions.

We discussed technical solutions to mitigate that issue, using cross-validation and regularization. However, as a final note, it's perhaps useful to consider that there is an inherent tension at play here. A model can be useful for two distinct reasons: to understand a phenomenon, or to make predictions. Adding more data will usually help make better predictions, but also introduces complexity. Conversely, simpler models may be less accurate, but help to understand how variables work together, and can validate whether things even make sense. Before building a model, ask yourself whether you would prefer an extremely accurate but opaque, black-box model, or a less-precise one, but one that you can explain to a colleague. This might help guide your decisions along the way!

USEFUL LINKS

- FSharp.Charting is a stable library, convenient for creating basic charts while exploring data from FSI: `http://fslab.org/FSharp.Charting/`

- Math.NET is an open-source library covering a broad range of mathematical and numeric analysis tools. In particular it contains essential linear algebra algorithms: `http://www.mathdotnet.com/`

- If you need higher performance from your algorithm, even if it requires a more-complex implementation, quantalea offers a very interesting .NET-to-GPGPU library, which is particularly F# friendly: `http://www.quantalea.net/`

- DiffSharp, while still evolving at the time of writing, is a promising auto-differentiation library that can simplify gradient computation considerably: `http://gbaydin.github.io/DiffSharp/`

CHAPTER 5

■ ■ · ■

You Are Not a Unique Snowflake

Detecting Patterns with Clustering and Principle Components Analysis

Sometimes, your day of machine learning begins with a very specific problem to solve. Can you figure out if an incoming email is spam? How accurately can you predict sales? You have been given your marching orders: You start with a question, look for what data is available, and get to work building the best model you can to answer that question.

Oftentimes, though, life is not quite that clear cut, and your day begins with a much fuzzier problem. All you have is data, and no clear question just yet. Perhaps someone came to you and simply asked, "Can you tell me something interesting about my data?" Perhaps you want to run some analyses on a dataset, but would like first to understand the hand you have been dealt. Perhaps that dataset is large, with many features, making it hard to grasp if there are obvious relationships between features. Manual data exploration is a painstaking and tedious process—it would be nice if we could offload some of the work to a machine and let it figure out if patterns exist in our data.

This is the domain of **unsupervised learning**. In supervised learning methods (such as classification or regression), we begin with a question and labeled data—that is, examples with an answer to the question—and we use that to learn a model that fits the data. By contrast, in unsupervised learning all we have is data, and we want the computer to help us find some structure in it. Hopefully that structure will be "interesting" in a human sense, and can be used to organize the individual elements in a meaningful way.

In this chapter, we will do the following:

- Introduce two classic data-analysis techniques, k-means clustering and principal component analysis, which both aim to automatically extract information from a dataset and to provide a simpler and more usable representation. We will apply these techniques to historical data from the StackOverflow website and see if the patterns that emerge are interesting.

- Sketch out how the same general idea—detecting patterns in data—can be used to make recommendations to users based on their past behavior and how similar it is to patterns we observed among other users.

■ **Note**   Some of the more complex charts from this chapter have been included in the source code package, to allow for a larger format viewing if necessary.

Detecting Patterns in Data

If you think about it for a second, you will realize this is not an easy task. How do you define "something interesting" about the data? There is no clear metric for interesting, so what are we asking the computer to do for us here, exactly?

There are many ways data can be "interesting." If we go by opposites, data that is not interesting is data where nothing stands out. In that sense, Figure 5-1 displays uninteresting data.

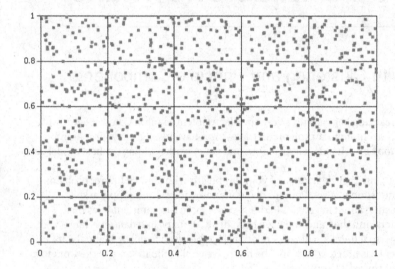

Figure 5-1. *Data without patterns*

By contrast, Figure 5-2 displays "something interesting." Instead of an even, homogeneous arrangement, there seems to be some organization. Observations are clumped into two groups, randomly scattered around two centers. This type of pattern is called **clusters**, and cluster analysis is the process of automatically identifying this type of structure in a dataset.

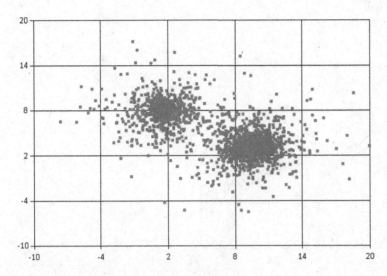

Figure 5-2. *Data organized in two clusters*

However, to paraphrase Leo Tolstoy, "all uninteresting datasets are alike; each interesting dataset is interesting in its own way." Clusters are only one of the many ways a dataset could be interesting. For instance, consider Figure 5-3. The data clearly displays an interesting pattern, with observations roughly following a straight line, but without clusters.

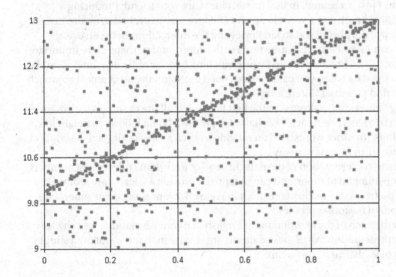

Figure 5-3. *Linear patterns*

Clusters and linear structures are two ways a dataset can be interesting, but there are virtually infinitely many ways data could exhibit patterns; for instance, consider Figure 5-4, where data appears to be organized in rings. It's somewhat clustered (we can distinguish three groups) and is somewhat similar to Figure 5-3 (data follows lines)—but is also pretty different.

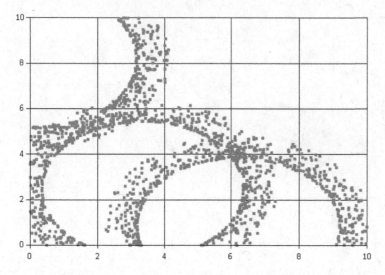

Figure 5-4. *Complex pattern*

Structure can come in many forms, and, as a result, there isn't one method that will work in every case. Each dataset is unique, and data mining is a bit of a dark art. Figuring out what works often simply takes trying different algorithms, as well as manipulating the data and transforming it into more appropriate features.

We humans are very good at detecting patterns. You didn't even have to think to figure out that there were patterns in some of the figures I just presented. In that frame, charts are your friend: Producing a scatterplot plotting one feature against another is a very cheap and effective way to eyeball structure in data.

At the same time, scatterplots will only bring you so far. Reviewing the interactions between every single variable pair in a dataset becomes quite painful quite fast. Furthermore, and perhaps more important, patterns might exist in the data that will be hard to pick up by just watching two variables at a time. So, while you should take the time to look at the data when you can, you also need a systematic, mechanical approach to just sift through the dataset and find potential "interesting facts."

Why do we care about finding "interesting patterns" in the first place? For all the examples we presented above, we can describe the dataset in a single sentence: "We have two groups," "Data follows a straight line," "Data is organized around three rings." In other words, we can provide a much more condensed description of the entire dataset. This is very useful, in at least two ways.

First, we now have a much better representation of the data. Instead of a random collection of numbers, the dataset can be described in a meaningful manner, and can potentially provide a vocabulary around it. As an example, if each of the data points from our clustered chart in Figure 5-2 represented customers, we could now start describing two types of customer profiles.

Second, just like we can describe each of these situations in English in a concise manner, we can also provide a concise mathematical representation. All of these datasets are similar in that they follow a simple mathematical structure, with a bit of statistical noise on top.

Our Challenge: Understanding Topics on StackOverflow

In this chapter, we will apply some classic unsupervised learning techniques to see if we can mine some information out of StackOverflow usage data. It is an interesting dataset in that its domain should be familiar to most developers. As a result, we will be able to try out algorithms and modifications and judge, in a non-scientific way, whether the approach is producing sensible results or not.

Specifically, we will look into whether we can identify patterns in the tags used in StackOverflow questions. Every question on StackOverflow is tagged with up to five words describing what topic it covers. Our goal will be to see if, when we look at many users and questions over time, and what tags individuals were most active in, we can see some structure and common combinations emerge.

For that purpose, I created a dataset by using the approach we discussed in Chapter 3—gathering data from the StackExchange API using the JSON type provider. The dataset, `userprofiles-toptags.txt`, can be downloaded from here: `http://1drv.ms/1ARuLg9`. I identified the 30 most common tags on StackOverflow at the time, and for each tag I retrieved the most active users, grouping together the users with the most answers and those with the most questions (top answerers and top askers, all-time and current month). This gave me a list of about 1,600 distinct StackOverflow users.

For each individual user, I then retrieved the top 100 tags they were active in over the year 2015, with the corresponding level of activity, and retained only the data pertaining to the 30 main tags. Finally, I rearranged data in the final dataset, with 30 columns (one for each tag), 1,600 rows (one for each user), and, for each row and column, the number of times that user had been active for that tag in 2015. Note that because I retrieved only the first 100 tags for a user, the information for each tag is not complete; if a particular user was active for, say, XML, but this was only his 101st most active tag, we would have recorded this as a zero.

HOW WAS THE DATASET CREATED?

We retrieved the 30 most popular tags on StackOverflow using `https://api.stackexchange.com/docs/tags`. At the time of creation, this produced the following list:

.net, ajax, android, arrays, asp.net, asp.net-mvc, c, c#, c++, css, django, html, ios, iphone, java, javascript, jquery, json, linux, mysql, objective-c, php, python, regex, ruby, ruby-on-rails, sql, sql-server, wpf, xml

We used the following methods to create a list of most active users by tag, and extract what tags they were most active in:

`https://api.stackexchange.com/docs/top-answerers-on-tags`: selects users with most answers, all time or most recent month

`https://api.stackexchange.com/docs/top-askers-on-tags`: selects users with most questions, all time or most recent month

`https://api.stackexchange.com/docs/tags-on-users`: for a selected set of users, returns the activity for most active tags

---

Getting to Know Our Data

Given the exploratory nature of our task, we will, once again, work from the F# scripting environment. Let's create a new solution with an F# library project, Unsupervised, and, for convenience, add the data file to the solution itself. The dataset is in the form of a text file, userprofiles-toptags.txt, and can be downloaded from the following link: http://1drv.ms/1M727fP. If you take a look at it from Visual Studio, you should see something like this:

```
UserID,.net,ajax,android,arrays,asp.net,asp.net-mvc,c,c#,c++,css,django,html,ios,iphone,java
,javascript,jquery,json,linux,mysql,objective-c,php,python,regex,ruby,ruby-on-rails,sql,sql-
server,wpf,xml
1,0,0,0,0,0,0,0,0,0,0,0,0,0,0,0,0,0,0,0,0,0,0,0,0,0,0,0,0,0,0
1000343,0,0,0,0,0,0,0,0,0,3,0,0,5,0,0,0,0,0,0,0,0,0,0,2,52,0,0,0,0,0,0
100297,0,0,0,26,0,0,0,0,0,0,99,62,0,0,0,29,0,182,0,26,0,0,4478,172,0,0,32,0,0,27
100342,0,0,0,0,0,1,0,0,0,0,0,3,0,0,0,16,5,0,0,0,0,0,0,0,1,7,0,0,0,0
```

The first row is a header describing the contents of each column. The first column contains the user ID, followed by 30 comma-separated columns, each of which contains the level of activity for that particular user and tag.

Before diving into algorithms, let's start with basic statistics to get a sense for the lay of the land. We'll begin with opening the Script.fsx file. We will read every line, drop the user IDs (which we don't really need), and parse each line into an array of floats. We could also keep the values as integers, but as we are likely going to perform operations such as averages, we might as well directly convert to an easy-to-work-with type. We will also keep the headers in a separate array so that we can later map columns to the proper tag name.

Listing 5-1. Reading the dataset in memory

```
open System
open System.IO

let folder = __SOURCE_DIRECTORY__
let file = "userprofiles-toptags.txt"

let headers,observations =

    let raw =
        folder + "/" + file
        |> File.ReadAllLines

    // first row is headers, first col is user ID
    let headers = (raw.[0].Split ',').[1..]

    let observations =
        raw.[1..]
        |> Array.map (fun line -> (line.Split ',').[1..])
        |> Array.map (Array.map float)

    headers,observations
```

Now that we have data, let's see how each variable looks by computing basic statistics, like the average, min, and max values. We are using two small tricks here. `Array.iteri` allows us to iterate over an array, capturing the current index as we go; as a result, we can iterate over the headers and use the current index, `i`, to extract the `i`th column from the observations. In the second trick, we use advanced formatters in `printfn` to enforce a consistent column width and number of decimals so as to make the output more readable. As an example, `printfn "%4.2f" 12.34567;;` uses the formatter %4.2f, which will keep only two digits after the decimal, and (unless it is insufficient) will pad the column to four characters.

Listing 5-2. Basic dataset statistics

```
printfn "%16s %8s %8s %8s" "Tag Name" "Avg" "Min" "Max"

headers
|> Array.iteri (fun i name ->
    let col = observations |> Array.map (fun obs -> obs.[i])
    let avg = col |> Array.average
    let min = col |> Array.min
    let max = col |> Array.max
    printfn "%16s %8.1f %8.1f %8.1f" name avg min max)
>
        Tag Name       Avg      Min       Max
            .net       3.5      0.0     334.0
            ajax       1.7      0.0     285.0
         android       7.1      0.0    2376.0
          arrays       6.4      0.0     327.0
         asp.net       2.6      0.0     290.0
// snipped for brevity
```

In simply scanning through the output, a few points stand out. First, every tag has a minimum of zero, which means that no user was active in every tag. Then, in every case, we have a low average that is fairly close to zero as compared to the maximum value. What this suggests is that for each tag, the bulk of users have low or no activity, and a few have very high activity. This is not entirely surprising, given that we gathered usage data for the top users for each tag. Instead of a classic bell-shaped distribution, where values are nicely spread out around the average, the activity level for each tag is split between two groups (either very active or very inactive users), with nothing in the middle.

Tables of numbers tend to be a bit too low level to discern bigger trends. Let's add `FSharp.Charting` via NuGet and plot each variable on a bar chart (Figure 5-5) to get a better feel for things.

Listing 5-3. Plotting average usage by tag

```
#r @"..\packages\FSharp.Charting.0.90.9\lib\net40\FSharp.Charting.dll"
#load @"..\packages\FSharp.Charting.0.90.9\FSharp.Charting.fsx"
open FSharp.Charting

let labels = ChartTypes.LabelStyle(Interval=0.25)

headers
|> Seq.mapi (fun i name ->
    name,
    observations
    |> Seq.averageBy (fun obs -> obs.[i]))
|> Chart.Bar
|> fun chart -> chart.WithXAxis(LabelStyle=labels)
```

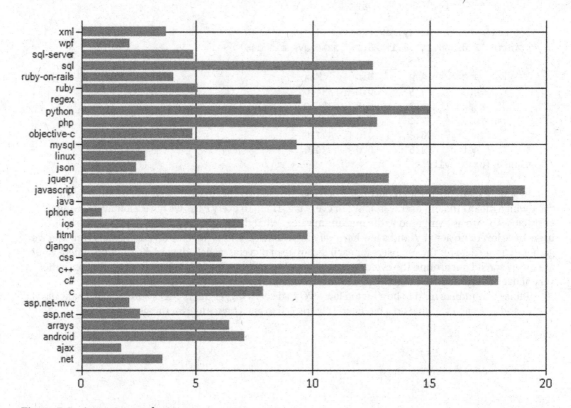

Figure 5-5. *Average usage by tag*

The chart shows a couple of tags to be significantly larger than the others (Javascript, Java, C#, Python, jQuery, PHP, SQL, and C++), followed by tags that are much smaller in comparison. This is useful information, but limited. Instead of isolated facts, we'd like a more comprehensive view that helps us understand what relationships might exist between these topics. This is what we'll look into in the next sections, first using k-means clustering to identify groups of users with similar behavior, and then using principal components analysis to better understand how variables are related to one another.

Finding Clusters with K-Means Clustering

What do we mean when we say, for instance, "This dataset has two clusters?" What we have in mind is something along these lines: Instead of being evenly spread around, the observations are concentrated in two areas. Another way to say this is, "In this dataset, there are roughly two types of observations, type 1 and type 2." The two high-density areas respectively contain observations of type 1 and 2—that is, observations that are fairly close to each other (see Figure 5-6).

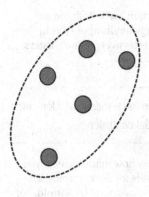

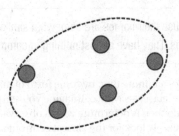

Figure 5-6. *Data clusters*

We can think of this in a slightly different, and perhaps easier, way. All the observations in a cluster are slight variations of an idealized underlying observation. This simplifies a lot the problem: Instead of having to detect the boundaries of a cluster, we can reduce a cluster to a prototypical representative for the entire group. These "fictional representatives" are called **centroids**.

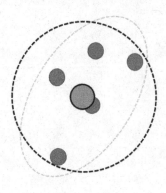

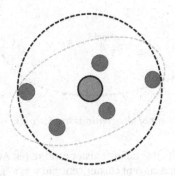

Figure 5-7. *Clusters and centroids*

Why centroids? If I want a good representative for a cluster, it should occupy a central position in the cluster so as to be far from none of the cluster observations. In this frame, an obvious candidate to determine the centroid of a cluster is the average of its constituents. Conversely, this makes for a very simple classification rule: If I want to determine which cluster an observation belongs to, I will simply look up all available centroids and pick the closest one.

Improving Clusters and Centroids

This is all well and good, but how do we find these amazing centroids? In this section, we'll flesh out an approach to updating centroids, in a way that defines better clusters. If we then repeatedly apply this update procedure, we'll have an algorithm that, starting from arbitrary centroids, will progressively refine clusters. This is the core of the **k-means clustering algorithm**.

■ **Caution**   Because their names are somewhat similar, people sometimes mix up the k-means and k nearest neighbors algorithms. They have almost nothing in common—beware of the potential confusion!

Let's assume for a minute that, by some form of magic, you happened to know how many clusters you should find in your dataset—say, two. Imagine you started with two random guesses for the centroids. The first thing you can do then is determine which observation from your dataset belongs to which centroid. For each observation, simply look for the closest centroid and assign the observation to it.

Figure 5-8 takes the fictional dataset from Figure 5-6, with the two "real" clusters marked by a light gray boundary. We start with two arbitrary centroids, A and B, and assign each data point to the closest centroid. The darker boundaries represent roughly what the clusters based on the current centroids look like.

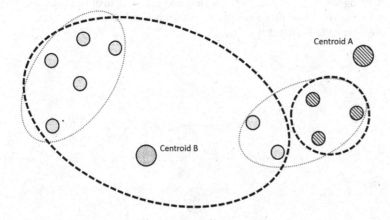

Figure 5-8. *Assignment of observations to centroids*

What we just did was define cluster candidates. All observations assigned to the same centroid form a possible cluster. If the current cluster centroid was a "good centroid," it would be located in the middle of that cluster. Let's adjust the centroid location (Figure 5-9) and move it toward the average position in the cluster, to the center.

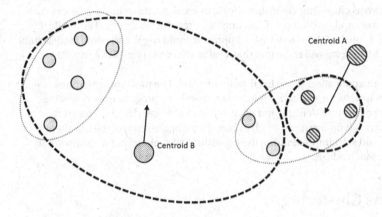

Figure 5-9. *Adjusting the centroids*

As we do that, note that a couple of interesting things happen. Moving the centroid toward the average location within a cluster will mean it tends to gravitate toward high-density areas, which concentrate more weight in a small area and act as "attractors." As an example, consider what is happening to Centroid B in Figure 5-10; it naturally moves towards the "real" cluster located on the left. As it does, it also moves away from isolated, fringe observations, such as the two on the right. This will tend to dislodge uncharacteristic elements from the cluster and give the data points a chance to be swallowed by another centroid.

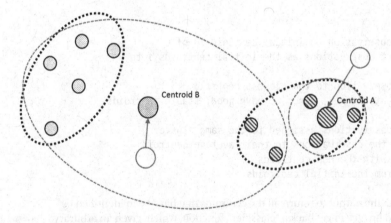

Figure 5-10. *Updated centroids and clusters*

Once that update has been performed, we can repeat the procedure and recompute which centroid each observation is assigned to, as well as the updated location of the centroids.

When should we stop? Note that if the same exact observations are assigned to the same clusters before and after the centroid locations have been updated, then the centroids won't move anymore. Each centroid is already occupying a location that is the average of its cluster, and updating it won't change its position.

This is essentially how the k-means clustering algorithm works: to break a dataset into k clusters, pick k arbitrary centroids, and progressively update their positions until they reach a stable one. Hopefully this explanation was enough to provide some insight as to why the approach could work, and could lead to stable centroids located in high-density clusters; we will leave it at that, and won't even try to prove whether it actually works.

The algorithm can be seen as an application of the fixed-point method. The procedure assumes that stable centroids exist, and tries to achieve self-consistency (so to speak) by progressively removing discrepancies between what cluster a centroid defines, and what centroid a cluster defines. There are still important questions that we have left unanswered, such as how do we figure out k or the number of clusters—but first, let's keep going and start implementing the algorithm in F#, assuming we know what value of k is correct, and see where that leads us.

Implementing K-Means Clustering

A few concepts emerged from the algorithm description: Given a collection of observations, we need to be able to assign each of them to one of k centroids, based on shortest distance, and we also need to reduce a cluster of observations into a centroid. So far nothing sounds particularly specific to our dataset, so let's try to write a general version of the algorithm, in its own separate module, and use it for the problem at hand by loading it in a script later.

This gives us a solid starting point. From the outside, the algorithm should look like this: We need to provide a collection of observations and a number of clusters k. We also need a definition for distance, so that we can assign an observation to the closest centroid, and a way to reduce observations from the same cluster into a single, aggregated observation, the updated centroid. In pseudo-code, here is an outline of what we are going to implement:

```
clusterize
     1. initialize
             assign every observation an initial centroid ID of 0
             pick k distinct observations as the initial centroids 1 to k
     2. search
             assign each observation to the closest centroid
             if no assignment changes, done: we have good, stable centroids
             else
                     group observations assigned to the same cluster
                     reduce the observations to their average centroid
                     repeat with the new centroids
     3. search, starting from the initial centroids
```

At a minimum, I would expect the output to return all the centroids that have been identified by the algorithm; as a bonus, it would be nice to get back a "classifier" function, which, given an arbitrary observation, will tell me directly what centroid it is assigned to.

Let's begin implementing. First, we need a new file—let's call it KMeans.fs—and then we can start working on a clusterize function. Before starting iteratively updating clusters and assignments, we need to initialize both of these and decide on how to represent them. Let's give each cluster an ID, which will simply be an integer, and define an assignment as an observation with a cluster ID attached. Of course, we could create dedicated types for both assignments and observations, but it doesn't really seem worth the effort—this is, after all, entirely internal to the algorithm implementation. So rather than create unnecessary types, we will simply use tuples here, in both cases storing the cluster ID in the first slot and the observation in the second.

We can then initialize the procedure in a couple of lines. Create a random number generator and pick k observations randomly as the starting candidates for centroids, with a cluster ID from 1 to k. This is not unreasonable: Picking existing observations guarantees that the centroid locations won't be completely unrealistic. At the same time, this also means that we are at risk of picking "bad" initial centroids. We'll ignore that issue for the moment and revisit it later.

Our first problem is to pick k distinct observations at random from our dataset, which we will use as starting centroids. Let's do it the easy way by picking random numbers in the interval from 0 to `size - 1`, and adding them to a set (which will automatically detect and eliminate duplicates) until the number of selected observations is k, the number of clusters we want. This is not perfect; in particular, if we were trying to pick a large set of distinct indexes, in comparison to the dataset size, this would be very inefficient. However, assuming the number of clusters is very small by comparison, this will do.

Listing 5-4. Selecting k observations as initial centroids

```
namespace Unsupervised

module KMeans =

    let pickFrom size k =
        let rng = System.Random ()
        let rec pick (set:int Set) =
            let candidate = rng.Next(size)
            let set = set.Add candidate
            if set.Count = k then set
            else pick set
        pick Set.empty |> Set.toArray
```

As for the assignments, we will give them an arbitrary starting centroid ID of 0, which doesn't match any real centroid ID. Given that all centroids have IDs greater than 1, this means that in our first pass, every observation is guaranteed to be assigned a different centroid, and the algorithm will at least complete a full update cycle.

Listing 5-5. Initializing the clustering algorithm

```
let initialize observations k =

    let size = Array.length observations

    let centroids =
        pickFrom size k
        |> Array.mapi (fun i index ->
            i+1, observations.[index])

    let assignments =
        observations
        |> Array.map (fun x -> 0, x)

    (assignments,centroids)
```

Now that we have a starting point, all we need to do is write the update procedure by assigning each observation to its closest centroid, which gives us a new assignment, and comparing it to the previous one. If no observation changes cluster, we are done (every cluster will remain the same, and so will the centroids), otherwise, group the observations by cluster ID, reduce them into their average centroid, and keep going. We will now define a recursive function search inside the clusterize function, generate initial values, and start recursively updating the centroids.

Listing 5-6. Recursive clusters update

```
let clusterize distance centroidOf observations k =

    let rec search (assignments,centroids) =
        // Centroid ID of the closest centroid
        let classifier observation =
            centroids
            |> Array.minBy (fun (_,centroid) ->
                distance observation centroid)
            |> fst
        // Assign each observation to closest centroid
        let assignments' =
            assignments
            |> Array.map (fun (_,observation) ->
                let closestCentroidId = classifier observation
                (closestCentroidId,observation))
        // Check if any observation changed cluster
        let changed =
            (assignments,assignments')
            ||> Seq.zip
            |> Seq.exists (fun ((oldClusterID,_),(newClusterID,_)) ->
                not (oldClusterID = newClusterID))

        if changed
        then
            let centroids' =
                assignments'
                |> Seq.groupBy fst
                |> Seq.map (fun (clusterID, group) ->
                    clusterID, group |> Seq.map snd |> centroidOf)
                |> Seq.toArray
            search (assignments',centroids')
        else centroids,classifier

    // start searching from initial values
    let initialValues = initialize observations k
    search initialValues
```

And that's it: We have a clustering algorithm! Given an array of observations and a value for k, if we provide a definition for the distance and reducer functions we want to use, we should get back clusters and a function that assigns any observation to the appropriate cluster.

Clustering StackOverflow Tags

Let's go back to our script file and see what happens if we cluster our dataset. We need a couple of elements in order to run our clustering algorithm: loading and opening the KMeans module in our script, observations, distance and reducer functions that work on observations, and a value for k, the number of clusters we are searching for.

Running the Clustering Analysis

Let's use the Euclidean distance and reduce a set of observations to their average. This is easily done with the following code, which goes into our script:

Listing 5-7. Defining distance and reduction for clustering

```
#load "KMeans.fs"
open Unsupervised.KMeans

type Observation = float []

let features = headers.Length

let distance (obs1:Observation) (obs2:Observation) =
    (obs1, obs2)
    ||> Seq.map2 (fun u1 u2 -> pown (u1 - u2) 2)
    |> Seq.sum

let centroidOf (cluster:Observation seq) =
    Array.init features (fun f ->
        cluster
        |> Seq.averageBy (fun user -> user.[f]))
```

We are now ready to search for clusters. We'll eliminate the observations where no tag is used (that is, where users have been entirely inactive on the selected tags during the period), pick, totally arbitrarily, a value of 5 for k—and call clusterize:

Listing 5-8. Clustering the dataset

```
let observations1 =
    observations
    |> Array.map (Array.map float)
    |> Array.filter (fun x -> Array.sum x > 0.)

let (clusters1, classifier1) =
    let clustering = clusterize distance centroidOf
    let k = 5
    clustering observations1 k
>
val clusters1 : (int * Observation) [] =
  [|(1,
    [|2.47860262; 1.063755459; 9.765065502; 5.454148472; 2.333624454;
      2.293449782; 5.173799127; 10.98689956; 4.822707424; 5.772052402;
      1.693449782; 7.274235808; 9.717030568; 1.220087336; 23.49956332;
      10.12751092; 5.999126638; 2.011353712; 2.509170306; 7.932751092;
      6.620087336; 12.78777293; 7.658515284; 7.425327511; 6.794759825;
      5.561572052; 9.624454148; 4.525764192; 1.031441048; 4.483842795|]);
    // snipped for brevity
    (2,
    [|0.0; 0.0; 19.0; 17.0; 19.0; 0.0; 0.0; 69.0; 0.0; 0.0; 0.0; 0.0; 0.0;
      0.0; 68.0; 0.0; 0.0; 0.0; 0.0; 4159.0; 0.0; 821.0; 17.0; 56.0; 0.0; 0.0;
```

```
        7054.0; 1797.0; 0.0; 0.0|])|]
val classifier1 : (Observation -> int)
```

As expected, we get back two things: an array of five clusters, each with an ID and a set of values representing the profile for the cluster for each of our tags. As an example, in the output above, (2, [|0.0; 0.0; 19.0; // snipped // 0.0|]) represents the cluster with ID 2; the average user in that cluster never used the tags .NET or ajax (the two first tags in our list), but used the Android tag 19 times. Note that, because we pick our initial centroids at random, it is very likely that you will observe different results for each run (we'll get back to that in a minute).

Analyzing the Results

Let's face it, it is hard to interpret the output in its current form. The first thing that would help would be to map each of the clusters and align the tag names with the numbers we have. Let's do this:

```
clusters1
|> Seq.iter (fun (id,profile) ->
    printfn "CLUSTER %i" id
    profile
    |> Array.iteri (fun i value -> printfn "%16s %.1f" headers.[i] value))


>
CLUSTER 4
            .net 2.9
            ajax 1.1
         android 6.1
          arrays 5.0
        asp.net 2.4
        // snipped for brevity
```

This is a bit better; at least we can start scanning through each of the clusters and looking for some sort of pattern to emerge. However, the information is still a bit overwhelming—let's see if a chart helps us visualize our output more clearly (see Figure 5-11):

```
Chart.Combine [
    for (id,profile) in clusters1 ->
        profile
        |> Seq.mapi (fun i value -> headers.[i], value)
        |> Chart.Bar
    ]
|> fun chart -> chart.WithXAxis(LabelStyle=labels)
```

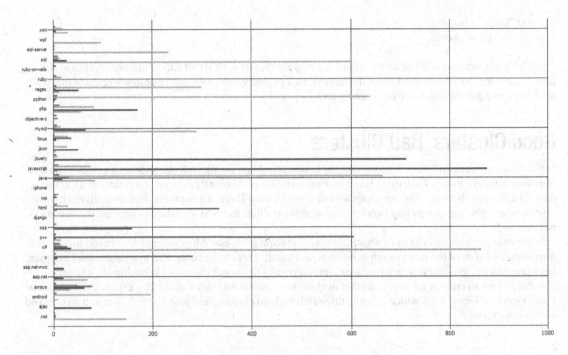

Figure 5-11. *Clusters profile (see source code package for details)*

The resulting chart is much easier to parse. In this case, what I see is that

- cluster 2 has a large spike for Java and Android, as well as Python and Regex (!);

- cluster 4 has strong spikes on Javascript, JQuery, html, and css, as well as PHP;

- cluster 5 is strong on C#, .NET, and WPF—and SQL, SQL Server, and MySQL;

- cluster 3 has spikes for C and C++, as well as a hint of Linux and Arrays; and

- cluster 1 has no discernible spike.

This is interesting. On one hand, the clustering algorithm did run, and produced clusters, and some of the associations that come up make sense. Seeing Java and Android together is not surprising. Seeing web-client technologies like Javascript, JQuery, and html in the same bucket, or database-related tags like SQL, MySQL, and SQL server together, is logical. Our algorithm does pick up relationships that are meaningful. At the same time, there appear to be some oddities, too: are Java, Python, and Regex really related? What about this strange bucket that mixes .NET and database developers?

Before going further, let's look at another piece of information. How big are each of these clusters?

```
observations1
|> Seq.countBy (fun obs -> classifier1 obs)
|> Seq.iter (fun (clusterID, count) ->
    printfn "Cluster %i: %i elements" clusterID count)
>
Cluster 4: 1137 elements
Cluster 2: 22 elements
Cluster 1: 23 elements
```

```
Cluster 5: 20 elements
Cluster 3: 15 elements
```

That's not very good. What we have here is one giant cluster with about 93% of our observations, and four clusters, each with less than 2% of the dataset. In a perfect world, we would like to see clusters that are somewhat comparable in size. What is going on?

Good Clusters, Bad Clusters

Let's take a step back and think for a minute about what could go wrong with our approach and how we can hopefully improve things. First, there is one obvious possibility: Maybe there is just no cluster at all in the data. In that case, there is really not much we can do—if it's not there, it's not there. However, given that we saw some sensible tag groups pop in our initial analysis, we'll go forward with the assumption that we are not doomed.

There are at least two ways our algorithm could go wrong: We could be looking for an inadequate number of clusters, or the features might be on scales too different to be compared in a meaningful manner. Let's take a closer look at these two problems, and hopefully figure out ideas for improving our clusters.

We picked an entirely arbitrary number of clusters to search for—what should we expect if that number is off? Consider Figure 5-12, which exhibits three rather clean clusters, and imagine now that you were asked to find two clusters.

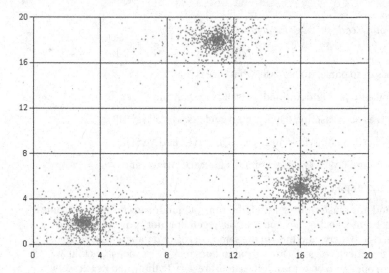

Figure 5-12. *Searching for insufficiently many clusters*

The algorithm will very probably identify two clusters, in one of three ways: One of the clusters will be "correct," and the other one will aggregate the remaining two clusters, like in Figure 5-13, for example.

This is actually fairly reasonable: If we can pick only two groups, picking one good one and making a mediocre one from the two remaining is as good as we can get. However, given that we pick our starting centroids at random, the clusters will depend almost entirely on which three random observations we started with. If we repeat the procedure multiple times, we will see three different results appear, combining the "true" clusters differently. In a situation where we have more than three clusters, we would expect to see more combinations appear.

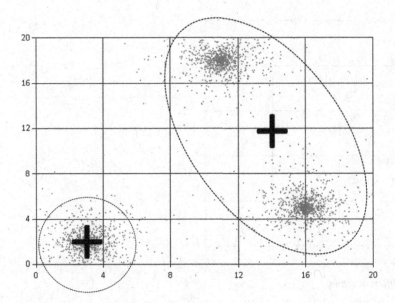

Figure 5-13. *Searching for two clusters out of three*

This problem sounds consistent with what we are observing here. If you ran the clustering function multiple times, you probably observed the following: The results are different from one run to the next, but there are consistent buckets that frequently appear together, but might also be lumped together with other ones. As an example, the combination Java and Android appears frequently, with or without Python.

If we want to address this issue, we need to increase the number of clusters to a value that actually works; that is, find a value for k that is close to the actual number of clusters.

We will revisit this question in the next section after looking at another way k-means clustering can go wrong. Consider the situation described in Figure 5-14. What we have here are two clusters, centered at {-2;0} and {2;0}, but with very different elongations on the X and Y axes. While the X values are primarily in the [-3;-1] and [1;3] ranges, the Y values vary all the way between -20 and 20.

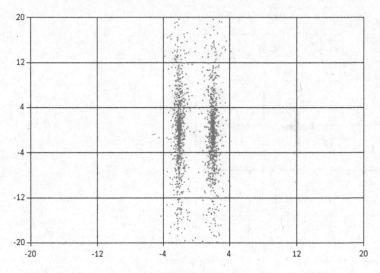

Figure 5-14. *Features with very different scales*

What would happen if we unleashed k-means on that dataset as-is, asking for two clusters? Again, there is an element of randomness, depending on what initial centroids we pick, but a plausible outcome is the following: We could quite easily get two clusters, one centered around {0;10}, the other around {0;-10}. Why is that?

The problem here is that the two features are on very different scales, and, as a result, whatever differences exist on the X axis (the first feature) will be completely dwarfed by the spread on the Y axis. In other words, using the distance on the raw data will give a very poor indication of how close or far apart two points are (see Figure 5-15).

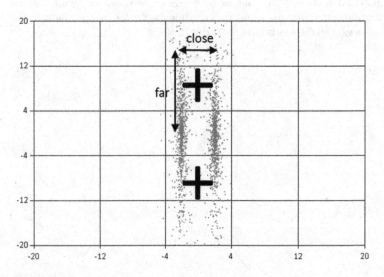

Figure 5-15. *Close points*

How can we address this issue? Simple: If the issue stems from features being on different scales, we need to transform the data so that differences of the same magnitude are comparable across all features. In other words, when an observation has a low or high value on a feature, the impact on the distance function should be comparable.

One common approach is to rescale each feature using the following formula: x' <- (x - min) / (max - min). As a result, every feature is spread on the interval from 0 to 1, with the smallest value being 0 and the largest 1, and the others are scaled linearly in between. As an illustration, if we applied this to our previous dataset, this is how the data would look (see Figure 5-16):

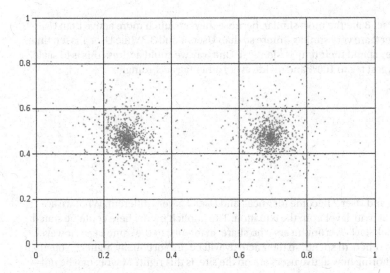

Figure 5-16. *Features, rescaled*

This is not the only way to rescale features; depending on the data, other methods can be more appropriate. We will see another way features can be rescaled a bit later. Feature scaling is a bit of a black art, and there isn't one unique way to do it. As a rule of thumb, ask yourself if the distance you are using is comparing comparable things.

Rescaling Our Dataset to Improve Clusters

Our initial clustering extracted some information that seemed sensible; it also had clear issues, which were consistent with having an inadequate number of clusters (we will get different results every time we run the algorithm), and discrepancies in feature scales. Before tackling the harder task of determining an adequate number of clusters to search for, let's begin with the simpler issue of rescaling the dataset.

You might have picked up on the fact that the spikes our initial clustering detects correspond to the tags with highest usage: Javascript, Java, C#, Python, and so on. In general, while the algorithm will produce different clusters from run to run, the same set of tags will show up. This makes sense, because high-volume tags will produce large differences in distance. This is not great, because what our algorithm is doing is essentially finding high-traffic tags, and won't be picking up more subtle differences on lower-traffic tags.

The big issue here is that the volume of activity on each tag is fairly different: The average usage of JavaScript is over 20 times higher than that of the iPhone tag. We could rescale features along the lines of we described earlier, and remap them to span the interval from 0 to 1. We will take a different direction instead. Here is how we could describe our dataset: We believe users can be categorized by a few interest profiles, but they have a widely different level of activity on StackOverflow. To compare their profiles directly, regardless of how active they are on the site, what we want is to eliminate the discrepancies due to activity levels. For instance, consider these three hypothetical users:

	JavaScript	C#
User 1	100	20
User 2	10	2
User 3	50	50

By raw distance, User 1 and User 3 are the most similar, because they are much more active than User 2. However, arguably, User 1 and User 2 are very similar—more so than Users 1 and 3. While User 1 is ten times more active than User 2, where they spend their time is identical. One way we could address this is to scale by user: For each row, scale the largest tag to 100% and divide every other tag accordingly.

	JavaScript	C#
User 1	100%	20%
User 2	100%	20%
User 3	100%	100%

If we do that, suddenly User 1 and User 2 become identical, and User 3 is very different. What we are really doing here is removing user activity level from the equation. The implicit model here could be stated like this: "There are a few archetypal StackOverflow users who share an interest in the same tags. However, some of them have more time than others to spend, so their activity will be proportionally higher." Note that this also means that we are now ignoring how active users are on the site. Is this right? Maybe, maybe not— there is no clear-cut answer to that question.

At any rate, let's try this out, still with a "bad" number of clusters. All we need to do, really, is to take our observations and divide each number by the largest value in that row.

Listing 5-9. Normalizing observations to similar activity

```
let rowNormalizer (obs:Observation) : Observation =
    let max = obs |> Seq.max
    obs |> Array.map (fun tagUse -> tagUse / max)

let observations2 =
    observations
    |> Array.filter (fun x -> Array.sum x > 0.)
    |> Array.map (Array.map float)
    |> Array.map rowNormalizer

let (clusters2, classifier2) =
    let clustering = clusterize distance centroidOf
    let k = 5
    clustering observations2 k
```

We still haven't dealt with what k should be, and, as a result, we are very likely still looking for too few clusters; results will still be unstable from run to run. However, even then, we should observe a couple of things. First, the cluster size is now much more balanced. Running the same code as before, here is what we get:

```
observations2
|> Seq.countBy (fun obs -> classifier2 obs)
|> Seq.iter (fun (clusterID, count) ->
    printfn "Cluster %i: %i elements" clusterID count)

>
Cluster 4: 480 elements
Cluster 5: 252 elements
Cluster 2: 219 elements
Cluster 1: 141 elements
Cluster 3: 125 elements
val it : unit = ()
```

Also, some associations appear more clearly now, such as the pair C/C++, or even pairs that didn't register before, like Python and Django, or Ruby and Ruby on Rails, where one of the elements had too little activity to make a difference in the distance (see Figure 5-17).

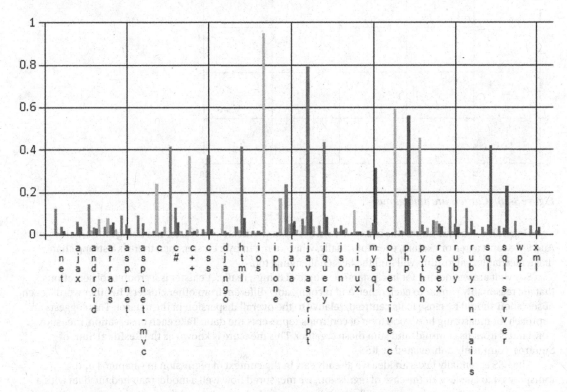

Figure 5-17. *Clusters after row normalization (see source code package for details)*

Identifying How Many Clusters to Search For

We still haven't addressed the crucial question of figuring out how many clusters we should search for. Unfortunately, as we discussed earlier, this is not an issue we can brush aside: Searching for too few clusters will cause unstable results. So, let's first figure out how to approach the problem, and then apply it to our dataset.

What Are Good Clusters?

I will reiterate once again that identifying clusters is not a trivial task, because there is some ambiguity about what a cluster is. Consider Figure 5-18: How many clusters do you see? You could make the case for three big clusters, or for seven clusters—and probably more combinations in between (for the record, this was generated with seven clusters).

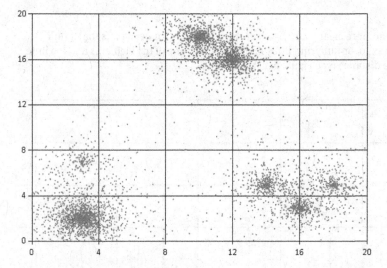

Figure 5-18. *Clusters are ambiguous*

Hopefully, at a minimum, this example conveys what we mean by a cluster not being entirely clear cut. And if we can't agree or explain, even informally, what we mean by a cluster, then there is a strong chance that a mechanical algorithm will find the task challenging, too.

So, what are we looking for in clusters? A couple of things, really. A cluster is a group of observations that are reasonably similar to each other, and recognizably different from other clusters. In other words, each observation should be close to its centroid, relative to the overall dispersion in the dataset. This suggests an approach for measuring how good a set of centroids represents the data: Take each observation, measure how far it is from its centroid, and sum these together. This measure is known as the **Residual Sum of Squares**, commonly abbreviated as **RSS**.

The RSS essentially takes an idea we already saw in the context of regression in Chapter 4 and transposes it to clusters. In the case of regression, we measured how well a model matched the data with a cost function, computing the square difference between each data point and the corresponding predicted value, and taking their sum. In our case now, each observation that belongs to a cluster is modelled as its centroid, and we measure how well our clusters fit the data by comparing each observation to the corresponding centroid.

How about we try different values of k and find the one that minimizes RSS? Well, there is a bit of a problem with that. Suppose we have a dataset with N observations—there is an obvious value that minimizes RSS, and that is k = N. If we create one centroid for each observation, we will of course get a perfect fit. Note also that if we have k centroids, adding one centroid will always decrease RSS (to be more precise, RSS will never increase).

This is useful in that it clarifies what we are after. What we want is an "efficient" summary of the data, once again following Occam's Razor principle. We want clusters that explain the data well, but are as simple as possible. Taking only RSS into account misses that second point: There is no penalty for complexity, and our clustering will over-fit and simply reproduce the dataset itself, without any form of summarization.

So, what should we do? The general answer is, if we had a measure for clustering quality, it should probably include RSS (how well the model fits the data), and a penalty term for complexity. Again, this is a tricky problem, and there is no silver bullet here. There are a few popular approaches. First, imagine that you computed the RSS for a value of k. Now compute the RSS for k + 1: If you are barely improving RSS, increasing the number of clusters is not economical. This method is known as the elbow method—look for places where the relative improvement in RSS degrades.

This general direction can be used to compute a numeric measure for how good a particular value of k is. The **Akaike Information Criterion**, or **AIC**, is a popular choice. It combines in one measure the RSS and a penalty term 2 * m * k, where m is the number of features and k the number of clusters. In other words, prefer models with fewer clusters, and be more conservative with models with many features. There are a couple of other classic measures (which we won't implement here), such as BIC (Bayesian Information Criterion) or Calinski-Harabasz, which follow roughly the same general principles.

Which one is right? Unfortunately, it depends. Again, clustering is a bit of an ambiguous task; all these methods are heuristics, and while they follow a similar general approach, they will not necessarily agree; identifying something that works will usually take a bit of trial and error. In the next section, we'll simply use the AIC, because it's particularly easy to implement.

Identifying k on the StackOverflow Dataset

Let's see how this works out on the dataset at hand. The first heuristic we will use to calibrate which value of k might work is a "rule of thumb" common in the industry, which suggests the following value for k:

```
let ruleOfThumb (n:int) = sqrt (float n / 2.)
let k_ruleOfThumb = ruleOfThumb (observations2.Length)
```

This approach is obviously way too simple to work well in every situation; the only thing it takes into account is how large the dataset is! On the other hand, it has the benefit of simplicity. I would recommend using it simply to get a rough sense for what range of values might be reasonable. In this case, the suggested value is 25, which we will use as an upper bound for k. Next, let's try out the AIC.

Listing 5-10. Akaike Information Criterion (AIC)

```
let squareError (obs1:Observation) (obs2:Observation) =
    (obs1,obs2)
    ||> Seq.zip
    |> Seq.sumBy (fun (x1,x2) -> pown (x1-x2) 2)

let RSS (dataset:Observation[]) centroids =
    dataset
    |> Seq.sumBy (fun obs ->
        centroids
        |> Seq.map (squareError obs)
        |> Seq.min)
```

```
let AIC (dataset:Observation[]) centroids =
    let k = centroids |> Seq.length
    let m = dataset.[0] |> Seq.length
    RSS dataset centroids + float (2 * m * k)
```

In order to figure out a decent value for k, we'll try out every single possibility between k = 1 and k = 25. Because the clustering itself is going to be unstable for low values of k, we will run the algorithm a couple of times for each value and average out the corresponding AIC so that we can cancel out potential flukes due to, for instance, unfortunate initial value selection:

```
[1..25]
|> Seq.map (fun k ->
    let value =
        [ for _ in 1 .. 10 ->
            let (clusters, classifier) =
                let clustering = clusterize distance centroidOf
                clustering observations2 k
            AIC observations2 (clusters |> Seq.map snd) ]
        |> List.average
    k, value)
|> Chart.Line
```

Figure 5-19 displays the result of our search, plotting average AIC values for various values of k. The AIC value decreases steadily as k increases from 1 to 5, keeps slowly going down until we reach k = 10, and starts climbing back up for larger values of k. This suggests we should use a value of k = 10, which minimizes AIC, and should give us our best shot at clean clusters. Note, however, that the curve is rather flat around 10.

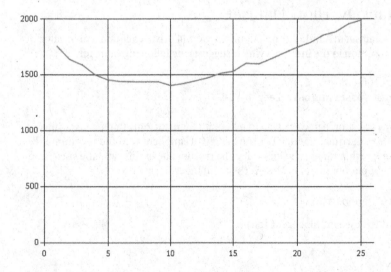

Figure 5-19. *Search for k-minimizing AIC*

Our Final Clusters

Now that we have selected a value of 10 for k, based on AIC, let's see what happens. We can now run the clustering algorithm multiple times so as to avoid flukes, and select the model that minimizes RSS for that specific value of k.

Listing 5-11. Final clusters

```
let (bestClusters, bestClassifier) =
    let clustering = clusterize distance centroidOf
    let k = 10
    seq {
        for _ in 1 .. 20 ->
            clustering observations2 k
    }
    |> Seq.minBy (fun (cs,f) ->
        RSS observations2 (cs |> Seq.map snd))
```

What's in our clusters? Let's check, then print out the tags with highest usage in each cluster. Note that just picking high values might not be a good idea in general; what we are really looking for are values that are significantly different from the rest of the observations. In general, picking large absolute differences from the average might be a better idea, but in our situation, with the averages being very low, we can safely simply look for unusually high values.

```
bestClusters
|> Seq.iter (fun (id,profile) ->
    printfn "CLUSTER %i" id
    profile
    |> Array.iteri (fun i value ->
        if value > 0.2 then printfn "%16s %.1f" headers.[i] value))

>
CLUSTER 5
          android 0.3
             java 0.5
CLUSTER 7
           django 0.3
           python 0.9
CLUSTER 4
             html 0.3
       javascript 0.9
           jquery 0.5
CLUSTER 6
             ruby 0.7
    ruby-on-rails 0.7
CLUSTER 10
                c 0.4
              c++ 0.8
CLUSTER 2
       javascript 0.3
            mysql 0.2
              php 1.0
```

157

```
CLUSTER 8
           .net 0.3
            c# 0.9
CLUSTER 9
          mysql 0.3
            sql 0.8
     sql-server 0.6
CLUSTER 1
            ios 1.0
     objective-c 0.6
CLUSTER 3
            css 0.9
           html 0.7
     javascript 0.5
         jquery 0.3
```

This looks pretty good. I suspect you can easily conjure a mental picture for each of the profiles, which correspond to clear development stacks. This is great: Without much effort, we managed to automatically extract meaningful information out of raw data. Without any understanding of what these tags mean, just by looking at the dataset and historical usage patterns, k-means figured out that Ruby and Ruby on Rails are related, or that some people we call DBAs focus mainly on SQL-related technologies.

There is probably more information we could squeeze out of the dataset using k-means; however, it is likely going to become increasingly hard to get new and interesting results if we continue in that direction, because our current results are pretty good already. What we will do instead is leave it at that for k-means, and introduce a completely different technique, Principal Component Analysis. We will apply it to the same problem so that we can compare and contrast the two methods.

Detecting How Features Are Related

For all its qualities, k-means clustering is not the end all be all. In particular, it doesn't provide a comprehensive picture of how the features work together. We can figure out some relationships by inspecting each cluster profile, looking for features that are markedly higher or lower than is typical, but this is a tedious manual process. The approach we will explore now, **Principal Component Analysis**, or **PCA** in short, is in a sense the complement to k-means: Where k-means provides a clear picture of individual profiles, but not much information regarding how features relate to each other, PCA is primarily about detecting some structure in features, instead of in individuals.

Covariance and Correlation

Patterns in data can take infinitely many shapes. While detecting all of them is hopeless, some patterns are both useful and easy to spot. One such example is the following: "Whenever quantity A increases, quantity B increases, too." This is what **covariance** and **correlation** are about.

The covariance between two measurements X and Y is defined as:

```
Cov(X,Y) = average [(X-average(X)) * (Y-average(Y))]
```

Once you start breaking this down, you see it is a reasonable way to go. If two values X and Y go up and down together, then when one is above its average, the other one should be, too, and the product will be positive. Similarly, when one goes below the average, so too should the other—and the product of their difference (both negative numbers now) will still be positive. By the same line of reasoning, you would expect two features moving in opposite directions to have a negative covariance.

■ **Side Note**   It is important to realize that a covariance (or correlation) of zero does not mean there is no relationship between features. It simply indicates that their relationship is not as simple as moving up and down together. As an example, data points describing a perfect circle will have a correlation of zero, even though their relationship is perfectly determined

Covariance is great, but it has one problem: It depends on the scale of the features and has no obvious scale itself, which makes interpreting it difficult. What is a high covariance? It depends on the data. Correlation is a modification of covariance, and addresses that problem. Formally, the correlation between features X and Y is defined as:

```
Corr(X,Y) = Cov(X,Y) / (stdDev(X) * stdDev(Y))
```

where stdDev stands for **standard deviation**. Depending on your level of comfort with statistics, this might look intimidating. It should not be—let's break this down a bit. Our issue with covariance was the scale discrepancy between X and Y. To make different features comparable, what we need is to reduce the terms (X-average(X)) and (Y-average(Y)) to similar scales. Dividing (X-average(X)) by its average value—the average distance between X and its average (quite a mouthful!)—would do just that, and that's exactly what the standard deviation, often denoted as sigma, is.

■ **Tip**   The standard deviation (and its square, the variance) is often described as a measure for the dispersion of a feature. Personally, I found the following description helpful: *The standard deviation sigma measures the average distance to the average.* If you took a random observation from your sample, the standard deviation is how far it would be from the sample average.

You can expand the covariance part and reorganize the formula a bit into this equivalent version, which helps us better understand how correlation works:

```
Corr(X,Y) = average [(X-avg(X))/stdDev(X) * (Y-avg(Y))/stdDev(Y)]
```

The term (X-average(X))/stdDev(X) takes the differences from the average from the covariance and rescales them by sigma so that the average difference is now 1.0. Both the X and Y terms are now on a comparable scale, and as a result (we won't prove it here), correlation has this pleasant property in that it goes from -1.0 to 1.0. A value of 1.0 indicates that X and Y always grow together in a perfect line, -1.0 indicates a perfect line in the opposite direction, and 0.0 indicates that no such relationship has been detected. The closer to 1.0 or -1.0 a correlation is, the stronger that pattern is—that is, the features move mostly together, with a certain level of uncertainty.

Incidentally, transforming a measurement X into (X-average(X))/stdDev(X) is a classic way to rescale a feature, and is known as a **z-score**. It is a bit more involved than the method we discussed earlier, where we simply converted values from [min;max] to [0;1], but it has some advantages as well. The transformed feature is centered on 0, so positive or negative values can be immediately interpreted as being high or low. If the feature is reasonably normal shaped, that is, bell-shaped around its mean, the result might be more "reasonable," too. While the min and max values are, by definition, outliers with extreme values, the standard deviation is typically a better metric by which to scale observations.

Correlations Between StackOverflow Tags

Let's go ahead and see how that works out on our dataset. For convenience, rather than adding code to our current script, we'll create a new script, PCA.fsx, and a module, PCA.fs, from which we will extract the principal component analysis code. In this section, we will also make use of linear algebra and statistics quite a bit, so rather than reinventing the wheel, let's add references to Math.NET Numerics and Math.NET Numerics for F# to our project via NuGet. Our script will start the same way as the previous one did, loading references to fsharp.Charting and reading headers and observations from the file.

As it turns out, Math.NET has a correlation matrix built in. The correlation function expects data to be presented in the form of features, and not observations—that is, instead of 1,600 observations with 30 values each, we need to transpose it into 30 rows, which correspond to the 30 features.

Listing 5-12. Computing the correlation matrix

```
#r @"..\packages\MathNet.Numerics.3.5.0\lib\net40\MathNet.Numerics.dll"
#r @"..\packages\MathNet.Numerics.FSharp.3.5.0\lib\net40\MathNet.Numerics.FSharp.dll"

open MathNet
open MathNet.Numerics.LinearAlgebra
open MathNet.Numerics.Statistics

let correlations =
    observations
    |> Matrix.Build.DenseOfColumnArrays
    |> Matrix.toRowArrays
    |> Correlation.PearsonMatrix

>

val correlations : Matrix<float> =
  DenseMatrix 30x30-Double
           1    0.00198997   -0.00385582      0.11219      0.425774   ..      0.172283    0.0969075
  0.00198997             1    -0.0101171     0.259896       0.16159   ..   -0.00783435     0.025791
 -0.00385582    -0.0101171             1    0.0164469   -0.00862693   ..   -0.00465378    0.0775214
// snipped for brevity
```

As expected, we get back a 30 x 30 matrix, where each cell corresponds to the correlation between two specific features. Reassuringly, the diagonal is all ones (a feature should be perfectly correlated with itself), and the matrix is symmetrical (the correlation between A and B, and B and A, should be identical). This isn't particularly usable, because there is just too much data, so let's take every tag pair, grab their correlation from the matrix, and extract the 20 largest ones in absolute value, because large positive or negative values indicate equivalently strong correlations:

```
let feats = headers.Length
let correlated =
    [
        for col in 0 .. (feats - 1) do
            for row in (col + 1) .. (feats - 1) ->
                correlations.[col,row], headers.[col], headers.[row]
    ]
    |> Seq.sortBy (fun (corr, f1, f2) -> - abs corr)
    |> Seq.take 20
    |> Seq.iter (fun (corr, f1, f2) ->
        printfn "%s %s : %.2f" f1 f2 corr)

>
ios objective-c : 0.97
ios iphone : 0.94
mysql sql : 0.93
iphone objective-c : 0.89
sql sql-server : 0.88
css html : 0.84
.net c# : 0.83
javascript jquery : 0.82
ajax javascript : 0.78
mysql sql-server : 0.76
html javascript : 0.73
html jquery : 0.71
ajax jquery : 0.70
ajax html : 0.66
ajax json : 0.60
javascript json : 0.56
asp.net c# : 0.53
c c++ : 0.50
ruby ruby-on-rails : 0.50
mysql php : 0.48
```

■ **Tip**   At the time of writing, there was no built-in descending sort in F#. As an alternative, you can sort by negation; for instance, in Seq.sortBy (fun (corr, f1, f2) -> - abs corr).

The results are very reasonable. We immediately see some groups of features that go hand in hand: iOS, objective-c, and iPhone; SQL, MySQL, and SQL-server—and so on and so forth. With very little effort, the correlation matrix extracted a lot of information from our dataset.

Identifying Better Features with Principal Component Analysis

We looked at the correlation matrix as a useful summary of relationships between features. Another way we can interpret it is as a signal that our dataset contains a lot of redundant information. As an example, iOS, objective-C, and iPhone have a correlation that is pretty close to 100%. What this means is that we could almost merge these three features into one—say, "iOS developer. Once you know one of the three is high (or low), you pretty much know the two others.

At the same time, some correlations are a bit trickier to handle. For instance, if you dive into the dataset a bit, you'll see that MySQL and SQL, SQL and SQL-Server, and MySQL and PHP are highly correlated. Does this mean that, by transitivity, PHP and SQL-Server go together? I doubt it—from my personal experience, I would read this as two different relationships, the DBAs on one side, and possibly the LAMP developers on the other. They happen to share one common interest in MySQL, but they are not one.

In this section, we will demonstrate principal component analysis (or in short, PCA), a data-mining technique that looks at the structure of the covariance or correlation matrix and uses it to reorganize data into a new set of features, combining the existing ones into composites that represent the data more efficiently and avoid redundancy.

Recombining Features with Algebra

A complete explanation on why PCA works would take us a bit far into algebra, without being all that useful in the end. We will try to convey the key points through an illustrative example, deliberately using some hand-waving at strategic moments, and letting readers who are so inclined dig deeper on their own.

What we are after here is a way to reorganize our dataset. Consider for a minute a dataset with, say, two features only, instead of our 30. One way to represent a transformation of our features is by using a 2 x 2 matrix. If we multiply an observation (a vector of two elements) by that matrix, we will get a new vector, which still has two features:

```
let observation = vector [ 2.0; 5.0 ]
let transform =
    matrix [ [ 1.0; 3.0 ]
             [ 2.0; 1.0 ] ]
transform * observation |> printfn "%A"

>
seq [17.0; 9.0]
```

Each of the rows in the transform matrix can be seen as weights. The first row, for instance, states that the first transformed feature combines 1.0 part of the first original feature and 3.0 parts of the second. If that transformation were the identity matrix (1s on the diagonal, 0s everywhere else), the transformation would simply return the original.

What we are looking for is a matrix of that form. Obviously, we can't pick just any arbitrary matrix; it would just rearrange the features, but without a reason a priori to produce anything particularly useful. So, what would we like to achieve here? In this particular situation, we would like the transformation to rearrange features so as to limit the information redundancy we spotted in the correlation matrix. We would also like a way to distinguish major trends in the dataset from unimportant differences.

This is the part where the heavy hand-waving takes place. As it turns out, there is a linear algebra technique that does just what we want: The factorization of a matrix into eigenvectors and eigenvalues. At a very high level, an N x X square matrix M can be uniquely decomposed into up to N pairs of eigenvalues and eigenvectors (a float, and a vector of N elements), each of which satisfies the following equation: M x eigenvector = eigenvalue x eigenvector. In other words, an eigenvector is a direction that just stretches M by an amplitude corresponding to its eigenvalue.

If we apply this technique to the covariance matrix, what should we get? First, each eigenvector represents a new feature built by combining the existing ones. Remember that the covariance matrix measures differences off the average from each feature; the eigenvector with largest eigenvalue represents a feature with the most stretch. Thus, in the case of the covariance matrix, it means the direction in which we observe the most joint variations from the center of the data. Stated differently, the eigenvector with the largest eigenvalue is a feature that combines existing features in a way that explains most of the differences we observe in our dataset. The second-largest eigenvalue isolates the next most informative combination, once the effect of the first feature has been removed, and so on and so forth.

A Small Preview of PCA in Action

So far, this has all been fairly abstract. Before going into implementing PCA and applying it to the full dataset, let's illustrate what we are after with a small example. We'll be using the code we are going to write soon, ignoring the details and simply showing what type of results to expect, to clarify a bit how PCA works.

The correlation analysis we performed earlier showed a strong relationship between two pairs of features: iOS and objective-c, and SQL and SQL Server. Let's ignore all the other features and run principal component analysis on just these four.

The analysis extracts four eigenvalues, with magnitudes of 98.73, 38.59, 5.69 and 0.61, totaling 143.61. What these values represent is how much of the original information each of the new features explains. For instance, the first and largest component suffices to capture 98.73 / 143.61 ~ 69% of the variation in the data, and the second 27%. In other words, using just the two main features—the two main principal components—we can reproduce over 95% of the information from the original dataset. The two last components, which account for less of 5% of the information, can probably be ignored, as they bring almost no additional information.

What do these new features look like? We just need to look at the eigenvectors to figure that out. Table 5-1 displays the eigenvectors as a table. Each column corresponds to one component, ordered by decreasing importance. Each row corresponds with one of the original features, and each value represents the "weight" of the original feature in the component.

Table 5-1. *Principal Components*

Feature	Component 1	Component 2	Component 3	Component 4
iOS	0.00	**-0.70**	0.00	-0.71
Objective-C	0.00	**-0.71**	0.00	0.70
SQL	**0.80**	0.00	-0.59	0.00
SQL Server	**0.59**	0.00	0.80	0.00

In this case, what we see is that Component 1 combines SQL and SQL Server, and Component 2 Objective-C and iOS. This is excellent: PCA essentially simplified our dataset from four to just two features, "iOS /Objective-C" and "SQL / SQL Server," with barely any information loss.

We can visualize that information by representing how the original features map onto principal components, as in Figure 5-20. This is particularly convenient as the number of features increases: It makes it possible to eyeball relationships between features that would be much harder to spot in a table of numbers.

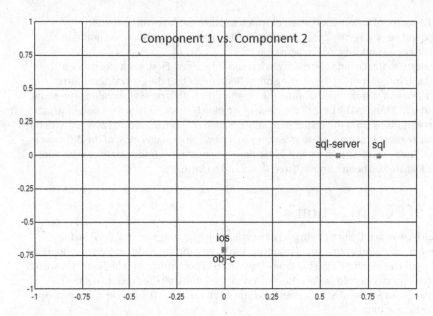

Figure 5-20. *Original features, projected onto principal components*

Another chart that is often useful visualizes the original observations after they have been converted from the original features into the principal components. As an example, Figure 5-21 shows that StackOverflow users typically don't care about both topics (except for one lone individual); people who are actively involved with SQL—that is, whose position is on the right of the chart—don't care about iPhone development, and vice versa.

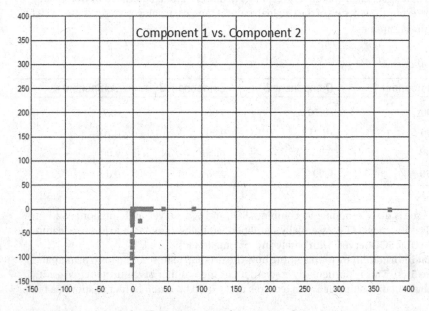

Figure 5-21. *Original observations projected on principal components*

Hopefully, this small example has given you a better sense of what to expect from PCA. Using a bit of linear algebra, we essentially managed to shrink our dataset by half, with barely any loss of information. Instead of four features originally, we ended up with two features–the two major principal components– which condensed information and provided a much clearer picture of our dataset. Now that we have seen what PCA can do for us, let's dive into how to implement it and then apply it to the full dataset.

Implementing PCA

The implementation itself is not overly complicated. We will move the general code into a separate code file called PCA.fs. PCA relies on the eigen decomposition of the dataset covariance matrix. There is no covariance matrix built into Math.NET, but it is easy enough to produce; we compute the covariance between every feature column, and avoid duplicating work by using the fact that the matrix is symmetrical (that is, the value at row r and column c is equal to the value found at row c and column r).

Listing 5-13. Computing the covariance matrix

```
namespace Unsupervised

module PCA =

    open MathNet
    open MathNet.Numerics.LinearAlgebra
    open MathNet.Numerics.Statistics

    let covarianceMatrix (M:Matrix<float>) =
        let cols = M.ColumnCount
        let C = DenseMatrix.create cols cols Matrix.Zero
        for c1 in 0 .. (cols - 1) do
            C.[c1,c1] <- Statistics.Variance (M.Column c1)
            for c2 in (c1 + 1) .. (cols - 1) do
                let cov = Statistics.Covariance (M.Column c1, M.Column c2)
                C.[c1,c2] <- cov
                C.[c2,c1] <- cov
        C
```

While we are at it, let's add another convenience function. PCA expects features to be centered and on a similar scale; to that effect, the dataset will typically be **normalized**, first by subtracting the average so that each feature has a zero mean, then shrinking it by the standard deviation to give it a spread of one around the mean.

Listing 5-14. Feature normalization

```
    let normalize dim (observations:float[][]) =

        let averages =
            Array.init dim (fun i ->
                observations
                |> Seq.averageBy (fun x -> x.[i]))
```

```
let stdDevs =
    Array.init dim (fun i ->
        let avg = averages.[i]
        observations
        |> Seq.averageBy (fun x ->
            pown (float x.[i] - avg) 2 |> sqrt))

observations
|> Array.map (fun row ->
    row
    |> Array.mapi (fun i x ->
        (float x - averages.[i]) / stdDevs.[i]))
```

There is barely anything left to implement for the principal component analysis itself. From a dataset consisting of rows of observations, we compute the covariance matrix and the eigen decomposition. For convenience, we also return a function (named "projector" later on) that takes in an individual observation and computes its representation in the new space as identified by PCA.

Listing 5-15. Principal component analysis

```
let pca (observations:float[][]) =

    let factorization =
        observations
        |> Matrix.Build.DenseOfRowArrays
        |> covarianceMatrix
        |> Matrix.eigen

    let eigenValues = factorization.EigenValues
    let eigenVectors = factorization.EigenVectors

    let projector (obs:float[]) =
        let obsVector = obs |> Vector.Build.DenseOfArray
        (eigenVectors.Transpose () * obsVector)
        |> Vector.toArray

    (eigenValues,eigenVectors), projector
```

Remember the transformation matrix we were describing earlier? This is exactly what we are doing here; we just need to transpose the eigenvectors matrix, because the factorization returns them as columns, and we need them as rows.

Applying PCA to the StackOverflow Dataset

Time to try it out in our script! Using our algorithm is as simple as this:

Listing 5-16. Running PCA on the StackOverflow dataset

```
#load "PCA.fs"
open Unsupervised.PCA

let normalized = normalize (headers.Length) observations

let (eValues,eVectors), projector = pca normalized
```

Let's take a look at the output. It is common to inspect the eigenvalues, which provide a sense of how much information each of the principal components (our new feature) contains. To do that, we will simply compute the total magnitude of the 30 eigenvalues we extracted, and then write out the percentage of the total each makes up, as well as how much of the total we cover by using only the most informative features up to that point.

Listing 5-17. Feature weight analysis

```
let total = eValues |> Seq.sumBy (fun x -> x.Magnitude)
eValues
|> Vector.toList
|> List.rev
|> List.scan (fun (percent,cumul) value ->
    let percent = 100. * value.Magnitude / total
    let cumul = cumul + percent
    (percent,cumul)) (0.,0.)
|> List.tail
|> List.iteri (fun i (p,c) -> printfn "Feat %2i: %.2f%% (%.2f%%)" i p c)

>
Feat  0: 19.14% (19.14%)
Feat  1: 9.21% (28.35%)
Feat  2: 8.62% (36.97%)
// snipped for brevity
Feat 28: 0.07% (99.95%)
Feat 29: 0.05% (100.00%)
```

This is consistent with our correlation matrix: The five top features explain over 50% of the dataset, and the top ten cover close to 80%. By contrast, the last ten features each cover less than 1% percent of the information.

■ **Caution**   It is customary to look at features in order of decreasing eigenvalue, but Math.NET returns the eigenvalues and eigenvectors in the opposite order. As a result, for instance, the most important principal component will be found in the last column of the eigenvectors matrix. Be careful!

Analyzing the Extracted Features

Can we take a look at these features? Each eigenvector directly maps the old features to a new feature, or principal component. All we need to do is to grab the eigenvector from the analysis results we obtained from the PCA earlier and map each of its values to the corresponding tag names. Listing 5-18 plots the original features against any pair of components; note how when we reconstruct component x, we retrieve the 30th – x column of eigenvectors, because the analysis returns them by increasing importance.

Listing 5-18. Plotting original features against extracted components

```
let principalComponent comp1 comp2 =
    let title = sprintf "Component %i vs %i" comp1 comp2
    let features = headers.Length
    let coords = Seq.zip (eVectors.Column(features-comp1)) (eVectors.Column(features-comp2))
    Chart.Point (coords, Title = title, Labels = headers, MarkerSize = 7)
    |> Chart.WithXAxis(Min = -1.0, Max = 1.0,
        MajorGrid = ChartTypes.Grid(Interval = 0.25),
        LabelStyle = ChartTypes.LabelStyle(Interval = 0.25),
        MajorTickMark = ChartTypes.TickMark(Enabled = false))
    |> Chart.WithYAxis(Min = -1.0, Max = 1.0,
        MajorGrid = ChartTypes.Grid(Interval = 0.25),
        LabelStyle = ChartTypes.LabelStyle(Interval = 0.25),
        MajorTickMark = ChartTypes.TickMark(Enabled = false))
```

We can then visualize the two main principal components by simply calling `principalComponent` 1 2;; in F# interactive. As an illustration, Figure 5-22 displays some of the largest features identified by the PCA, components 1 versus 2 and components 3 versus 4. Unsurprisingly given the correlation matrix, the main feature very clearly maps to SQL, MySQL, and SQL-Server, against everything else; let's call that one "DBAs." The second feature is less obvious to interpret, and seems to oppose WPF, and to a lesser extent C#- and .NET-related technologies such as ASP.NET and ASP.NET MVC, to many other things, in particular Python/Django and Ruby. Feature 3 isn't entirely obvious either, but seems to oppose web and non-web, with Ruby on Rails, Django, HTML, and Javascript on one side. Feature 4 clearly pits Python and Ruby against each other.

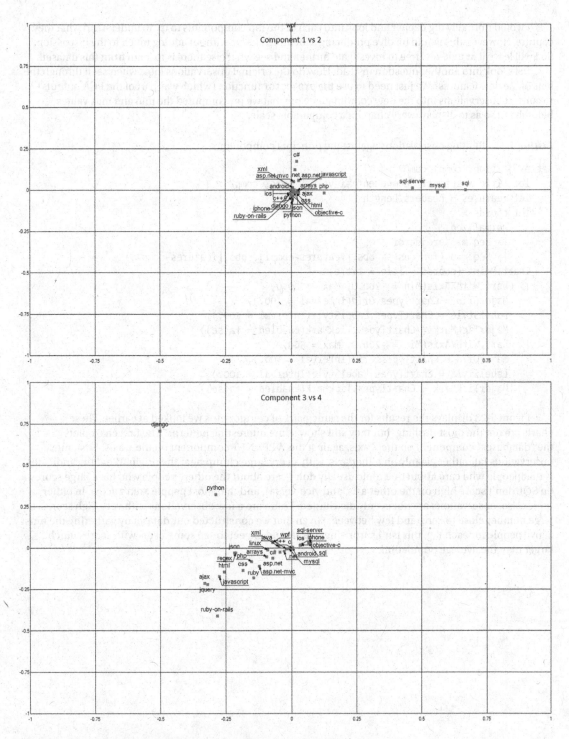

Figure 5-22. *Main components (see source code package for details)*

I would normally dig deeper and look into each of the top components to try to understand what they capture. However, this would involve producing a lot more charts, without adding much to the discussion. So I will leave it at that–feel free to investigate further and see what else there is to learn from this dataset!

Let's look into another question instead: How do the original observations look, when seen through the lens of the new features? We just need to use the `projector` function (which was part of the PCA outputs) to convert observations into the new coordinates. Note that we precomputed the min and max values beforehand so as to display every chart on a comparable scale.

Listing 5-19. Plotting observations against the principal components

```
let projections comp1 comp2 =
    let title = sprintf "Component %i vs %i" comp1 comp2
    let features = headers.Length
    let coords =
        normalized
        |> Seq.map projector
        |> Seq.map (fun obs -> obs.[features-comp1], obs.[features-comp2])
    Chart.Point (coords, Title = title)
    |> Chart.WithXAxis(Min = -200.0, Max = 500.0,
        MajorGrid = ChartTypes.Grid(Interval = 100.),
        LabelStyle = ChartTypes.LabelStyle(Interval = 100.),
        MajorTickMark = ChartTypes.TickMark(Enabled = false))
    |> Chart.WithYAxis(Min = -200.0, Max = 500.0,
        MajorGrid = ChartTypes.Grid(Interval = 100.),
        LabelStyle = ChartTypes.LabelStyle(Interval = 100.),
        MajorTickMark = ChartTypes.TickMark(Enabled = false))
```

Figure 5-23 displays the results for the same pairs of components we looked at earlier. These charts are not the most thrilling, but they still show some interesting patterns. The first chart plots the "databases" component on the X axis, against the WPF/.NET component on the Y axis. First, most observations fall rather cleanly on either axis, with a very large clump near the origin. What this indicates is that people who care about one topic usually don't care about the other (people who have large scores on SQL don't score high on the other axis, and vice-versa), and that most people aren't active in either topic. Also, observations are not evenly distributed: There are a few observations with very high scores, a large number close to zero, and few between. Given that we constructed our dataset by gathering the most active people for each tag, this isn't surprising: We should expect to see some users with scores much larger than the average population.

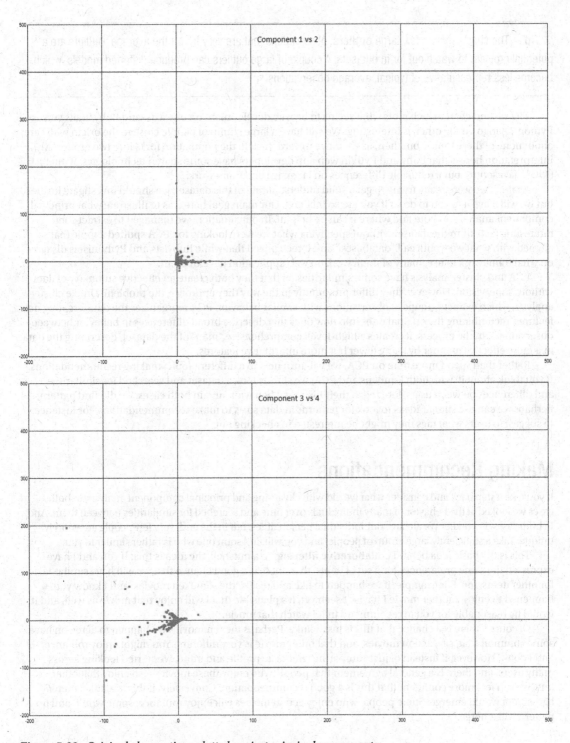

Figure 5-23. *Original observations plotted against principal components*

■ **Tip**   The charts show a few large **outliers**, observations that are very far off the average. Outliers are a potential problem to watch out for in datasets. A couple of large outliers can produce distorted models, which become less representative of typical, average observations.

The second chart, which plots what seems to be web development on one axis, and Ruby/Rails versus Python/Django on the other, is interesting. We still have a large clump of people close to the origin who care about none of these topics, but then, as we move toward the left, the population forks into two groups. My interpretation here is that Ruby and Python web app developers have some shared technologies of interest (JSON, javascript), but irreducible differences on language and framework.

Again, if we were really trying to get a solid understanding of this dataset, we should investigate further, but we will leave it to you to do so if you are so inclined. Our main goal here was to illustrate what principal component analysis is about and where it can be helpful. In our situation, we managed to extract some interesting facts from the dataset without specifying what we were looking for. PCA spotted a topic that aligned with what we would call "databases," and it recognized that while Rubyists and Pythonistas disagree on what framework to use, many of them work on web application development.

PCA and cluster analysis have some similarities, in that they both create an effective summary of data without supervision. However, they differ profoundly in the way they approach the problem. Unlike cluster analysis, which extracts groups of observations with similar behavior, PCA reorganizes the data, creating new features, recombining the original ones into new ones that describe broad differences in behavior between observations. In the process, it creates a high-level, comprehensive "map" of the dataset, describing the data in a more effective manner by using fewer but more informative features.

Rather than spend more time on PCA, we will turn next to a different topic: making recommendations. If you think about it, with both k-means and PCA, we simply took a dataset and searched for similarities and differences between users, looking at their historical behavior–and in both cases, we did find patterns. Perhaps we can use similar ideas to look for patterns in data so as to make recommendations–for instance, to suggest to users what tags they might be interested in checking out.

Making Recommendations

If you take a step back and consider what we did with clustering and principal component analysis, in both cases we looked at the behavior of many individuals over time and searched for similarities between them. And, in both cases, it worked. We all have our individual personalities, but in the end, very few people are entirely unique. Take a sufficiently large group of people, and you will find someone who is rather similar to you.

This is the basic idea behind **collaborative filtering**. In a nutshell, the idea is this: If you and I have expressed the same preferences for a set of items, then there is a good chance that we will have similar tastes for other items, too. For example, if we happen to like and dislike the same ten movies, and I know you happened to enjoy another movie I haven't seen yet, it's plausible that I will enjoy that movie as well, and it would be reasonable for you to recommend that I watch that movie.

Of course, there is a chance that this is just a fluke. Perhaps the ten movies we happen to agree on have some common trait, say, action movies, and that other movie is very different. You might enjoy romance, and I don't. However, if instead of just comparing your taste profile and mine, we started looking across many users, and there is a general agreement that people who enjoy these movies also enjoy that other one, we can feel more confident that this is a good recommendation. Conversely, if this is a fluke, then no agreement would emerge: Some people who enjoy action movies will enjoy romance, some won't, and no pattern will emerge.

Note that we could also take the question in a different direction. Instead of looking at it from the direction of users (do these two persons have similar taste profiles?), we could look at it from a movie perspective, and compare the movie profiles. If people who rated movie A tend to rate movie B the same way, for instance, then based on what you thought of movie A, it would be reasonable to make a guess on what you will think about B, and make a recommendation based on your predicted level of interest.

A Primitive Tag Recommender

Let's apply this idea to our StackOverflow dataset. This example will be a bit artificial, and is intended mostly as a sketch outlining how one might approach the problem. What we will do here is extract 100 "test" users from our dataset and try to predict which of the 10 last tags they might be interested in, based on the 20 first tags. In other words, let's imagine that these are relatively new users, and the only thing we know is what tags they have been active in so far. Based on their history, can we suggest tags? Given that we also know what they actually did for the 10 remaining tags, we will be able to validate our guesses by comparing them to the true behavior.

Let's try out recommendations based on user profiles. Our approach here will be simple: take a user, and, for the 20 tags we know, compare his (or her) profile with the known users and determine how similar they are. Then, predict the level of interest for the 10 remaining tags by computing the average interest level of known users for these tags, weighted by how similar they are to the target user.

If we are to compute a weighted average using similarity, we need two things. First, we need a measure that increases with profile similarity: If I found someone who is very similar to you, I want to take into account that person's preferences much more than others when trying to predict what you might like or not like. Then, we need a similarity value that is always positive so that we can compute a weighted average.

Can we use distance to compute similarity? The classic Euclidean distance matches one criterion–it is always positive–but not the other: The closer two profiles are, the smaller the distance becomes. That's not too hard to fix, though. If instead of the distance we take its inverse, we now have a quantity that increases as distance decreases. However, there is one small issue: If two profiles are identical, the distance will be zero, and the inverse infinite. Let's tweak this a bit, and measure similarity by:

```
Similarity(X,Y) = 1.0 / (1.0 + Distance (X,Y))
```

Now identical items will have a similarity of 1.0 (or 100%, if you prefer), and the farther apart users are, the smaller the similarity is, with a limit of 0.0. If you think this sounds like guesswork more than science, you would be right, at least to an extent. Just like there is no obvious unique choice for what distance to use, or how to scale features, defining the right similarity depends on the data. In the end, the "right" one will be the one that works best, as determined by cross-validation.

Implementing the Recommender

We will explore this in a new script file so as not to clutter our two existing scripts. We'll start the same way we did for the two other methods, opening in memory the userprofiles-toptags.txt file, extracting observations and headers, and filtering out observations that contain only zero values.

In order for the user profiles to be comparable, we need to address the same issue we encountered in clustering; that is, the widely different levels of activity between users. Let's start by rescaling observations so that the largest tag has a value of 100%, and the smallest 0%, and extract out 100 observations–our test subjects that we will use for cross-validation.

Listing 5-20. Preparing the dataset

```
let scale (row:float[]) =
    let min = row |> Array.min
    let max = row |> Array.max
    if min = max
    then row
    else
        row |> Array.map (fun x -> (x - min) / (max - min))

let test  = observations.[..99]  |> Array.map scale
let train = observations.[100..] |> Array.map scale
```

Before diving into the prediction part, we need a couple of helpers: a similarity function, which will use distance. For convenience, we will also write a weights function, which will take an array of floats and rescale them so that they sum up to 100% and can be used in a weighted average, and a split, which will separate the 20 first tags from the 10 "unknown" ones.

Listing 5-21. Similarity and utility functions

```
let distance (row1:float[]) (row2:float[]) =
    (row1,row2)
    ||> Array.map2 (fun x y -> pown (x - y) 2)
    |> Array.sum

let similarity (row1:float[]) (row2:float[]) =
    1. / (1. + distance row1 row2)

let split (row:float[]) =
    row.[..19],row.[20..]

let weights (values:float[]) =
    let total = values |> Array.sum
    values
    |> Array.map (fun x -> x / total)
```

▓ **Tip**   The ||> operator can be used with functions that operate on two collections at once, such as Array.
map2 or Array.zip. Instead of passing two arguments to the function, they can be fed in as a tuple with the
"double-pipe-forward" operator, which looks more consistent in a pipeline of operations.

We are now ready to dive into the prediction part. Given a user history, we will retain only the part we are supposed to know (the 20 first tags), and then we will compute its similarity with every user in the training set. Once that is done, we will take the last ten columns (which we are attempting to predict), and for each of them we will compute the sum-product of the similarities with the known usage levels, which will generate an array of ten values–the predicted interest level for the ten tags of interest.

Listing 5-22. Computing predictions for a user

```
let predict (row:float[]) =
    let known,unknown = row |> split
    let similarities =
        train
        |> Array.map (fun example ->
            let common, _ = example |> split
            similarity known common)
        |> weights
    [| for i in 20 .. 29 ->
        let column = train |> Array.map (fun x -> x.[i])
        let prediction =
            (similarities,column)
            ||> Array.map2 (fun s v -> s * v)
            |> Array.sum
        prediction |]
```

We are now ready to make predictions. Let's try it out on our first test subject:

```
let targetTags = headers.[20..]
predict test.[0] |> Array.zip targetTags
>
val it : (string * float) [] =
  [|("objective-c", 0.06037062258); ("php", 0.1239587958);
    ("python", 0.1538872057); ("regex", 0.06373121502); ("ruby", 0.1001880899);
    ("ruby-on-rails", 0.09474917849); ("sql", 0.07666851406);
    ("sql-server", 0.05314781127); ("wpf", 0.02386000125);
    ("xml", 0.03285983829)|]
```

For each of the 10 tags, we get a predicted interest level ranging from 0% to 100%. In this case, our top candidate is Python, at 15%, followed by PHP (12%) and Ruby (10%). Is this prediction any good? We can compare it to what really happened:

```
> test.[0] |> split |> snd;;
val it : float [] =
  [|0.0; 0.0; 0.03846153846; 1.0; 0.0; 0.0; 0.0; 0.0; 0.0; 0.0|]
```

If we were to recommend one tag, based on the largest predicted level of interest, 15.4%, we would have suggested the third tag (Python), which indeed is a tag the user was active in. This is good. At the same time, we would have missed this users' true favorite, Regex, which came in at about 6% in our predictions, and was not anywhere close based on the top-scoring recommendations.

Validating the Recommendations

We can't decide if our recommender is any good just by looking at one single example. Let's assume that we would use our recommender the following way: compute the predicted interest in each unknown tag and propose the tag with the highest forecasted level. One way we could measure how good our recommendations are is by whether the user actually showed an interest in the recommended tag. This is a bit of a weak evaluation; for instance, in the previous example we would count "Python" as a good recommendation, even though we missed a much better recommendation, "Regex." At the same time, this isn't a bad recommendation, in that we proposed something that might be actually of interest to our user.

Even though this might not be the best possible measure, it is fairly easy to do, so we will keep it at that. We will take every one of the 100 test subjects and simply count as positives every case where the prediction matches a tag where the user was active. We just need to grab the actual levels of activity for each of the ten tags we are interested in, predict levels for each of them, grab the largest, and check whether, for the recommended tag, the observed level was indeed greater than 0. We will count as a success every time this is the case, and compute the proportion of correct calls.

Listing 5-23. Percentage correct recommendations

```
let validation =
    test
    |> Array.map (fun obs ->
        let actual = obs |> split |> snd
        let predicted = obs |> predict
        let recommended, observed =
            Array.zip predicted actual
            |> Array.maxBy fst
        if observed > 0. then 1. else 0.)
    |> Array.average
    |> printfn "Correct calls: %f"
```

According to this metric, we get 32% correct recommendations. Let's face it–that isn't overly impressive. However, we don't really have a baseline to compare it against. The most naïve prediction we could make would be to simply predict the tag with the highest average rating and completely ignore any similarity between users. Let's do a quick-and-dirty evaluation of that approach.

Listing 5-24. Naïve recommendation accuracy

```
let averages = [|
    for i in 20 .. 29 ->
        train |> Array.averageBy(fun row -> row.[i]) |]

let baseline =
    test
    |> Array.map (fun obs ->
        let actual = obs |> split |> snd
        let predicted = averages
        let recommended, observed =
            Array.zip predicted actual
            |> Array.maxBy fst
        if observed > 0. then 1. else 0.)
    |> Array.average
    |> printfn "Correct calls: %f"
```

Using a naïve recommendation, our percentage accuracy drops to 13% correct calls. While this doesn't make our 32% great, it proves the point that our similarity-based approach is doing something right.

We will leave our recommendation engine as is, and won't try to improve it further. I am fairly certain we could make it much better, but I don't think we would gain much insight in the process. I'll finish instead with a couple of considerations that might be worth keeping in mind, in case you want to explore the problem further, either on that dataset or on another one.

First, our sample is not the most typical case for using that approach. In the prototypical scenario, you know how people rated certain items and don't know what they did for others; for instance, what movies a person watched and how they rated them, from terrible to awesome. This is a bit different from our situation, in two ways: In that situation, we know if an item has been rated or not, and all ratings have a consistent scale. By contrast, our dataset has vastly different scales for each user because we measure activity, and we don't have a clear distinction between empty values (the user has never seen this tag) or uninteresting tags (the user has had opportunities to view that tag but isn't interested). As a result, comparing users' or tags' similarity is made a bit complicated.

In a more typical situation, we would face slightly different challenges. A row would have mostly unknown values (all the items the user hasn't rated yet), and comparing that user with others would require comparing them only across common items, which is more involved that simply computing a distance between two complete rows. This also points at a limitation with the collaborative filtering approach, which is perhaps less obvious in our example. When a brand new user shows up in our system, there is no history available for that user, and therefore we have nothing usable with which to produce a recommendation. This is known as the "cold-start" problem. If you play a bit further with our model, you'll see more or less the following: By default, the recommender will predict Python, which is the most popular tag among our ten target tags. Only in situations where we have a strong, well-defined user profile does the engine produce different recommendations. This is a result you would expect in general: With limited information, engines will recommend broadly popular items, and will only start producing "interesting" picks for users who provided a lot of information.

A final note on this subject: In order to produce a recommendation, we had to scan through every single user. This is an obviously expensive operation, which hints at obvious scaling problems. First, we could have tried to approach the problem by feature, instead of by user, and try to detect similarity between 30 tags, instead of 1,600 users; we could even precompute similarities between columns, which would reduce quite a bit the amount of computations.

So What Have We Learned?

In this chapter, we introduced unsupervised learning. In supervised learning methods (such as classification or regression), algorithms are geared toward answering a specific question, guided by a training set of examples to learn from. By contrast, unsupervised learning is about automatically identifying interesting features or structure in "plain" data, without explicit guidance from the user. In the process of exploring unsupervised techniques, we discussed quite a few topics. Our goal was to take a dataset and see if, instead of manually exploring the data in the hopes of spotting interesting patterns, we could apply more mechanical methods to systematically extract and summarize information from the data.

We applied two complementary techniques to the data: clustering with the k-means algorithm, and principal component analysis. They share similar traits: both attempt to reduce the dataset into a more condensed representation by finding patterns in the data and simplifying information, grouping similar elements together based on a certain notion of distance. The two approaches differ in what type of patterns they are looking for. K-means clustering tries to group observations in clusters, so that, ideally, items within the same cluster are close to each other, and clusters themselves are as different as possible. K-means identifies centroids, which are essentially "archetypes," and are sufficient to describe a large class of observations.

By contrast, principal component analysis doesn't focus on similarities between the observations themselves, but rather on what traits vary together, and how observations differ from the average. By inspecting the covariance matrix, it identifies features that move together and attempts to provide an alternate representation, grouping together features that either typically evolve in the same or in opposite directions, and organizing them in a way that emphasizes the largest differentiating factors between observations.

In both cases, a key benefit is a simpler, more compact description of the dataset. In the case of clustering, instead of many unique observations, we can describe the dataset in terms of a few archetypes, which exhibit a consistent behavior. In the case of PCA, instead of multiple unrelated features, we get a couple of new features, the principal components, which strongly differentiate observations. As a result, instead of a multitude of hard-to-interpret facts, we can start developing an understanding of these dimensions that is more meaningful and easier to reason with than the raw data is. These methods allow us to develop a vocabulary to talk about the data more efficiently, and perhaps to gain a better understanding of how the data "works" and how we can derive insight out of it.

At the same time, both techniques are simply searching for specific types of patterns in data. There is no guarantee that such patterns actually exist, and, even if they do, there is no guarantee that they will be interesting to us. We might find clusters that are of no practical interest; they could be nonactionable, or state trivially obvious facts, for instance.

Another aspect we discussed was the notion of distance and the importance of thinking about scale. Clustering groups observations that are close, and in that frame, it is crucial to supply the algorithm with a meaningful distance. In that context, we ended up preprocessing our observations so as to reduce them to comparable user profiles. PCA groups features that have similar variations from the average, which leads us to a discussion on normalization and correlations, two notions that revolve around the idea of rescaling measures so that their variations are comparable.

Finally, we sketched out how similar ideas could be used, not to extract information from a dataset, but to produce recommendations. In all three cases, we looked at multiple individuals and how they behaved, and realized that in spite of individual differences, collectively there existed some patterns. In the last example, starting from the assumption that people who have behaved in a similar fashion in many situations will likely behave similarly in others, we explored how we could approach making recommendations by detecting similarities and applying them in order to determine what behavior was likely to occur in unknown cases.

CHAPTER 6

■ ■ ■

Trees and Forests

Making Predictions from Incomplete Data

One of my nieces' favorite games is a guessing game. One person thinks of something, and the other player tries to figure out what that something is by asking only yes or no questions. If you have played this game before, you have probably seen the following pattern in action: first ask questions that eliminate large categories of possible answers, such as "Is it an animal?", and progressively narrow down the focus of the questions as you gather more information. This is a more effective strategy than asking from the get-go, say, "Did you think about a zebra?" On the one hand, if the answer is "yes," you are done, as there is only one possible answer. On the other hand, if the answer is "no," you are in a rather bad spot, having learned essentially nothing.

Decision trees are classifiers that operate in a fashion similar to that game. They mimic the way we humans make diagnoses by asking a series of questions, trying to eliminate bad answers quickly, and deciding what question to ask next, based on everything we have learned so far. In that context, features can be thought of as questions one can ask about the characteristics of an observation. A decision tree will learn from a training set, analyzing it to determine which feature provides the most information, given everything that is known at that point about the observation it is trying to classify.

In this chapter, we will work on a classic dataset and progressively learn increasingly powerful classifiers, starting from decision stumps and expanding into decision trees and forests. Along the way, we will do the following:

- Learn how to construct flexible decision trees that can handle virtually any type of data, including situations where data is missing. We will also see how F# types like discriminated unions and options can be used to model tree-like structures very effectively.

- Introduce entropy as a way to measure how much information a dataset contains, and use it to compare features and decide which ones should be selected.

- Discuss the risks of over-fitting, as well as ways to address it. In particular, we will explore more-advanced methods of cross-validation, such as k-folds, and how the same ideas can lead toward ensemble methods, a general approach that aggregates multiple simple predictors into a robust one.

Our Challenge: Sink or Swim on the Titanic

The dataset we will be working with in this chapter is a classic. Using the list of passengers who embarked the Titanic, and some demographic information about each of them, our goal will be to predict their fate. Both the dataset and the problem are interesting, for a couple of reasons. First, the question at hand is typical of a large class of problems, once you get past its somewhat macabre nature. "Will that visitor click this link on the website?" or "Which customers will pick the small, medium, or large order?" are essentially the same problem: Using what information you have about individuals and how they behaved in the past, you are trying to build a classification model to predict one outcome from a limited set of possible ones.

Then, the data itself is quite typical of real-world situations, in that it is messy. It contains a mix of different types of features, from numeric (how much did the passenger pay for their ticket?) to categorical (was the passenger male or female?), with everything in between (passenger name and title). Some of the data is missing as well. Ideally, we'd like a classifier that is flexible enough to handle all these variables without too much of a hassle.

Finally, the data is interesting by itself, for obvious historical reasons. The Titanic disaster has fascinated people over time, and while there is little practical use in creating a predictive model for a one-time accident that occurred nearly a century ago, the dataset provides an opportunity to see what type of insight one can gain by analyzing its data.

Getting to Know the Dataset

The specific dataset we will use comes from the Kaggle competition "Titanic: Machine Learning from Disaster": https://www.kaggle.com/c/titanic-gettingStarted. Variants can easily be found online (, for instance, http://www.encyclopedia-titanica.org). However, we thought it would be fun to use the Kaggle reference dataset; that way, you can try out your skills and see how you fare. For convenience, we uploaded the same dataset on OneDrive here: http://1drv.ms/1HUh1ny.

The dataset is a CSV file, titanic.csv, nicely organized with a header row describing what each of the 12 available columns is. Of course we could write a bit of code to parse it, but why not use the CSV type provider? Let's create a solution with an F# project Titanic, add the titanic.csv file to that project, and add the fsharp.data NuGet package to the project.

We are now ready to begin exploring the data. In the script.fsx file, let's add a reference to FSharp.Data (the specifics of the path might vary, depending on the current latest version of the package), create a Titanic type by looking at our sample data, and add a type alias Passenger so that we can refer to each row of the dataset in a more intuitive way. We can now read our dataset.

Listing 6-1. Using the CSV type provider to read the Titanic dataset

```
#r @".\packages\FSharp.Data.2.2.2\lib\net40\FSharp.Data.dll"
open FSharp.Data

type Titanic = CsvProvider<"titanic.csv">
type Passenger = Titanic.Row

let dataset = Titanic.GetSample ()
```

The CSV type provider created a nice type for us, complete with properties, giving us all the benefits of types when exploring our data. We can now get to work. If our goal is to predict who survives or dies, a first step is to get a baseline for that value. Let's first count how many passengers are in each category, and then figure out the probability for an individual passenger to survive, by adding the following code to our script and running it in the F# Interactive:

```
dataset.Rows
|> Seq.countBy (fun passenger -> passenger.Survived)
|> Seq.iter (printfn "%A")
```

```
dataset.Rows
|> Seq.averageBy (fun passenger ->
    if passenger.Survived then 1.0 else 0.0)
|> printfn "Chances of survival: %.3f"

>
(false, 549)
(true, 342)
Chances of survival: 0.384
```

We have 891 passengers, out of which only 342 survived; in other words, without any additional information, each passenger has only a 38.4% chance of surviving (or, equivalently, a 61.6% chance of not making it off the ship alive). If we want to refine the predictions, we need to find features that will help us identify passengers with an over 50% chance of surviving. Anything else, while informative, won't directly make a material difference in our predictions, because it would not change our decision from the default case.

Taking a Look at Features

With that frame in mind, let's start looking at features. What we are looking for here is a quick way to slice passengers into different groups, and then to compute the survival rate for each group. Computing the survival rate is straightforward: Given a sample of passengers, simply compute the ratio of passengers who survived, divided by the total passengers in that sample. We can then simply group the passengers according to different criteria–say, sex or class–and display the survival rate for each group.

Listing 6-2. Computing the survival rate for different groups

```
let survivalRate (passengers:Passenger seq) =
    let total = passengers |> Seq.length
    let survivors =
        passengers
        |> Seq.filter (fun p -> p.Survived)
        |> Seq.length
    100.0 * (float survivors / float total)

let bySex =
    dataset.Rows
    |> Seq.groupBy(fun p -> p.Sex)

bySex
|> Seq.iter (fun (s,g) ->
    printfn "Sex %A: %f" s (survivalRate g))

let byClass =
    dataset.Rows
    |> Seq.groupBy (fun p -> p.Pclass)
```

```
byClass
|> Seq.iter (fun (s,g) ->
    printfn "Class %A: %f" s (survivalRate g))
>
Sex "male": 18.890815
Sex "female": 74.203822
Class 3: 24.236253
Class 1: 62.962963
Class 2: 47.282609
```

Clearly, both of these features are highly informative. As it turns out, with a 74% chance of surviving, being a lady on the Titanic was a very good idea. Similarly, first class passengers had a fair chance of making it off alive (63%), whereas the poor sods in third class had much grimmer prospects, with a 24% chance of surviving. To paraphrase George Orwell, "All passengers are equal, but some passengers are more equal than others." There are some fairly obvious sociological interpretations here, but I will leave that to you: After all, the data shows what is, but says nothing about why that is.

Building a Decision Stump

This is enough information for us to implement a super simple classifier, as well as a procedure to train it. Take sample data, break the sample into different groups along the lines of what we just did, and, for each group, predict the most frequent label. This type of model is called a decision stump, the shortest possible tree you could build. It is the building block of trees, and is a minimal classifier, which commonly appears as a building block in other models.

How could we go about building a stump based on passenger sex, for example? First, I would take all passengers from my sample and break them into groups according to the value of my chosen feature, in this case, their sex value ("male" or "female"). Then, for each group, I would look up the value of my chosen label, in our case whether they survived or not, and identify the most frequently appearing one for each group. We can then build a classifier (the stump): Take a passenger as input, compute the feature value, look that value up in the groups, and return the groups' most frequent label (see Figure 6-1).

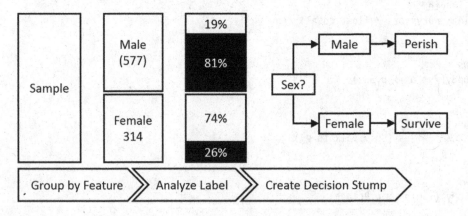

Figure 6-1. *Building a decision stump for survival using sex as a feature*

■ **Note**   In previous chapters, we used the term *class* to describe the predictions of a classifier. Here, we will use *label* instead, which is also common. In our case, it is convenient, because the passenger class is a feature of our dataset, and using class for both would introduce some potential ambiguities.

We can actually make this process entirely generic if we make both the feature and the label into functions that extract a value from an observation. Suppose that instead of passengers I had a sequence of items of generic type 'a; then a feature is simply a function that, when given an 'a, returns a value 'b; similarly the label takes an 'a and gives you back another type 'c. In our particular case, 'a will be a Passenger, 'b a string (taking value "male" or "female"), and 'c a Boolean (survived, or not). The only additional requirement on our types is that 'b and 'c need to support equality, because we need to group and count by both feature and label value.

So, how does our implementation look? Pretty much the way we described it:

Listing 6-3.   Learning a decision stump

```
let mostFrequentLabelIn group =
    group
    |> Seq.countBy snd
    |> Seq.maxBy snd
    |> fst


let learn sample extractFeature extractLabel =
    // group together observations that have the
    // same value for the selected feature, and
    // find the most frequent label by group.
    let groups =
        sample
        |> Seq.map (fun obs -> extractFeature obs, extractLabel obs)
        |> Seq.groupBy fst
        |> Seq.map (fun (feat,group) -> feat, mostFrequentLabelIn group)
    // for an observation, find the group with
    // matching feature value, and predict the
    // most frequent label for that group.
    let classifier obs =
        let featureValue = extractFeature obs
        groups
        |> Seq.find (fun (f,_) -> f = featureValue)
        |> snd
    classifier
```

Note that, largely for illustrative purposes, I didn't put any type annotations on the two functions in Listing 6-3. If you run that code in F# Interactive, or simply hover for the definition for learn, you'll see the following:

```
val learn :
  sample:seq<'a> ->
    extractFeature:('a -> 'b) -> extractLabel:('a -> 'c) -> ('a -> 'c)
    when 'b : equality and 'c : equality
```

This is a bit intimidating, so let's parse it. What this says is that learn is a function that, when given a sample of observations (a sequence of 'a), a function to extract a feature value 'b from an observation 'a ('a -> 'b), and a function to extract the label value 'c from an observation 'a ('a -> 'c), will give you back a function 'a -> 'c, a function that will take an observation and return a label, which is exactly what we expect from a classifier. If all the details of this function signature are not clear, don't fret, as it's not hugely important. The reason I brought it up is that it illustrates the power of the F# type-inference system. We only described how we wanted to process the input, without much specification, and F# correctly created a function with generic types, and even deduced that we needed to support equality for both the extracted labels and the feature values.

Training the Stump

How do we go about training a stump? We need to create a specification for what we want to use for labels and features and define them as functions that fit our dataset. Calling learn will create a function that is a full-fledged classifier, which we can immediately run and evaluate (ignoring cross-validation for the moment).

Listing 6-4. Training and evaluating a stump

```
let survived (p:Passenger) = p.Survived
let sex (p:Passenger) = p.Sex

let sexClassifier = survived |> learn (dataset.Rows) sex

printfn "Stump: classify based on passenger sex."
dataset.Rows
|> Seq.averageBy (fun p ->
    if p.Survived = sexClassifier p then 1.0 else 0.0)

>
Stump: classify based on passenger sex.
val it : float = 0.7867564534
```

Running this on the full sample, we get 78.6% correct predictions, markedly better than our initial 61.6%. We can equally easily create a model based on passenger class, as follows:

Listing 6-5. A stump with multiple prongs

```
let classClassifier = survived |> learn (dataset.Rows) (fun p -> p.Pclass)

dataset.Rows
|> Seq.averageBy (fun p ->
    if p.Survived = classClassifier p then 1.0 else 0.0)
```

As expected, with 67.9% correct, this is an improvement over having no model, albeit a more modest one than that what we observed in the previous case. The reason I ran this example was not really about improving performance, though. It illustrates two interesting aspects. First, unlike the first example, this stump had three branches and not just two. A stump (and a decision tree later on) can accommodate more than binary choices. Then, note that our two features have different types: Sex returns a string, and class integers. The type-inference system automatically handled this for us.

Features That Don't Fit

Obviously, such a simple model, using only one feature to make predictions, is only going to carry us so far, and the obvious question at that point is, "How can we combine multiple features into one single model?" This is where we will be headed next, trying to improve our predictions by putting together more of the dataset information and combining multiple stumps to form a decision tree. Before looking into more-complex models, however, we need to address a few issues. Our decision-stump approach is fairly flexible, but it has some limitations.

How About Numbers?

Among our features, consider this one: fare. After all, if passenger class is informative, there is a good chance that the price they paid for their ticket is, too. Let's check that out, by computing the survival rate for various ticket prices.

Listing 6-6. A feature with continuous numeric values

```
let survivalByPricePaid =
    dataset.Rows
    |> Seq.groupBy (fun p -> p.Fare)
    |> Seq.iter (fun (price,passengers) ->
        printfn "%6.2F: %6.2f" price (survivalRate passengers))
>
  7.25:   7.69
 71.28: 100.00
  7.93:  44.44
 53.10:  60.00
// snipped for brevity...
  5.00:   0.00
  9.85:   0.00
 10.52:   0.00
```

The numbers are right, but this doesn't seem like a good way to approach this feature. The fare was broken into 248 different individual cases, most of them with a 0% or 100% survival rate. If we follow this model, passengers who paid 39.4000 for their ticket have a 100% chance of surviving; those who paid 39.6000 only 50%; and those who paid 39.6875 have a 0% chance of making it alive. This is clearly silly.

Our problem here is that fare and, say, class are not of the same nature. Class takes discrete states (you are in first, second, or third class; there are no other choices) whereas fare could, in principle, take infinitely many values. Another way these two features differ is that fare represents an actual number; for instance, you can add two fares together, or subtract one from another, whereas the sum of passenger classes doesn't make any sense.

The issue here is that our stump can handle only categorical features; how can we incorporate continuous data? One approach is to reduce the problem to a known problem, and transform fare into a categorical feature. For instance, we could create a new feature, "fare level," with two levels, Cheap or Expensive, depending on whether the fare was below or above the average.

Listing 6-7. Converting fare into discrete bins

```
let averageFare =
    dataset.Rows
    |> Seq.averageBy (fun p -> p.Fare)

let fareLevel (p:Passenger) =
    if p.Fare < averageFare
    then "Cheap"
    else "Expensive"

printfn "Stump: classify based on fare level."
let fareClassifier = survived |> learn (dataset.Rows) fareLevel

dataset.Rows
|> Seq.averageBy (fun p ->
    if p.Survived = fareClassifier p then 1.0 else 0.0)

>
val it : float = 0.6621773288
```

The results are not very good, but that's not the point: We now have a way to reduce a continuous feature into a discrete one. This approach, known as **discretization**, is very general, too: Divide the feature into any number of consecutive intervals and assign observations to a "bin."

We solved a problem, but we also found another one: Out of the many ways we could discretize a continuous feature, which one should we pick? This question boils down to the following: Given two features (in this case two discretizations of the same underlying feature), which one should we pick to gain the most information? We will tackle that question in the next section, after we deal with another problem–missing data.

What about Missing Data?

Let's consider another one of the features we have at our disposal. Suppose that we wanted to use Embarked (the port of origin for each passenger) as a feature in our model. Let's look at the survival rate by port of origin.

Listing 6-8. A feature with missing values

```
let survivalByPortOfOrigin =
    dataset.Rows
    |> Seq.groupBy (fun p -> p.Embarked)
    |> Seq.iter (fun (port,passengers) ->
        printfn "%s: %f" port (survivalRate passengers))

>
S: 33.695652
C: 55.357143
Q: 38.961039
 : 100.000000
```

Apparently, boarding in Cherbourg, France (C) gave you a slightly better chance of survival than did Queenstown (Q) or Southampton (S). But what is this anonymous category with a 100% survival rate?

What it is, is missing data. For every passenger, we know the sex and class, but for some, we don't know where they embarked. This problem is real and very common. Unfortunately, in real life, most datasets you will be given will have some issues, missing values being the most likely one. So, what should we do about it? One tempting option would be to eliminate incomplete records. However, you might end up discarding a lot of valuable information that way, especially if multiple features in your dataset are missing data.

Yet we can't keep an empty string as a valid port of embarkation! At the very least, we should clearly mark that this is missing data, so that we can decide how to deal with it later. We could create a dedicated discriminated union here, but this seems like overkill when we have the Option type available to us, with its two cases, Some<'T> or None.

In that frame, one option (sorry for the pun) is to slightly modify the way we define a feature and require that it explicitly define what a missing value is by returning an Option, with None indicating missing data. As a consequence, the learning function now needs to be explicit about the strategy used to handle that situation. The code snippet in Listing 6-9 illustrates one way to go about it. The main changes from our previous version are that we filter out the examples with missing values from our sample, and then create a branch for these cases only, storing them as a Map for convenience. In the case that a missing value comes in, we will simply predict the most common label in the sample.

Listing 6-9. Incorporating missing values

```
let hasData extractFeature = extractFeature >> Option.isSome

let betterLearn sample extractFeature extractLabel =
    let branches =
        sample
        |> Seq.filter (extractFeature |> hasData)
        |> Seq.map (fun obs -> extractFeature obs |> Option.get, extractLabel obs)
        |> Seq.groupBy fst
        |> Seq.map (fun (feat,group) -> feat, mostFrequentLabelIn group)
        |> Map.ofSeq
    let labelForMissingValues =
        sample
        |> Seq.countBy extractLabel
        |> Seq.maxBy snd
        |> fst
    let classifier obs =
        let featureValue = extractFeature obs
        match featureValue with
        | None -> labelForMissingValues
        | Some(value) ->
            match (branches.TryFind value) with
            | None -> labelForMissingValues
            | Some(predictedLabel) -> predictedLabel
    classifier

let port (p:Passenger) =
    if p.Embarked = "" then None
    else Some(p.Embarked)

let updatedClassifier = survived |> betterLearn (dataset.Rows) port
```

■ **Note**   Pattern matching on an `Option` result in the classifier function makes for a logical flow that is very easy to follow. However, filtering examples with missing values, and then extracting out the actual values, is pretty ugly. The Seq module contains a function, Seq.choose, which does both in one shot, but requires the original sequence to contain options, which is unfortunately not the case in our example.

Measuring Information in Data

We now have an approach for creating a classifier for a population using a single feature, regardless of its type or whether it has missing values. This is great, but we can't limit ourselves to using only one feature at a time, ignoring the information potentially available in the other features we have at our disposal.

We will expand our model along the same lines as in the game of 20 questions. We will proceed by turns; at each turn, you can ask a single "question" about the observation from a list of features: Is the passenger a man or woman? Is he travelling first, second, or third class? Based on the answer to these questions, you then need to make a decision: Do you have enough information to make a prediction (survive or not), or, given the answer you got ("the passenger is a man"), do you want to ask another question that could improve your odds of producing the right answer?

The key issue here is how to measure and compare information so that we can decide which sequence of questions is best. This is what we'll discuss in this section.

Measuring Uncertainty with Entropy

In and of itself, a feature is not informative; the information lies in the possible answers you might get and how they help you decide which label is the most likely. To measure how informative a question is, I need to consider how much better off I would be by knowing the answer. Would I be better off knowing "the passenger is a man," or "the passenger travelled first class?"

Now, what we really care about is not whether the passenger is a man or a woman, but rather, if I told you that he is man, how certain would you be about him surviving? The worst thing I could tell you is, "If the passenger is a man, he has a 50% chance of surviving." This is essentially as good as saying that the information is worthless. Conversely, if men had either a 100% chance of surviving–or the opposite–you would be done: This is perfect information, and no additional question would improve on that.

The intuition here is that the more evenly distributed a population is, the less information we have: No guess is better than the other. Information theory has a measure defined exactly for this: entropy (Shannon entropy, to be specific). If you have a sample population, its entropy is measured as:

```
entropy(sample) = sum [ - p(x) * log p(x) ]
```

where p(x) is the proportion of x in the sample, that is, the probability to observe an item of value x.

■ **Note**   What base you pick to compute the logarithm with doesn't really matter, as long as you stay consistent. Different bases result in different units (bits, nats, etc.), but will not affect how samples are ordered. For that reason, we will use log, the natural logarithm, because it is the easiest to use from F#.

Let's implement this in F# to see a bit better how it works. Given a data sample, we'll count how many elements we have in each category, divide by the total, and compute p log p. Note that x log(x) is undefined for x = 0; we'll replace it by its right-limit, zero, and end up with the following:

Listing 6-10. Shannon entropy of a sample

```
let entropy data =
    let size = data |> Seq.length
    data
    |> Seq.countBy id
    |> Seq.map (fun (_,count) -> float count / float size)
    |> Seq.sumBy (fun f -> if f > 0. then - f * log f else 0.)
```

■ **Tip** F# has a built-in function id for identity, that is, a function that returns its input as output. This can be useful in cases like Listing 6-10, where we want to find unique elements in a sequence and count how many of each we have.

Let's quickly explore how entropy behaves by running a couple of examples in F# Interactive:

```
> [1;1;1;2;2;2] |> entropy;;
val it : float = 0.6931471806
> [1;1;1;1;1;1] |> entropy;;
val it : float = 0.0
```

Entropy is largest when the sample is the least informative (every label is equally represented), and decreases toward zero for a perfectly organized (and predictable) sample. Figure 6-2 contrasts a couple of examples, with very different characteristics, and illustrates how entropy maps our intuitive notion of order, or purity: The higher our sample purity is, the easier it is to guess, and the lower its entropy. As a side note, entropy can also handle more than two labels, which makes it a convenient metric.

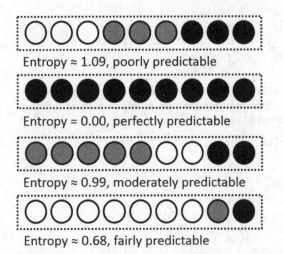

Entropy ≈ 1.09, poorly predictable

Entropy = 0.00, perfectly predictable

Entropy ≈ 0.99, moderately predictable

Entropy ≈ 0.68, fairly predictable

Figure 6-2. *Comparing sample information with entropy*

Information Gain

Shannon entropy gives us a measure for how usable the information in a sample is–the lower the entropy, the better the information. This is useful, but is not exactly what we are after. What we want is the following: If we have a sample and need to pick one of two questions (the features) to ask about it, which one should we select?

To make that decision we will use the notion of information gain. Let's start with its mathematical expression, and then discuss why this makes sense. Suppose you have a sample, and that by observing feature F you can break that sample into n groups: sample(1), ..., sample(n). The entropy gain for feature F is then

```
gain = entropy(sample) - (proba(sample(1)) * entropy(sample(1)) + ... proba(sample(n)) *
entropy(sample(n)))
```

Why would this formula make sense? The first part, `entropy(sample)`, simply represents the current entropy–that is, how good our information about the raw sample is. You might have recognized that the second part is an average, the average entropy we would get by splitting the sample according to our feature.

Before diving into implementing this, let's illustrate the idea on a few graphical examples. In each image, we will consider a fictional sample of passengers, where survivors are rendered in white, and black otherwise, and passenger gender is represented with the classic Mars and Venus symbols.

In Figure 6-3, we have the ideal situation. We start with a sample that is as bad as it gets for making a prediction (half survivors, half casualties). If we split the sample according to sex, we end up with two perfect groups, one entirely survivors, the other all dead. In this case, sex is a perfect feature to use; if we asked the passenger sex, we would know exactly their fate–and the entropy gain would be as high as possible.

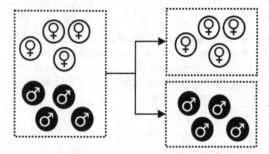

Figure 6-3. *Perfect information gain*

By contrast, Figure 6-4 represents the worst scenario. We begin with a sample with no information, and, after splitting on sex, we have two samples that still contain no information. In this case, sex is entirely uninformative, and the corresponding information gain would be zero.

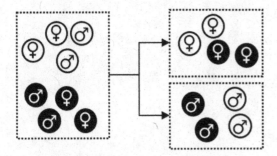

Figure 6-4. *Zero information gain*

Note that entropy gain is about how much information we gain by splitting on a feature (or asking a question), and not entropy itself. For instance, Figure 6-5 shows a situation where, after splitting on sex, we get two decently informative samples (in either case, male or female, we can make a guess on the result with 75% confidence), but no improvement from the original situation, and, just like in the previous case, no gain in entropy.

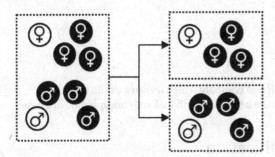

Figure 6-5. *Good information but not gain*

The other component of interest in entropy gain is group size. Consider Figure 6-6, which depicts two similar but slightly different situations. In both situations, splitting our sample by sex gains us information. However, the bottom situation is better than the top one. In the top case, if we learn the passenger is a male, we have perfect information, but there is only a 25% chance of hearing that answer. By contrast, in the second case, we have a 75% chance of learning the passenger is female, and gaining perfect information. We will be done much faster in one case than in the other using the same feature, and that aspect will again be reflected by the way the information gain is constructed, because it will take into account entropy by group, weighted by the size of each group.

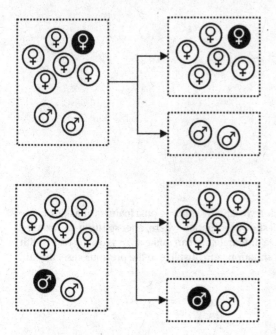

Figure 6-6. *Information gain by group*

In other words, entropy gain gives us a metric by which to compare which features would be most advantageous to use, if we wanted to efficiently learn about the labels, and could ask only one question at a time.

Implementing the Best Feature Identification

We have the first part of this already; the only thing we need is the average entropy if we split a sample on a given feature. That is fairly straightforward, as the only thing we need to pay attention to is potential missing data in our sample. We simply filter out any observation with no value for the feature, group by feature value, and compute the weighted average of entropy by group.

Listing 6-11. Average entropy after feature split

```
let splitEntropy extractLabel extractFeature data =
    // observations with no missing values
    // for the selected feature
    let dataWithValues =
        data
        |> Seq.filter (extractFeature |> hasData)
    let size = dataWithValues |> Seq.length
    dataWithValues
    |> Seq.groupBy extractFeature
    |> Seq.sumBy (fun (_,group) ->
        let groupSize = group |> Seq.length
        let probaGroup = float groupSize / float size
        let groupEntropy = group |> entropy extractLabel
        probaGroup * groupEntropy)
```

Let's see how that works out, by computing the information gain for various features in F# interactive.

Listing 6-12. Comparing information gain for different features

```
let survived (p:Passenger) = p.Survived

let sex (p:Passenger) = Some(p.Sex)
let pclass (p:Passenger) = Some(p.Pclass)
let port (p:Passenger) =
    if p.Embarked = ""
    then None
    else Some(p.Embarked)
let age (p:Passenger) =
    if p.Age < 12.0
    then Some("Younger")
    else Some("Older")

printfn "Comparison: most informative feature"
let h = dataset.Rows |> entropy survived
printfn "Base entropy %.3f" h

dataset.Rows |> splitEntropy survived sex |> printfn "  Sex: %.3f"
dataset.Rows |> splitEntropy survived pclass |> printfn "  Class: %.3f"
dataset.Rows |> splitEntropy survived port |> printfn "  Port: %.3f"
dataset.Rows |> splitEntropy survived age |> printfn "  Age: %.3f"

>
Comparison: most informative feature
Base entropy 0.666
  Sex: 0.515
  Class: 0.608
  Port: 0.649
  Age: 0.660
```

The clear winner here is sex, which has the lowest entropy, and is therefore the most informative feature; class seems to have some potential, too, but port and age don't show any obvious improvement. This gives us a decision stump, and two groups, male and female; we can repeat the same procedure again.

Listing 6-13. Comparing information gain in sub-groups

```
let bySex = dataset.Rows |> Seq.groupBy sex

for (groupName, group) in bySex do
    printfn "Group: %s" groupName.Value
    let h = group |> entropy survived
    printfn "Base entropy %.3f" h

    group |> splitEntropy survived sex |> printfn "  Sex: %.3f"
    group |> splitEntropy survived pclass |> printfn "  Class: %.3f"
    group |> splitEntropy survived port |> printfn "  Port: %.3f"
    group |> splitEntropy survived age |> printfn "  Age: %.3f"
>
```

```
Group: male
Base entropy 0.485
   Sex: 0.485
   Class: 0.459
   Port: 0.474
   Age: 0.462
Group: female
Base entropy 0.571
   Sex: 0.571
   Class: 0.427
   Port: 0.555
   Age: 0.565
```

If you run this, you'll see first that splitting again on Sex would produce zero gain, which is reassuring (we used that information already). You will also see that the features are ordered differently for each group–in this case, the best one is still class for both, but you could very well end up with different features for each branch. Finally, note also that we always end up with at least the same entropy level after a split, which implies that if we just added more features and kept going recursively, we would never be worse off, and would probably keep breaking our sample into smaller and smaller groups, regardless of whether the split was really meaningful. So, we'll need to think about a stopping rule to decide when going further down is just not worth it anymore.

From a coding standpoint, you might have thought to yourself that the code above is screaming for some refactoring. Manually writing each feature is very tedious, and being able to define a list of features would be much more satisfactory. Unfortunately, we have a bit of a problem here. If you consider the features, say, sex and pclass, you'll notice that their types differ. Sex produces a string option, whereas pclass returns an int option, and as a result, we can't include them in the same list.

So, what should we do? A couple of options are available, none of which are excellent. We'll go for simplicity here and force features to produce a string option. While we are at it, it would be convenient for features to have a name, too. If we defined a type for features like type Feature<'a> = string * 'a -> string option, for instance, we could treat them similarly and analyze them in a much more coherent manner.

Listing 6-14. Analyzing a list of features

```
let survived (p:Passenger) = p.Survived

let sex (p:Passenger) = Some(p.Sex)
let pclass (p:Passenger) = Some(p.Pclass |> string)

let features =
    [   "Sex", sex
        "Class", pclass ]

features
|> List.map (fun (name, feat) ->
    dataset.Rows
    |> splitEntropy survived feat |> printfn "%s: %.3f" name)
>
Sex: 0.515
Class: 0.608
```

Using Entropy to Discretize Numeric Features

As a special case where this approach can come in handy, let's revisit the question we discussed earlier, namely how to reduce a feature that is continuous, such as age or fare, into a set of discrete cases.

In the previous section, we created a feature for age where passengers younger than 12 years old were considered "Younger," the others being "Older." Why 12, and not 5, 42, or any other value? We picked that value completely arbitrarily. It might work, but it is not very scientific or data driven.

Instead of relying on intuition, we could try to approach the problem using entropy. What we are looking for is a threshold for age that is as informative as possible. Rephrased in entropy parlance, we would like a value that maximizes the entropy gain. This is not very complicated: Simply take every possible age value from the dataset and identify the one that yields the largest information gain by creating a feature for each possible cut-off value:

```
let ages = dataset.Rows |> Seq.map (fun p -> p.Age) |> Seq.distinct
let best =
    ages
    |> Seq.minBy (fun age ->
        let age (p:Passenger) =
            if p.Age < age then Some("Younger") else Some("Older")
        dataset.Rows |> splitEntropy survived age)
printfn "Best age split"
printfn "Age: %.3f" best

Best age split
Age: 7.000
```

This approach isn't perfect. Binning continuous variables is a bit of a dark art, and there is no silver bullet. This one has the benefit of being fully automated; as a result, you could generate stumps from the data without manual intervention.

■ **Note** One limitation of this method is that it assumes having two categories is a good way to discretize the value, which may or may not be appropriate. One way to address this issue is by recursively applying the same procedure and inspecting whether any of the bins identified can be profitably split further. However, this is potentially tricky, because as the bins become smaller, the risk increases to create artificial divisions. We'll leave it at that, but mention the search term "minimum description length" for readers interested in exploring that question further.

Growing a Tree from Data

We have now the two key elements needed to build a decision tree. With decision stumps, we have minimal units, which can be trained to process an observation in different branches, based on a feature. With entropy, we can measure how useful a particular feature is, given a sample of observations. All we need now is to combine stumps into a full tree. Starting with a collection of features and a training set, we will identify the most informative feature, create a stump for each outcome, and repeat the operation for each branch.

The code we are going to write is fairly general, so, in a fashion similar to that in Chapter 2, let's extract it into its own separate module. We will add a file to our solution, say, Tree.fs, start moving some of our general code there, and use that file in our scripts, which will be focused exclusively on the specific problem of crafting a model for the Titanic dataset.

Modeling the Tree

Let's start with the end result, the tree. The main difference between a stump and a full tree is that while each branch of the stump gives us a final, definite answer, a tree is more complex: It can give us a final answer, but it can also keep going and lead us down to another stump, with a follow-up question to ask.

Most of the time, when you hear a domain description that involves an "or" statement ("it can be this or that"), the F# solution will involve a discriminated union. This works perfectly well here: A tree is either an answer or a stump leading to another tree. The code in Listing 6-15 maps our description of the problem rather directly.

Listing 6-15. Modeling a decision tree as a discriminated union

```
namespace Titanic

module Tree =

    type Feature<'a> = 'a -> string Option
    type NamedFeature<'a> = string * Feature<'a>
    type Label<'a,'b when 'b:equality> = 'a -> 'b

    type Tree<'a,'b when 'b:equality> =
        | Answer of 'b
        | Stump of NamedFeature<'a> * string * Map<string,Tree<'a,'b>>
```

A couple of quick comments here: First, even though in the Titanic case the labels are strings, this isn't necessarily always the case. In Chapter 1, for instance, the classes were integers. We made the labels generic here so that our tree can handle more general situations. Then, the Tree data structure is a bit complex–let's explain it a bit. What it says is that a tree results in one of two things: either we reached an answer (a final leaf, which contains the label value 'b), or it leads to a Stump. In that case, we need to know three things: what feature the stump was built with (NamedFeature<'a>), what value to use for the feature when its value is missing (a string), and, for each of the possible values we expect to see for the feature (the "branches" of the stump), what comes next, either an Answer or another Stump.

How would we use this to make a decision? What we want is the following: Given a passenger and a tree, if the tree is an Answer, then we are done. Otherwise, use the feature attached to the Stump to get another feature value for the passenger and keep searching in the corresponding tree. If the value is None, we encountered missing data, and will use the default specified in the Stump. We also decided that in case an unknown value was encountered, we would treat it as default, too. You could argue that in that case, the tree should throw an exception; feel free to do that, but it will come at the cost of potential issues.

Listing 6-16. Using a tree to make a decision

```
let rec decide tree observation =
    match tree with
    | Answer(labelValue) -> labelValue
    | Stump((featureName,feature),valueWhenMissing,branches) ->
        let featureValue = feature observation
        let usedValue =
            match featureValue with
            | None -> valueWhenMissing
            | Some(value) ->
```

```
        match (branches.TryFind value) with
        | None -> valueWhenMissing
        | Some(_) -> value
    let nextLevelTree = branches.[usedValue]
    decide nextLevelTree observation
```

Constructing the Tree

Almost done! The last thing we need to do is to build up the tree from a sample and an initial collection of features. We will simply find the most informative feature for the sample, create a stump for it, and recursively keep going until we have either no features left, or too little data left to use.

Listing 6-17 does just that; it's a bit lengthy, but not particularly complex. There are two tricky bits that are perhaps worth noting. First, features are passed in as a Map<string,Feature>; on the one hand, this makes it easy to access a feature by a name, and add or remove features. On the other hand, when using a Map as a sequence, elements appear as KeyValuePair. Also, we don't want a branch for missing values in a stump: These will be handled by the default value case.

Listing 6-17. Growing a tree from a sample and features

```
let mostFrequentBy f sample =
    sample
    |> Seq.map f
    |> Seq.countBy id
    |> Seq.maxBy snd
    |> fst


let rec growTree sample label features =

    if (Map.isEmpty features)
    // we have no feature left to split on:
    // our prediction is the most frequent
    // label in the dataset
    then sample |> mostFrequentBy label |> Answer
    else
        // from the named features we have available,
        // identify the one with largest entropy gain.
        let (bestName,bestFeature) =
            features
            |> Seq.minBy (fun kv ->
                splitEntropy label kv.Value sample)
            |> (fun kv -> kv.Key, kv.Value)
        // create a group for each of the values the
        // feature takes, eliminating the cases where
        // the value is missing.
        let branches =
            sample
            |> Seq.groupBy bestFeature
            |> Seq.filter (fun (value,group) -> value.IsSome)
            |> Seq.map (fun (value,group) -> value.Value,group)
        // find the most frequent value for the feature;
        // we'll use it as a default replacement for missing values.
```

197

```
        let defaultValue =
            branches
            |> Seq.maxBy (fun (value,group) ->
                group |> Seq.length)
            |> fst
        // remove the feature we selected from the list of
        // features we can use at the next tree level
        let remainingFeatures = features |> Map.remove bestName
        // ... and repeat the operation for each branch,
        // building one more level of depth in the tree
        let nextLevel =
            branches
            |> Seq.map (fun (value,group) ->
                value, growTree group label remainingFeatures)
            |> Map.ofSeq

        Stump((bestName,bestFeature),defaultValue,nextLevel)
```

Most of our work is done here. We can now learn a tree from a dataset and a collection of features. Let's try this out! Now that our algorithm is becoming stable, perhaps it's time to move our exploration to a new script file.

Listing 6-18. First Titanic tree

```
#r @".\packages\FSharp.Data.2.2.2\lib\net40\FSharp.Data.dll"
#load "Tree.fs"

open System
open FSharp.Data
open Titanic
open Titanic.Tree

type Titanic = CsvProvider<"titanic.csv">
type Passenger = Titanic.Row

let dataset = Titanic.GetSample ()

let label (p:Passenger) = p.Survived

let features = [
    "Sex", fun (p:Passenger) -> p.Sex |> Some
    "Class", fun p -> p.Pclass |> string |> Some
    "Age", fun p -> if p.Age < 7.0 then Some("Younger") else Some("Older") ]

let tree = growTree dataset.Rows label (features |> Map.ofList)

dataset.Rows
|> Seq.averageBy (fun p -> if p.Survived = decide tree p then 1. else 0.)

>
val tree : Tree<CsvProvider<...>.Row,bool> =
  Stump
```

```
  (("Sex", <fun:features@17-2>),"male",
   map
     [("female",
       Stump
         (("Class", <fun:features@18-3>),"3",
          map
            [("1",
              Stump
                (("Age", <fun:features@19-4>),"Older",
                 map [("Older", Answer true); ("Younger", Answer false)]));
// snipped for brevity
val it : float = 0.8058361392
```

The good news is that running this code produces a tree, and a clear improvement, with about 80% correct calls. There is some bad news, too. First, the output tree is ugly as hell. Also, we have completely ignored all we have preached so far, and didn't use cross-validation at all to evaluate our work. We need to fix that.

■ **Caution**   In a fashion similar to the naïve Bayes classifier we discussed in Chapter 2, what a decision tree learns is directly based on how frequently items are found in the training set. As a consequence, it is important to bear in mind that if the dataset is significantly distorted from the "real" population, and doesn't reflect its true composition, the predictions are likely to be entirely incorrect.

A Prettier Tree

The tree we receive back is barely readable, at best; let's write a simple function to display it in a more human-friendly format. Essentially, we are going to recursively walk down the tree, increasing indentation every time we hit a new depth level, and printing out feature and branch names as we go.

Listing 6-19. Rendering the tree

```
let rec display depth tree =
    let padding = String.replicate (2 * depth) " "
    match tree with
    | Answer(label) -> printfn " -> %A" label
    | Stump((name,_),_,branches) ->
        printfn ""
        branches
      |> Seq.iter (fun kv ->
          printf "%s ? %s : %s" padding name kv.Key
          display (depth + 1) kv.Value)
```

Here is the result for the previous tree we grew:

```
? Sex : female
  ? Class : 1
    ? Age : Older -> true
    ? Age : Younger -> false
  ? Class : 2
    ? Age : Older -> true
    ? Age : Younger -> true
```

```
  ? Class : 3
    ? Age : Older -> false
    ? Age : Younger -> true
? Sex : male
  ? Class : 1
    ? Age : Older -> false
    ? Age : Younger -> true
  ? Class : 2
    ? Age : Older -> false
    ? Age : Younger -> true
  ? Class : 3
    ? Age : Older -> false
    ? Age : Younger -> false
```

You could clearly do something fancier, but in my opinion this is largely sufficient to see what the model is telling us; for instance, that a female traveling third class, younger than seven years old, had a better chance of surviving than an older female in the same class.

Incidentally, I think this is one of the key appeals of decision trees: Their results are very understandable by humans. A tree is something you can present to a person with a limited mathematical background, and they will still get it. While trees have their limits, too, as we will see in a second, the ability to just look at a model output and make sense of it is not to be underestimated.

Improving the Tree

We wrote a completely generic algorithm, ready to use any dataset and build a decision tree out of it, using any list of features you please, in the best possible order. Does this mean we are done?

Not quite. While the most complicated blocks are in place, some things can go wrong with our tree-growing algorithm. As it stands now, we are almost guaranteed to over-fit the training data and learn a fragile model that will perform poorly when trying to predict new data.

Why Are We Over-Fitting?

Let's illustrate with an egregious example the type of problems that might occur, and consider building a model on a single feature, the passenger ID. Of course, this is a preposterous model: Observing the unique ID of passengers we don't have in our training sample shouldn't help us predict their fate. And yet, if you grow a tree using that feature, you will get the following model:

Listing 6-20. Overfitting on passenger ID

```
let idExample = [ "ID", fun (p:Passenger) -> p.PassengerId |> string |> Some ]

let idTree = growTree dataset.Rows label (idExample |> Map.ofList)

dataset.Rows
|> Seq.averageBy (fun p -> if p.Survived = decide idTree p then 1.0 else 0.0)
|> printfn "Correct: %.3f"

idTree |> display 0

>
Correct: 1.000
```

```
? ID : 1 -> false
? ID : 10 -> true
? ID : 100 -> false
// snipped for brevity
? ID : 97 -> false
? ID : 98 -> true
? ID : 99 -> true
```

This is obviously wrong on many levels. There is nothing wrong with the math, mind you; it's just that the result, from a practical standpoint, is entirely useless. If we use this model against new data, those new IDs will obviously not be in the tree, and as a result the prediction will be the default, uninformed one–and yet, this model is 100% correct on modeling and predicting the training set.

We already have encountered this last issue, and hopefully by now you are thinking to yourself, "Of course–he should have used cross-validation," and you would be right. We will use cross-validation ahead, but I thought it was useful to make this point, first, because it is a very simple illustration of how things can go terribly wrong, and second, because over-fitting is a particularly important issue to keep in mind for trees.

Unlike other algorithms we considered earlier, a tree is learning recursively. As a result, instead of learning all the features at once on the full training set, it learns one feature at a time, on samples that are smaller and smaller as the algorithm progresses.

This is a bit problematic, when you consider how entropy works. First, information doesn't disappear; in the worst possible case, splitting by a feature will gain us no information. As a result, in the current implementation, we will always add every single feature we have to the tree, even when it doesn't add any information. Then, because entropy is based on proportions, it will draw the same conclusions when analyzing both small and large samples, as long as their composition is identical. This is a bit problematic, too: I would not have the same confidence in conclusions derived from a sample containing 10 observations versus a sample with 100,000.

Limiting Over-Confidence with Filters

Let's begin first by addressing the easier issues. We want to avoid learning with too much confidence based on insufficiently conclusive samples. One simple way to do that is to add filters to our tree-growing algorithm so as to eliminate weak candidates as we progress down the tree.

Let's consider the two cases we identified already. We are currently picking the feature that has the highest conditional entropy; we can improve the algorithm by keeping only features that have a strictly positive entropy gain. In order to perform that operation, I need a few pieces of data: a feature, obviously, but also a sample and a label, to compute the entropy and split entropy, and check that the entropy is better (that is, strictly lower) after the split.

If I were to just hard-code this rule in the algorithm, I would modify our existing code along these lines:

```
let rec growTree sample label features =

let features =
    features
    |> Map.filter (fun name f ->
        splitEntropy label f sample - entropy label sample < 0.)
```

This works, but it is not open for extension, to use SOLID parlance. What if we want more flexibility, for instance by retaining only features that pass a user-defined threshold, say, at least 5% entropy improvement over previous value? How about the other issue we discussed, that is, drawing conclusions from insufficiently large samples?

The code above hints at a potential solution; in Map.filter, we are applying a "feature filter," a function that checks whether a feature passes a condition for a given sample and a label. Instead of hard-coding this, we can simply pass a collection of filters to our algorithm, keeping only features where all filters are satisfied. Let's modify the growTree code in the Tree module, and also add a couple of built-in filters.

Listing 6-21. Injecting feature filters into the tree algorithm

```
let entropyGainFilter sample label feature =
    splitEntropy label feature sample - entropy label sample < 0.

let leafSizeFilter minSize sample label feature =
    sample
    |> Seq.map feature
    |> Seq.choose id
    |> Seq.countBy id
    |> Seq.forall (fun (_,groupSize) -> groupSize > minSize)

let rec growTree filters sample label features =

    let features =
        features
        |> Map.filter (fun name feature ->
            filters |> Seq.forall (fun filter -> filter sample label feature))

    if (Map.isEmpty features)
    // snipped for brevity
```

Applying this updated algorithm using the same features as previously, but passing in [entropyGain; leafSize 10] as a filter, this is the tree I get:

```
? Sex : female
    ? Class : 1 -> true
    ? Class : 2 -> true
    ? Class : 3
        ? Age : Older -> true
        ? Age : Younger -> false
 ? Sex : male
    ? Class : 1 -> false
    ? Class : 2 -> false
    ? Class : 3
        ? Age : Older -> false
        ? Age : Younger -> false
```

Our decision tree lost some depth from our previous version. This is good: Using filters leads to dropping some spurious branches, and as a result, we have a tree that is both more readable and more reliable. Note also that all the branches under male lead to the same conclusion. Does this indicate an issue with our algorithm? Not necessarily: Entropy will decide to split when it finds a significant difference between branches, regardless of whether that difference is material to our decision. For instance, a 51% and a 99% chance of surviving are significantly different, but the difference is not material to the conclusion, which remains the same. Depending on what you want, you could improve the tree in two different ways, either by adding probabilities to the final branches or by collapsing together stumps that contain identical answers into a single answer.

From Trees to Forests

We limited some of the most obvious over-fitting risks by injecting a bit of common sense into the algorithm, but the solution was rather crude. Over-fitting is particularly problematic for trees because of their recursive nature; however, it is a general problem in machine learning. By learning from one training sample, there is an inherent risk of learning that one sample too well. The filters we applied on our tree and the regularization methods we mentioned in an earlier chapter both address that issue with one strategy: limiting how much the algorithm is allowed to learn by applying a form of penalty.

In this section, we will introduce another way to think about this question, with a very different angle on how to resolve the problem. If you think about it, one of the reasons over-fitting is an issue is that we rely on a single training set and try to squeeze as much information as possible from it, taking the risk of learning a model that is too specific to that particular dataset. Instead of arbitrarily limiting what we can learn, perhaps we could try to learn from a diverse set of data in order to avoid over-reliance on a single model.

Deeper Cross-Validation with k-folds

Let's start by revisiting the question of how good our model is. Our dataset contains 891 passengers; that isn't much to go on in the first place. If we used, say, the first 75% for training and the remaining 25% for validation, we are left with less than 700 examples to train our classifier–and around 220 to try the model on so as to evaluate its performance. And, just like training a model on too little data can result in fragile results, evaluating it on too little data may result in spurious values from time to time. Because of the luck of the draw, some validation samples will be atypical and produce spurious quality metrics.

One way this problem can be limited is by doing the following: Instead of choosing one single and arbitrary validation sample, we can construct multiple training/validation samples and repeat the same process on each of them. For instance, we could divide our sample into k slices and create k combinations by using one slice for validation and the remaining k - 1 for training. As an example, instead of simply splitting our sample into 2/3 for training and 1/3 for validation, we could construct three alternate pairs by dividing our dataset into three equal slices, leaving one of them out for validation (see Figure 6-7).

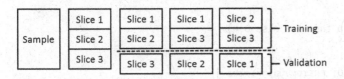

Figure 6-7. *Constructing three training/validation combinations from one sample*

So, why would we do that? It might seem pointless: Instead of one model and quality metric, we now have three slightly different models, with probably three different quality metrics, and a decision problem. Which of our three models is the best, and which evaluation should we trust? How is this helpful?

It is helpful if we change perspective a bit. We know that the validation metric we are getting will be incorrect no matter what: It is an estimate. In that frame, getting an idea of how wrong that estimate might be is as useful as the estimate itself. Rather than hanging everything on one incorrect number, we can now get a sense for how changes in the data could impact our model and how volatile the quality could be.

This approach is known as **k-fold**. Choosing k entails a bit of a trade-off. At the extreme, if we increase k to its largest possible value, the dataset size, we'll end up with k different models, validated on a single example each, which is commonly referred to as "leave-one-out." Obviously, the larger k becomes, the more expensive the operation will be, because more models need to be trained. Also, as k increases, each of the models shares more common data, and can therefore be expected to behave more like a model that would use the dataset in its entirety.

Let's try it out on our model here. First, we need to generate k pairs of training and validation samples. The following implementation, while not pretty, does the job: For each of the k values, it computes the start and end index of the validation slice and returns a list of k sample pairs, each of which contains the training and validation parts in a tuple.

Listing 6-22. Generating k training/validation pairs from a sample

```
let kfold k sample =

    let size = sample |> Array.length
    let foldSize = size / k

    [ for f in 0 .. (k-1) do
        let sliceStart = f * foldSize
        let sliceEnd = f * foldSize + foldSize - 1
        let validation = sample.[sliceStart..sliceEnd]
        let training =
            [|
                for i in 0 .. (sliceStart - 1) do yield sample.[i]
                for i in (sliceEnd + 1) .. (size - 1) do yield sample.[i]
            |]
        yield training,validation
    ]
```

Let's try out a k-fold analysis of our basic tree, with k = 10:

Listing 6-23. Evaluating ten folds

```
let folds = dataset.Rows |> Seq.toArray |> kfold 10
let accuracy tree (sample:Passenger seq) =
    sample
    |> Seq.averageBy (fun p ->
        if p.Survived = decide tree p then 1.0 else 0.0)

let evaluateFolds =
    let filters = [ leafSizeFilter 10; entropyGainFilter ]
    let features = features |> Map.ofList
    [for (training,validation) in folds ->
        let tree = growTree2 filters training label features
        let accuracyTraining = accuracy tree training
        let accuracyValidation = accuracy tree validation

        printfn "Training: %.3f, Validation: %.3f" accuracyTraining accuracyValidation
        accuracyTraining, accuracyValidation]
>
Training: 0.802, Validation: 0.697
Training: 0.788, Validation: 0.843
Training: 0.796, Validation: 0.775
Training: 0.797, Validation: 0.764
Training: 0.803, Validation: 0.798
Training: 0.798, Validation: 0.843
Training: 0.804, Validation: 0.787
```

```
Training: 0.805, Validation: 0.775
Training: 0.788, Validation: 0.843
Training: 0.794, Validation: 0.787
val evaluateFolds : (float * float) list =
  [(0.8017456359, 0.6966292135); // snipped // ; (0.7942643392, 0.7865168539)]
```

There are a couple of interesting results here. First, while not hugely different, the average accuracy on training is around 79.7%, about 0.6 points higher than on validation (79.1%). Then, the quality measurements on the validation samples are much more variable than those on the training samples. While the accuracy for training ranges from 78.8% to 80.5%, the validation results vary all the way from 69.7% to 84.3%. This is not surprising, because each of the validation samples is smaller, and thus more variable. These results are very useful in that they convey a much better picture of what we should expect from our model. Had we performed a basic cross-validation only, we would have seen only one of the ten results we produced with k-fold; depending on which of the training/validation pairs we happened to select, we could have reached different conclusions—either overly optimistic, or pessimistic. By contrast, with k-fold, we can conclude that our model is likely not over-fitting (the average errors on training and validation are very close). We also get a much more refined sense for how good or bad our model might be: We should expect to be correct in about 79.1% of the cases, but the standard deviation—the average error around that value—is of 4.5 percentage points.

Hopefully, this simple example illustrates how, by simply creating multiple samples from our original dataset, we managed to get a much better picture of our model quality. This technique is mainly useful for evaluating whether changes in a model are actual improvements; in the next section, we'll see how similar ideas can be used to improve the model itself.

Combining Fragile Trees into Robust Forests

With k-folds, we saw that resampling our training set allowed us to extract more information from it without having to add new observations. Instead of putting all of our eggs in a single basket (or all our observations in a single training set), we generated multiple training samples, which gave us a better overall picture of how sensitive to changes in data our model really was.

This is a result that I find both obvious and fascinating. Fascinating, because on the surface it appears as if we created additional information out of thin air. Using the exact same amount of information we initially had, we managed to squeeze out apparently new and better information. Obvious, because this is simply a change of focus. Fundamentally, we are dealing with uncertainty, and the best description for uncertainty is a distribution. By constructing multiple, random samples from our original data, we can mimic the type of variability that exists in the phenomenon we are trying to predict, and thus replicate (and measure) the resulting variability in the outputs.

This same idea can be taken further and be used to produce potentially more robust prediction models as well. Rather than trying to find the one and perfect model, we could embrace accidents, accept that inputs are volatile, and create a multitude of models based on different training sets. Some of them will be right, and some will be wrong, but if we look at all their predictions taken together, it is highly unlikely that they will all be simultaneously incorrect. For instance, we could take a majority vote and hope for a "wisdom of the crowds" effect, where a couple of odd predictions will be canceled out by a majority of reasonable ones. This general approach is known as "ensemble methods," an approach that studies how multiple weak prediction models can be combined into an overall model that is stronger than the sum of its parts.

In the specific case of decision trees, one way to go about it would be to simply generate multiple training sets from the original dataset by uniformly sampling observations at random, with replacement, potentially repeating the same observation multiple times. That approach is known as "bagging" (short for *bootstrap aggregating*). The intuition here is that this will mitigate the risks of over-fitting, because each model will be trained on a different sample. Each model might still pick up artifacts from the data, but different ones, and they will likely cancel each other out when taken together.

Decision trees, as we implemented them, have another issue that is less obvious. Because the procedure progresses one feature at the time, some features might mask the impact of others. Imagine that a feature is heavily related to another one (say, what class you travel in and how much you paid for your ticket), but contains a bit of information on its own. Once the tree picks up the first one, it is quite possible that the second one will not be selected, because the remaining information is not sufficiently strong by itself. As a result, by picking from all the features in order of entropy, we take the risk of systematically ignoring features that could convey some usable information.

In a fashion similar to bagging, we could address that issue by randomly sampling features. In at least some cases, the "hidden" feature will be present without the competing one, and will have a chance to participate in that tree if it turns out to be informative.

These two ideas can be combined into one. Instead of creating a single decision tree, we will create a multitude of simpler trees, a forest, each using a randomly selected training sample and a subset of features. Instead of relying on a single tree, we will take a majority vote from among all of them. Each individual model will be weaker than a decision tree using all the data at once, but, perhaps paradoxically, taken together they will provide more reliable predictions.

Implementing the Missing Blocks

Extending our current code to make a forest instead of a tree is rather straightforward. Basically, we only need to add three elements: randomly selecting features from a list (without repetition), randomly selecting examples from the original sample (with repetition), and combining the predictions of multiple trees into a majority vote. We will add all the necessary code to the Tree.fs file, and then try it out on the specific Titanic example.

Let's start with the second element. If we assume our initial sample is an array, the picking with repetition is as simple as selecting a random index, as many times as we need:

```
let pickRepeat (rng:Random) proportion original =
    let size = original |> Array.length
    let sampleSize = proportion * float size |> int
    Array.init sampleSize (fun _ -> original.[rng.Next(size)])
```

Picking with no repetition is a bit trickier. One possibility is to shuffle the entire collection and pick the first elements. Another possibility is to process the collection recursively, deciding one by one if an element should be selected. If I want to pick n elements out of N, the head of the list has an n/N chance of being selected. If it is selected, I now have n - 1 elements to select from N - 1 left; in the other case the chances were n over N - 1. Here we go:

```
let pickNoRepeat (rng:Random) proportion original =

    let size = original |> Seq.length
    let sampleSize = proportion * float size |> int

    let init = ([],size)
    original
    |> Seq.fold (fun (sampled,remaining) item ->
        let picked = List.length sampled
        let p = float (sampleSize - picked) / float remaining
        if (rng.NextDouble () <= p)
        then (item::sampled,remaining-1)
        else (sampled,remaining-1)) init
    |> fst
```

Finally, the prediction from a forest is simply the most frequent decision resulting from its trees:

```
let predict forest observation =
    forest
    |> Seq.map (fun tree -> decide tree observation)
    |> Seq.countBy id
    |> Seq.maxBy snd
    |> fst
```

Growing a Forest

Let's put all of this together: The only thing needed is a function that will create a user-defined number of trees. We will also wrap things tighter and directly return a function that can be used to make predictions. While an individual tree is useful because it can be inspected, we are not going to look into hundreds of trees in the hopes of detecting patterns and whatnot.

Listing 6-24. Creating a forest from decision trees

```
let growForest size sample label features =

    let rng = Random ()

    let propFeatures =
        let total = features |> Seq.length |> float
        sqrt total / total

    let featSample () = pickNoRepeat rng propFeatures features
    let popSample () = pickRepeat rng 1.0 sample
    let filters = [ leafSize 10; entropyGain ]

    let forest = [
        for _ in 1 .. size ->
            let sample = popSample ()
            let features = featSample () |> Map.ofList
            growTree filters sample label features ]

    let predictor = predict forest
    predictor
```

We simplified the function signature by pre-selecting reasonable defaults for filters; we also selected default proportions for what sample proportion to use for the population (100%) and for the features (square root of the number of features). Providing a fine-grained version wouldn't be very complicated; it just takes writing a fully expanded signature of that function and calling it from the simplified "default" version.

Trying Out the Forest

Now that we have the algorithm in place, let's try it out and compare the results with the tree we ended up with earlier. We will create a list of features, and, using the same ten training/validation pairs as before, we will train a forest of 1,000 trees (each time using a slightly different combination of features and observations), and then compute the algorithm's accuracy on both the training and validation sets.

Listing 6-25. Testing out the forest

```
let forestFeatures = [
    "Sex", fun (p:Passenger) -> p.Sex |> Some
    "Class", fun p -> p.Pclass |> string |> Some
    "Age", fun p -> if p.Age < 7.0 then Some("Younger") else Some("Older")
    "Port", fun p -> if p.Embarked = "" then None else Some(p.Embarked) ]

let forestResults () =

    let accuracy predictor (sample:Passenger seq) =
        sample
        |> Seq.averageBy (fun p ->
            if p.Survived = predictor p then 1.0 else 0.0)

    [for (training,validation) in folds ->

        let forest = growForest 1000 training label forestFeatures

        let accuracyTraining = accuracy forest training
        let accuracyValidation = accuracy forest validation

        printfn "Training: %.3f, Validation: %.3f" accuracyTraining accuracyValidation
        accuracyTraining,accuracyValidation ]

forestResults ()
>
Training: 0.803, Validation: 0.753
Training: 0.800, Validation: 0.775
Training: 0.808, Validation: 0.798
Training: 0.800, Validation: 0.775
Training: 0.798, Validation: 0.798
Training: 0.792, Validation: 0.854
Training: 0.800, Validation: 0.775
Training: 0.812, Validation: 0.764
Training: 0.792, Validation: 0.854
Training: 0.804, Validation: 0.820
val it  : (float * float) list =
  [(0.8029925187, 0.7528089888); // snipped //; (0.8042394015, 0.8202247191)]
```

The results are, on average, a tiny bit better than those with the tree, but nothing particularly impressive. However, what is more interesting here is that there is much less of a discrepancy between the accuracy measured on the training and validation sets. Furthermore, the accuracy on the validation set is also more consistent. In the case of the tree, accuracy varied all the way from 69.7% to 84.3%; for the forest, we get a much narrower range, from 75.3% to 85.4%. This is great: What this means is that, typically, a forest is much less prone to over-fit, and the model will generalize well; that is, its performance on new data it hasn't seen before should not be significantly different from how well it does on the training data.

> ■ **Note** One additional benefit of forests over plain trees is that they make it possible to train on the full dataset without having to set aside a validation set. Each observation will be used in only some of the generated trees, so one could use all the trees that didn't include that example for training, and use them as a forest to predict the label of that example, and then check whether the prediction is correct. Repeating that procedure over every example will produce the so-called "out of bag estimates," which is a form of cross-validation. The idea is simple, but the implementation a bit tedious, so we won't include it here, and will leave it as the proverbial "exercise to the reader."

So, What Have We Learned?

We covered quite a bit of territory in this chapter.

First, we presented decision trees. Part of the appeal of decision trees probably lies with how intuitive they are. In the end, a tree is nothing more than a sequence of questions, designed to produce a diagnosis as quickly as possible. They mimic the way humans make decisions, and are also very convenient to interpret, even by nonspecialists. As silly as it might sound, this can be invaluable. Chances are, once you are finished developing a machine learning model, you will need to convince someone else that it works; that conversation is much easier to have when your model "makes sense" on an intuitive level.

However, there are also technical reasons for why trees are a tool worth having in your tool belt. The Titanic dataset we used as a basis is typical, in that it is messy. It contains different types of features, from numeric (fare) to categorical (male/female), and some of the observations have missing values—and yet, it was fairly easy to build a model that handled all these potential issues without much of a problem. Trees are flexible and are applicable to virtually any dataset.

Beyond the cases we just mentioned, trees can be used to classify using more than two labels, and this works without any particular tricks. It is an interesting contrast to many classic classifiers, which are intrinsically binary and require an additional level of complexity to handle three or more labels. For that matter, with a bit of additional effort, trees can even be used to handle regression problems.

As an added bonus, trees are directly based on probabilities; the ability to produce not only predictions, but the corresponding probabilities, is very convenient. The flip side is that the model quality will be sensitive to the training-sample quality. If the training sample doesn't replicate the composition of the general population reasonably well, the learning algorithm will base its conclusion on incorrect information, in a fashion similar to the naïve Bayes model we discussed in Chapter 2.

Along the way, we needed a consistent way to quantify how much information there was in a feature so that we could decide which of the features we should focus on. We introduced Shannon entropy, a measure for how much impurity a dataset contains (and how reliably predictions can be made about it), and expanded into conditional entropy, which measures how likely we are to be in a better information state after asking a question.

We also demonstrated another way entropy can be useful, by discretizing numerical features. Trees, by construction, operate on categorical features; that is, features that distinguish between a limited set of discrete cases. As a result, any input that is numerical needs to be reduced to discrete bins, and entropy provides a way to decide what appropriate cutoff values to use so as to extract the maximum information.

Finally, we also discussed how decision trees, because of their recursive nature, have a natural tendency to over-fit. By construction, trees add features progressively, operating on smaller and smaller samples as the algorithm progresses, thus potentially including features based on insufficiently conclusive data, and ending up with a brittle model. This led us to an exploration of two ideas related to over-fitting: cross-validation using k-folds, and random forests. With k-folds, we saw how creating multiple combinations of training and validation samples allowed us to generate a range of values describing the quality of a model, providing us with a deeper understanding of how reliable a model could be, and how much it might be affected by small changes in training data.

Building on the same ideas, we implemented a simple version of a random forest, a classifier that belongs to a broader class of models known as ensemble methods. Instead of relying on a single tree, we trained many of them, using randomly selected training data and features for each of them, and combining their predictions into one majority vote. That somewhat paradoxical approach, where we choose to ignore some of the data available to us, is in many ways close to the idea of "wisdom of the crowds." By creating multiple smaller and less accurate models, each using a slightly different source of information, we managed in the end to create an overall model that is very robust, because many independent models are unlikely to all be wrong simultaneously, and this model is, in some ways, more than the sum of its individual parts.

USEFUL LINKS

You can find the Kaggle "Titanic: Machine Learning from Disaster" page here: `https://www.kaggle.com/c/titanic`. It is a fun opportunity to test your skills against real competition, and there are also a couple of interesting tutorials.

If you are interested in learning more about random forests, Leo Breiman (who created the algorithm) has a page full of useful information here: `https://www.stat.berkeley.edu/~breiman/RandomForests/cc_home.htm`.

CHAPTER 7

■ ■ ■

A Strange Game

Learning from Experience with Reinforcement Learning

Imagine you are a creature in the middle of a large room. The floor is covered with colorful tiles everywhere you look, for as far as you can see. You feel adventurous and take a step forward onto a blue tile. Zing! You feel a burst of pain. Maybe blue tiles are bad? On your left is a red tile, on your right a blue tile. Let's try red this time. Tada! This time, good things happen. It would seem red tiles are good, and blue are bad. By default, you should probably avoid blue tiles and prefer red ones. Or maybe things are slightly more complicated, and what matters is the particular configurations of tiles. There is only one way to know—trial and error. Try things out, confirm or invalidate hypotheses, and in general, do more of the things that seem to work, and less of the ones that seem to fail.

The real world is certainly more complicated than the universe of colored tiles I just described. And yet, if you think about it, our life is not that different from that of our fictional creature. We evolve in a vast universe, where we encounter new, unknown situations. When such a situation arises, we try things out. Sometimes, the result is immediate. I remember very vividly the day I put my finger into a power socket; I learned very promptly that this wasn't a good decision. Some lessons take longer to learn; for instance, usually, when you behave nicely to people, they tend to respond in kind. When you are disrespectful, it generally works poorly. But it isn't always true, and it sometimes takes time to observe the effects of your actions, which makes drawing conclusions less obvious.

In this chapter, we will take a look at how we could actually build a brain for our creature, so that it learns to behave in a somewhat reasonable way as it accumulates experience. In and of itself, programming a creature to move around in a maze of colors is probably not that close to what most developers do. However, first, it is a fun problem—and then, it is a simple, representative version of a large class of similar problems, which will allow us to explore a few interesting questions and techniques which are more widely applicable. We will do the following:

- Write a very simple game that simulates the behavior of a creature discovering a world it knows nothing about. Using reinforcement learning, we will build up a basic strategy to allow the creature to learn from the outcomes of its actions, and make better decisions as it accumulates experience,

- Analyze the shortcomings of our initial approach, and refine the learning algorithm accordingly, along two main directions. We will see how to overcome short-sighted decision making, by taking into account both immediate rewards and longer-term consequences, and how we can improve learning, by injecting some randomness into the decision making process and encouraging exploration.

Building a Simple Game

As a warm up, let's begin with building a simple game, following the scenario outlined earlier, and, starting from a brainless creature, let's see how we can model the world and make it, if not smart, at least not entirely stupid. Once we get a handle of how things work, we will step it up and go for a more complex version.

The point here is not to create a shiny block-buster video game; at the same time, having an actual game, where you can see things happen, is fun, so we will go very old school, and do a retro console-based game. So let's begin by creating a new F# project, of type Console Application, which we will name SimpleGame. Once you have created that project, you should see a file named Program.fs, with the following contents:

```
// Learn more about F# at http://fsharp.net
// See the 'F# Tutorial' project for more help.

[<EntryPoint>]
let main argv =
    printfn "%A" argv
    0 // return an integer exit code
```

This is a minimal console application, which you can already run or debug by pressing the F5 key. At that point, the program will simply run the main function (the entry point of the application), start a window, and immediately finish execution and shut down the window. Let's try to make that program more interesting!

There are a couple of different aspects to the game. We need to model the rules, to deal with rendering into the console, and run games as a program. Once we have these pieces wired up, we will also need to build the "brains" of our creature.

Modeling Game Elements

So let's begin with a bit of modeling. Our game will have a single creature, evolving on a terrain of square tiles. "Creature" sounds a bit demeaning, so let's call it a Hero from now on, which is both more flattering and shorter. At each turn, the Hero can do three things: keep going straight, turn left, or turn right. In order to be able to track down what is happening to the Hero, we will need two additional pieces of information: its position, for instance from the top and left sides of the world, and its direction.

This fits very nicely with F# discriminated unions. Let's add a file Game.fs, which we will move on top of the list of project files, and start a module Game.

Listing 7-1. Modelling the Game elements

```
namespace Game

module Game =

    type Dir =
        | North
        | West
        | South
        | East
```

```
type Act =
    | Left
    | Right
    | Straight

type Pos = { Top:int; Left:int }

type Hero = { Position:Pos; Direction:Dir }
```

Pretty easy so far. Next we need a world. To keep things simple, our world will be square, and have no edges, so that if for instance you went all the way north, you would end up passing the limit and re-appearing in the southernmost position. This simplifies things a bit, because we don't have to deal with situations where we reached the "end of the world": wherever the Hero is, he can always take any of the three actions available.

Our world is a simple one—each cell will either be empty, or contain a treasure, or a trap. We could model that a couple of ways; for now we will use a map (roughly an immutable dictionary) to hold the cells, and we will only store non-empty cells. For good measure, let's also immediately create a record to hold the entire "state of the world," and a record to hold the size of that world.

Listing 7-2. Modelling the Game world

```
type Cell =
    | Treasure
    | Trap

type Board = Map<Pos,Cell>

type GameState = { Board:Board; Hero:Hero; Score:int }

type Size = { Width:int; Height:int }
```

Modeling the Game Logic

Now that we have our building blocks, we can start defining how the world works, with a couple of functions. The first thing we need is to be able to move our Hero around: Given his position and direction, where will he (or she) be next on the board? We cannot simply increase or decrease the position, because once we go over the edge of the world, we should reappear on the other side, so to speak. Let's create our own custom modulus operator %%%, which handles negative numbers the way we want to, a function to "adjust" a position and return its equivalent, staying within the bounds of the board size, and we are set—we can now write a function moveTo, which will transform a position into the next, when moving along one of the four possible directions.

Listing 7-3. Moving in the Game world

```
let inline (%%%) (x:int) (y:int) =
    if x >= 0 then x % y
    else y + (x % y)

let onboard (size:Size) (pos:Pos) =
    { Top = pos.Top %%% size.Height;
      Left = pos.Left %%% size.Width; }
```

```
let moveTo (size:Size) (dir:Dir) (pos:Pos) =
    match dir with
    | North -> { pos with Top = (pos.Top - 1) %%% size.Height }
    | South -> { pos with Top = (pos.Top + 1) %%% size.Height }
    | West -> { pos with Left = (pos.Left - 1) %%% size.Width }
    | East -> { pos with Left = (pos.Left + 1) %%% size.Width }
```

We are nearly done with modeling. On the Hero side, what we need is to apply the decision (left, right or straight) to get the next position. That's straightforward.

Listing 7-4. Implementing the Hero's movements

```
let takeDirection (act:Act) (dir:Dir) =
    match act with
    | Straight -> dir
    | Left ->
        match dir with
        | North -> East
        | East -> South
        | South -> West
        | West -> North
    | Right ->
        match dir with
        | North -> West
        | West -> South
        | South -> East
        | East -> North

let applyDecision (size:Size) (action:Act) (hero:Hero) =
    let newDirection = hero.Direction |> takeDirection action
    { Position = hero.Position |> moveTo size newDirection; Direction = newDirection }
```

Finally, we need to model what happens to the world. For now, whenever the Hero visits a position, if there is nothing, nothing happens; if there is a treasure, pocket 100 points, if there is a trap, lose 100 points, and the trap or treasure is gone. Again, that is fairly straightforward. The function computeGain looks for a potential cell on the board at the Hero's position, and the corresponding gain if there is one, and updateBoard takes the current board, and removes the cell at the Hero's position, if any.

Listing 7-5. Updating the world

```
let treasureScore = 100
let trapScore = - 100

let computeGain (board:Board) (hero:Hero) =
    let currentPosition = hero.Position
    match board.TryFind(currentPosition) with
    | Some(cell) ->
        match cell with
        | Treasure -> treasureScore
        | Trap -> trapScore
    | None -> 0
```

```
let updateBoard (board:Board) (player:Hero) =
    let currentPosition = player.Position
    board
    |> Map.filter (fun position _ -> position <> currentPosition)
```

And... we are done with modeling. Next up, let's get that game running!

Running the Game as a Console App

Let's wire up the most basic things that could possibly work. The game needs to run a loop: Ask the Hero to make a decision, update the world accordingly, render it—and start again. We also need some code to initialize the world.

In the Program.fs file, let's modify a bit the default code, and create a Program module, with the same namespace Game we used for the Game modeling part:

```
namespace Game

open System
open System.Threading
open Game

module Program =

    [<EntryPoint>]
    let main argv =

        0 // return an integer exit code
```

Now that we have the shell for a console application, let's add in the initialization. There is nothing really tricky here. We need to decide on a size for our world, and an initial location for our Hero. We also need some traps and treasures for our world, to spice up our Hero's adventures! Let's go and randomly fill the Map, so that each position has a 50% chance of containing something, with equal chance a Trap or Treasure.

Listing 7-6. Initializing the game world

```
module Program =

    // world initialization
    let size = { Width = 40; Height = 20 }
    let player = { Position = { Top = 10; Left = 20 }; Direction = North }

    let rng = Random ()

    let board =
        [   for top in 0 .. size.Height - 1 do
                for left in 0 .. size.Width - 1 do
                    if rng.NextDouble () > 0.5
                    then
                        let pos = { Top = top; Left = left }
                        let cell = if rng.NextDouble () > 0.5 then Trap else Treasure
```

215

```
                    yield pos, cell ]
    |> Map.ofList

let score = 0
let initialGameState = { Board = board; Hero = player; Score = score }

[<EntryPoint>]
let main argv = // etc...
```

The other missing part is a way for the Hero to make decisions. For now we will keep him brainless: like a headless chicken, he will randomly decide at each turn whether to go Straight, Left or Right (we'll have plenty of time later in this chapter to fix that).

Listing 7-7. Initial Hero decision making

```
let initialGameState = { Board = board; Hero = player; Score = score }

// decision function
let choices = [| Straight; Left; Right |]
let decide () = choices.[rng.Next(3)]

[<EntryPoint>]
let main argv = // etc...
```

Now to the main loop. Let's not worry about rendering for now (we'll look at it in the next section) —just to make sure that something is happening, we'll print out the current score at each step. In that case, our loop should look along the lines of what's shown in Listing 7-8.

Listing 7-8. Running the game in a loop

```
[<EntryPoint>]
let main argv =

    let rec loop (state:GameState) =

        let decision = decide ()

        // world update
        let player = state.Hero |> applyDecision size decision
        let board = updateBoard state.Board player
        let gain = computeGain state.Board player
        let score = state.Score + gain

        // world rendering
        printfn "%i" score

        let updated = { Board = board; Hero = player; Score = score }

        Thread.Sleep 20
        loop (updated)
```

```
    // start the game
    let _ = loop (initialGameState)

    0 // return an integer exit code
```

At that point, if you run the code, you should see numbers being printed on screen. The Hero is making decisions and moving around the world, and the score is changing—but without any graphical display, this is thoroughly unexciting. Let's fix that, and add some graphics to our game.

Rendering the Game

The last piece we need is rendering the game. This is pretty straightforward—let's create another file, Rendering.fs, move it above Program.fs, and put all the rendering code in a new module. Our "graphics" will be relying on System.Console, using Console.SetCursorPosition to determine where we want to draw, and Console.ForegroundColor to set the drawing color. The only subtlety here is that in addition to representing the Hero and the world he evolves in, we also want to print out the current score. For that purpose, we will move all coordinates by an offset of two lines down, so we can use the top two lines on the Console display to write out the score.

Listing 7-9. Rendering the game

```
namespace Game

open System
open Game

module Rendering =

    let offset (pos:Pos) = (pos.Left, pos.Top + 2)
    let writeAt (left,top) color (txt:string) =
        Console.ForegroundColor <- color
        Console.SetCursorPosition (left,top)
        Console.Write txt

    let prepareDisplay size =
        Console.SetWindowSize(size.Width, size.Height+2)

    let renderPlayer (before:Hero) (after:Hero) =
        writeAt (offset (before.Position)) ConsoleColor.Black "•"
        writeAt (offset (after.Position)) ConsoleColor.Yellow "•"

    let renderBoard (before:Board) (after:Board) =
        after
        |> Map.iter (fun pos item ->
            if (before |> Map.containsKey pos)
            then
                match item with
                | Treasure ->
                    writeAt (offset pos) ConsoleColor.Blue "@"
                | Trap ->
```

```
            writeAt (offset pos) ConsoleColor.Red "+"
        else writeAt (offset pos) ConsoleColor.Black " ")

let renderScore score =
    writeAt (0,0) ConsoleColor.White (sprintf "Score: %i    " score)
```

One thing I want to point out here is how, by design, F# leads us toward a virtuous path. We have all seen projects starting with the best of intentions, and quickly devolve into a massive pile of spaghetti code, where everything depends on everything else. Most people would agree that while the rendering code depends on the domain model, changing the rendering should not ripple through the domain. F# type inference system, which requires that code has to be used top-to-bottom (I can only call code that has been written above the current line), naturally enforces a good separation of concerns, and makes dependencies immediately visible. The Rendering module is placed below the Game module in the project, because it depends on it—and I cannot create unhealthy code cycles between these two areas.

The only thing left to do now is to incorporate the rendering code in the game loop. Include open Rendering in the Program.fs file, and in the loop function from Listing 7-8, replace the printfn "%i" score with Listing 7-10.

Listing 7-10. Rendering the game in the main loop

```
let score = state.Score + gain

// world rendering
renderScore score
renderPlayer state.Hero player
renderBoard state.Board board

let updated = { Board = board; Hero = player; Score = score }
```

At that point, we are ready to run the game. If you do so, you should see something close to what's shown in Figure 7-1.

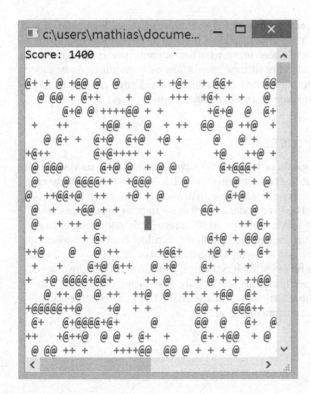

Figure 7-1. *Running the game*

■ **Note**   The actual game uses a different color theme, against a black background.

Our hero, represented by a little yellow rectangle, is moving around forever without much purpose, hitting traps (+) and treasures (@) randomly. This game will certainly not win any prizes at gaming conventions, but now we have a baseline, and a way to visualize what is going on.

Building a Primitive Brain

It is now time to give our Hero a bit of a brain. Nothing fancy to start with—just a minimal brain to learn from his mistakes and successes. Once we have that primitive approach down, we will see what we learn in the process, and try to make him even smart, or at least, less silly.

Initially, our Hero knows nothing about the world he evolves in. He has no notion that traps are to be avoided, and treasures sought. We could try to build his brain explicitly, with clever, pre-programmed routines, to give him a predetermined strategy. However, we will take a different route, for at least two reasons. First, writing such a predetermined strategy is both difficult and fragile. Difficult, because it isn't quite obvious how such a strategy should be designed in the first place. Fragile, because if we decide at some point to change the game a bit, say, modify the rewards attached to treasures, or maybe add a different type of element to the game, such as another type of trap, we would have to re-write our entire strategy.

Then, it is a bit of a waste. Whenever the Hero moves around, he is accumulating valuable experience, and should be able to learn by himself things that work, and things that don't. It would be much more interesting to build a learning routine, which observes what action has been taken, what the outcome was, and progressively does more of the good stuff, and less of the bad. This is, after all, more or less how we learn things. As an added benefit, this would also address the previous problem mentioned: if we relied on experience, rather than hard-code a strategy, our Hero would be able to learn and adapt when we modify the game.

Modeling the Decision Making Process

So how could we approach this? If we stick to our vocabulary, here is what we want: our Hero moves around the world, taking decisions at each step. Every time, he is in a certain state (what he can see from the world), performs an action (straight, left or right), and observes a result (the gain or loss of that action), and the new state he ends in. A reasonable approach would be to consider each of these steps as experiences, and try to learn from each of them what the result of an action might be. As the adage (of debated source) goes, "insanity is doing the same thing over and over again, and expecting different results;" conversely, wisdom might be to do over and over again things that work, and avoid repeating failures.

Let's decompose the problem, and establish a bit of vocabulary. For our game, we will assume that the Hero is somewhat short-sighted, and can only see his immediate vicinity, as depicted in Figure 7-2. In that frame, it would make sense to define State, the information available to the Hero, as his immediate surroundings—the eight cells around him—and his current direction.

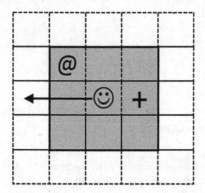

Figure 7-2. *Defining the State*

What we need is a way to learn what decision the Hero should make, given the information he has at the moment, his State. In this case, the Hero can choose between doing three things: go Left, Right, or Straight. Let's call these each of these combinations a *strategy*—so when the Hero is in a particular state, he has three strategies available to choose from:

```
{ Current State; Go Left }
{ Current State; Go Right}
{ Current State; Go Straight }
```

What makes a strategy good or bad? Our goal is for the Hero to score big, so a good strategy should yield a high score. How could we go about predicting the gain of a *strategy*, then? If you consider a game as it unfolds, you can see it as a succession of moves of the form:

```
State0 -> Action1 -> Reward1 -> State1 -> Action2 -> Reward2 ...
```

We can re-organize this, and see a game as a sequence of "experiences":

```
{ State0; Action1; Reward1; State1 }
{ State1; Action2; Reward2; State3 }
...
```

■ **Note**   We included the end-state in each experience. We will not use that information in the beginning, but it will become useful later on in the chapter.

As we run the game, the Hero will be accumulating experience each time he makes a decision. Initially, some decisions will be good, some will be bad. What we would like is to use that experience to learn a winning strategy, so that when he finds himself in conditions he has encountered before (a known *state*), he can predict the *reward* he should expect from each of the three strategies available to him, and pick the best decision accordingly (the decision corresponding to the strategy with highest expected value).

Learning a Winning Strategy from Experience

The only thing we need at that point is a learning process to evaluate strategies. One possibility would be to keep track of all the accumulated *experience*; when the Hero enters a *state*, we could then simply look for every situation where the same *state* was encountered in the past, and compute (for instance) the average reward for each of the *decisions* taken. This is clearly impractical: we would end up accumulating a lot of data, and the program would slowly grind to a halt.

A more effective approach would be to maintain a single record for every strategy we tried, that is, a *state* and *decision* combination, and progressively build up an estimate for how good or bad that strategy is, based on all our accumulated *experience* so far. When we encounter a known *state*, all we have to do is look up for the three possible matching *strategies* in our catalog of strategies, which we'll call the *brain*, and select the strategy with highest value.

We almost have an algorithm ready to go. The only thing left is to deal with two small problems. The first one is rather obvious: what should the Hero do when he encounters an unknown state? What I would do in his shoes is simply take a random action, and see what happens.

The second is a bit more intricate: what should the Hero do when taking the same action twice? In our particular situation, we know that doing the same thing twice in the same conditions will result in the same outcome—so we could just take the action once, measure the gain, and stop learning. However, the only reason we can say that is because we know how the game is implemented; and nothing guarantees that this will remain the case. We could, for instance, decide that treasures and traps will materialize randomly in the world, or that the reward attached to a treasure or a trap will change over time. In that case, such an approach would be pretty bad: we would rely on one single experience, which might be highly unusual, to form our strategy, and stop learning altogether afterward.

A better and more robust approach (which is advised outside of the realm of this game, too) is to keep learning all the time. Mimicking what we did in previous chapters, there is a simple way to do that: progressively refine our estimate for what rewards we should expect from a strategy, using a **learning rate** α (between 0 and 1) to decide how aggressively to update the strategy value. Whenever we take a certain action in a state, update the value of that strategy according to the scheme:

$$Value(Strategy) \leftarrow (1-\alpha) \times Value(Strategy) + \alpha \times gain$$

Before diving into the implementation, two quick comments. First, whenever I am presented with a formula that involves a rate, I like to use this "weird old trick" to interpret what the formula is saying: set the value to 0 and 1, and see what's left. In this case, setting α to 0 implies "never learn," and keep whatever your initial estimate was intact. Conversely, setting α to 1 implies "forget everything you learned": whatever your previous estimate for the strategy value was, ignore it and replace with the latest value observed (the gain you just obtained). Any value for the learning rate α in between balances these two extremes: the closer to 0, the slower it adjusts, the higher the value, the faster it reacts to a new observation.

CAN WE CHECK THAT THIS WORKS?

We can verify informally that this process converges to the correct value on a small example. Suppose the gain was always 100. Using an initial estimate of 0, and a learning rate of 0.5, repeating our update procedure converges fairly quickly from 0 to 100, which is the correct value:

```
> let vs = Seq.unfold (fun x -> Some(x, 0.5 * x + 0.5 * 100.)) 0.
vs |> Seq.take 20 |> Seq.toList;;
val it : float list =
  [0.0; 50.0; 75.0; 87.5; 93.75; 96.875; 98.4375; 99.21875; 99.609375;
   99.8046875; 99.90234375; 99.95117188; 99.97558594; 99.98779297; 99.99389648;

  99.99694824; 99.99847412; 99.99923706; 99.99961853; 99.99980927]
```

Implementing the Brain

Just as we separated the rendering code in its own module, it makes sense to clearly separate the learning algorithm in its own area. So let's add a new file Brains.fs to our project, with a Brains module, move it right below Game.fs, and let's start modeling.

Listing 7-11. Modeling the Brain

```
namespace Game

open System
open Game

module Brains =

    // My current direction and surrounding cells
    type State = Dir * (Cell option) list
```

```
type Experience = {
    State: State;         // where I was
    Action: Act;          // what I did
    Reward: float;        // what reward I got
    NextState: State; }   // where I ended

// one possible course of action I can take
// when I am  in that State
type Strategy = { State:State; Action:Act; }

// Strategies I tried, and what reward
// I should expect from them
type Brain = Map<Strategy,float>
```

The model maps pretty much word-for-word our description of the problem. We have a State, putting together the current direction and a list of Cell options, denoting that some cells might be empty, Experience, and a Brain, which maps each possible Strategy (a State and the Action that could be taken) to an estimated reward.

It makes sense to refactor a bit our code, and move the random decision function we had in the Program itself (Listing 7-7), into the Brain as well:

```
let rng = Random ()
let choices = [| Straight; Left; Right |]
let randomDecide () = choices.[rng.Next(3)]
```

Let's get into the learning process. What we want here is to incorporate a new Experience and update the Brain accordingly. This is fairly straightforward: we need to extract out the Strategy that was taken in that Experience, look for the corresponding entry in our brain, and apply the learning rate α to it. Note how we use brain.TryFind, which returns an option, and thus allows us to very cleanly handle both cases (the key exists or doesn't), with a simple pattern match (see Listing 7-12).

Listing 7-12. Updating the Brain with a new experience

```
let alpha = 0.2 // learning rate
let learn (brain:Brain) (exp:Experience) =
    let strat = { State = exp.State; Action = exp.Action }
    match brain.TryFind strat with
    | Some(value) ->
        brain.Add (strat, (1.0-alpha) * value + alpha * exp.Reward)
    | None -> brain.Add (strat, (alpha * exp.Reward))
```

■ **Note** Map.Add is actually "add or update." If the key is not found, a new item is added; if the key is already there, the original value is replaced.

Now that our Hero has a brain, he can make decisions. What we need is the following: when entering a certain State, if our Brain has never seen it before, we will take a random decision; otherwise, out of the three possible strategies (move Straight, Left or Right from the current State) we will pick the strategy with the largest value, assuming a value of 0 for strategies that haven't been evaluated yet. A bit more code there, but still pretty tight.

Listing 7-13. Making a decision using the Brain

```
let decide (brain:Brain) (state:State) =
    let knownStrategies =
        choices
        |> Array.map (fun alt -> { State = state; Action = alt })
        |> Array.filter (fun strat -> brain.ContainsKey strat)
    match knownStrategies.Length with
    | 0 -> randomDecide ()
    | _ ->
        choices
        |> Seq.maxBy (fun alt ->
            let strat = { State = state; Action = alt }
            match brain.TryFind strat with
            | Some(value) -> value
            | None -> 0.0)
```

We are almost ready to plug in our brain. The last missing bit is a function that extracts the visible state, given the Hero's location on the board. The purpose of the following three functions is simply to extract the Hero's direction, and the eight cells around him, identified by the list of eight offsets, where (–1,0) for instance represents –1 cell from the top and 0 from the left, that is, one move north on the current row.

Listing 7-14. Extracting the current state

```
let tileAt (board:Board) (pos:Pos) = board.TryFind(pos)

let offsets =
    [   (-1,-1)
        (-1, 0)
        (-1, 1)
        ( 0,-1)
        ( 0, 1)
        ( 1,-1)
        ( 1, 0)
        ( 1, 1) ]

let visibleState (size:Size) (board:Board) (hero:Hero) =
    let (dir,pos) = hero.Direction, hero.Position
    let visibleCells =
        offsets
        |> List.map (fun (x,y) ->
            onboard size { Top = pos.Top + x; Left = pos.Left + y }
            |> tileAt board)
    (dir,visibleCells)
```

Testing Our Brain

That's it, we have a brain! Let's plug it into the existing Program module. The first change is that instead of making a random decision, we are now using a Brain—so we will pass it into the recursion state, and start each loop by extracting the current state and making a decision. The other minor modification is that of course we need to do some learning at some point; that's easily done, by making the changes shown in Listing 7-15.

Listing 7-15. Incorporating learning in the game loop

```fsharp
let rec loop (state:GameState,brain:Brain) =

    let currentState = visibleState size state.Board state.Hero
    let decision = Brains.decide brain currentState

    // world update
    let player = state.Hero |> applyDecision size decision
    let board = updateBoard state.Board player
    let gain = computeGain state.Board player
    let score = state.Score + gain

    // learning
    let nextState = visibleState size board player
    let experience = {
        State = currentState;
        Action = decision;
        Reward = gain |> float;
        NextState = nextState; }
    let brain = learn brain experience
```

Finally, when we start the game, we need to provide it a brain, which will be initially empty:

```fsharp
let _ = loop (initial,Map.empty)
```

And we are ready to go—if you run this, you should see a similar game as before, but with a Hero who apparently is making fewer mistakes over time. So... ship it?

Hold your horses! First, where is the data? We are scientists here, and I would like a bit more evidence than a fuzzy statement like "it apparently makes less mistakes" to evaluate whether our brain is doing something right. The easiest way to perform that evaluation is probably to run a head-to-head comparison (sorry for the pun), seeing how the two approaches fare on games of equal length. Because both approaches involve an element of randomness, we will want to run that comparison on a few runs. If we relied on one game only, we would face the risk to observe unusual results, out of sheer luck. Running a bunch of games mitigates that risk.

This creates another small inconvenience, though. Obviously, the more runs we want to run and record, the longer this will take. With 20 milliseconds between each frame rendering (at least), a 500-turns game will take at least 10 seconds. Run a few of these, and we are quickly talking minutes here. Can we reduce things a bit? Well, there are obvious things we could do, like going headless (sorry again—no more puns, I promise). Remove all the rendering bits, and run the game with no graphics, simply recording the final score, which is all we care about, at least for our purposes here.

That sounds like a perfect case for a script. We won't really ship that experiment in production, and it seems a bit silly to create another console app just for this. Let's add a script file to our project, copy-paste the entire contents of Program.fs—and modify it a bit, so that it runs as a script (see Listing 7-16).

Listing 7-16. Simulating the effectiveness of different brains

```fsharp
#load "Game.fs"
open Game.Game
#load "Brains.fs"
open Game.Brains
open System
```

```
let size = { Width = 40; Height = 20 }
let player = { Position = { Top = 10; Left = 20 }; Direction = North }

let rng = Random ()

let board =
    [   for top in 0 .. size.Height - 1 do
            for left in 0 .. size.Width - 1 do
                if rng.NextDouble () > 0.5
                then
                    let pos = { Top = top; Left = left }
                    let cell = if rng.NextDouble () > 0.5 then Trap else Treasure
                    yield pos, cell ]
    |> Map.ofList

let score = 0
let initialGameState = { Board = board; Hero = player; Score = score }

let simulate (decide:Brain -> State -> Act) iters runs =

    // Loop now includes the iteration count
    let rec loop (state:GameState,brain:Brain,iter:int) =

        let currentState = visibleState size state.Board state.Hero
        let decision = decide brain currentState

        // world update
        let player = state.Hero |> applyDecision size decision
        let board = updateBoard state.Board player
        let gain = computeGain state.Board player
        let score = state.Score + gain

        // learning
        let nextState = visibleState size board player
        let experience = {
            State = currentState;
            Action = decision;
            Reward = gain |> float;
            NextState = nextState; }
        let brain = learn brain experience

        let updated = { Board = board; Hero = player; Score = score }

        if iter < iters
        then loop (updated,brain,iter+1)
        else score

    [ for run in 1 .. runs -> loop (initialGameState,Map.empty,0) ]

// Simulating different brains
printfn "Random decision"
```

```
let random = simulate (fun _ _ -> Game.Brains.randomDecide ()) 500 20
printfn "Average score: %.0f" (random |> Seq.averageBy float)

printfn "Crude brain"
let crudeBrain = simulate Game.Brains.decide 500 20
printfn "Average score: %.0f" (crudeBrain |> Seq.averageBy float)
```

I won't comment much on this, because it is very close to our original code from Program.fs. The first interesting difference is that we added a number of iterations to the recursive loop state, so that each game only runs for a finite, known length. The second one is that instead of hard-coding the decision function in the loop, we are actually injecting it in as an argument, a function which must fit the signature decide:Brain -> State -> Act. This essentially defines an interface for decisions—and we can finally test out our two strategies, by passing in our two possible decision methods.

When I ran this on my machine, here is what I saw:

```
Random decision
average: 855
Crude brain
average: 2235
```

Results will vary every time you run the script; however, you should typically observe that things go better with a brain than without, which is good. Also, if you look into the details of each run, you will see that there is quite a bit of variability in the results; with or without brain, some games turn into epic failures. In other words, first, we have confirmation that our brain is doing something right—but we also see that doing the right thing doesn't guarantee good results every single time. You win some, you lose some, but overall, in the long run, you are better off taking that strategy.

Can We Learn More Effectively?

We established that our simplistic brain is working better than nothing. That is a success. At the same time, describing our Hero's behavior as intelligent would be quite a stretch. We went from "dumb as bricks" to "not entirely stupid," but not much better. For instance, you might notice that from time to time, he ends up walking a straight line, forever, even though there is still plenty of treasure to loot not that far off. On the one hand, it's certainly a solid tactic to avoid traps; on the other hand, it's certainly not the best possible behavior, because it is completely sacrificing potential gains.

Suppose we wanted a smarter Hero—can we do better? Hopefully yes—but to do that, we need to think a bit about what we mean by learning and knowledge, to understand better what isn't quite right about our current model, and how it can be improved.

Exploration vs. Exploitation

As a software engineer, here is a question you are probably faced with on a regular basis: should I use the same techniques I am familiar with and know well, or should I try this new fancy idea I have never used before, which I hear is interesting, but might completely fail?

This is in a nutshell the tension between exploration and exploitation; you could choose to exploit a known strategy, which you have tried before, with predictable results, or you could explore new possibilities, hoping to learn new strategies that work even better than what you currently do, but with a risk of failure, where you would actually perform worse than what the conservative, "business as usual" approach would have given. As software engineers, all exploitation, and we would still be coding on punch cards; all exploration, and we would be entirely changing our stack and process all the time.

This is also why our Hero ends up chasing his tail from time to time. The only exploration our Hero does is when he is forced to do so, because he has never encountered a situation, and has no default choice to fall back to. However, once he found a strategy that had a positive outcome, he will go to it over and over again, and never try anything else.

This suggests a first direction we can take to improve our brain: give the Hero a bit of an adventurous spirit, and make him try out from time to time random strategies, even though a decent one is readily available. The simplest way we can do that is called **ε-learning**: each turn, with a small probability ε, we will take a random decision, regardless of what we already know, and explore. This will help make sure that we are not settling for a comfortable strategy, when a much better one might be available.

Is a Red Door Different from a Blue Door?

Being silly is repeating the same mistakes, over and over again. Being smart is recognizing that some situations are similar enough that they should be treated the same. The first time I try to open the door to my kitchen, which happens to be red, I might fumble until I figure out how it works, and next time I see it, at a minimum, I should be able to repeat what worked the last time. However, when I see the door to the living room, which happens to be blue, even though the circumstances are slightly different (it's a blue door, and a different room), I would probably try the same thing that worked in the kitchen.

Behaving in an intelligent manner involves recognizing similar states, abstracting them, and applying what was learned to a broader context. What makes us smart is that we recognize not only "the red kitchen door," but also "a door." Thankfully, we are not learning from scratch how to operate a new door every time we see one.

Our Hero and his current brain are suffering from a bit of a lack of abstraction. Specifically, if you think about it, our game is symmetrical. As an illustration, the two situations displayed in Figure 7-3 are virtually identical, except for the fact that one "state of the world" has been rotated 90 degrees to the right:

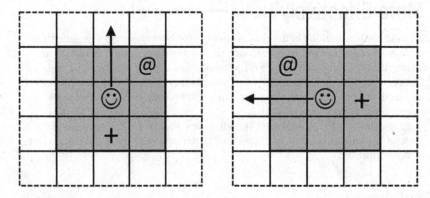

Figure 7-3. Rotated states are identical

In our currently implementation, the two states represented are distinct, and constitute two different entries in the brain. If we reduced them to 1 single state—together with the two other equivalent states— we would gain on two levels. First, our brain would use much less memory; just as I don't have to exactly remember how every single door I opened works, the Hero would need only 25% of his brain to achieve the same result. Then, he would also learn much faster, because whatever applies to one state would immediately be usable in three other situations.

The only thing we need to achieve that is to rotate and re-align the visible state, so that it is oriented toward the Hero's line of sight. Note, however, that we are also cheating here, to an extent. The beauty of the initial approach was that we really made no assumption whatsoever about how the world worked; we simply created a state from whatever we could observe, treated it as a black-box—and it worked. Here, we are using some knowledge we have about the mechanics of the game, which isn't completely a black-box anymore. A harder problem, which we will not touch here, would be to build a brain which recognizes by itself what states are equivalent, and potentially reduce the relevant states even more. This would lead us a bit too far, so we will leave that discussion out.

Greed vs. Planning

The behavior of our Hero can be currently described as greedy—look around, and pick the decision that will give me the biggest possible reward, right now. It's not working too badly for him—but greed is not always the best policy. A classic example, from the real-world realm, is the decision to go to college to get a higher education, rather than get a job that doesn't require that degree of qualification. The difficulty here is that a greedy approach would lead to go for a low-paying job and start making money right now, rather than incur the cost of education, which (hopefully) would open more interesting and better paid prospects a couple of years later.

There is nothing wrong with either choice, but our Hero would never even consider going to school. He is just deciding in the instant, without any consideration for the future—and yet, usually, planning ahead and taking into account short term gains with long term situation is part of what is considered intelligent decision making. Going for broke all the time is a risky proposition!

What we would like is a brain which balances these two aspects. In its current form, the only thing we take into account to evaluate a strategy is how much immediate gain it yields:

$$Value(Strategy) \leftarrow (1-\alpha) \times Value(Strategy) + \alpha \times gain$$

We could make the situation more balanced by including not only the immediate gain, but also the value of where we end up as a result of the strategy, using a formula like this one for our update:

$$Value(Strategy) \leftarrow (1-\alpha) \times Value(Strategy) + \alpha \times \big(gain + \gamma \times Value(best\ choice\ in\ next\ state) \big)$$

Once again, γ is a coefficient between 0 and 1. The current model is simply a special case where γ is set to 0, and whatever happens next is completely ignored. Conversely, setting γ to 1 would essentially state that our immediate gain is exactly as important as where we end up. Anything in between strikes a compromise between short-term gain and long-term planning. This equation is known as **q-learning**: it generalizes our initial approach, so that the procedure we use to determine the value of taking each of the possible decisions in a state strikes a compromise between immediate rewards and long-term gains, and produces a behavior which is less of a "blindly go for broke" strategy.

■ **Note**   If you are familiar with dynamic programming, the preceding formula probably looks familiar; q-learning is essentially an application of dynamic programming. Similarly, if you have done some economics, you might think of γ as analogous to a discount rate—the "interest rate" at which you discount future rewards, over immediate ones.

A World of Never-Ending Tiles

We will try out all these improvements to the learning process. But, to make things a bit more interesting, first we will modify a bit the game itself. The current game is so simple, most of the ideas we discussed wouldn't make a difference, because the games are too short: once every trap or treasure has been consumed, there is nothing left to learn. We need a more challenging world for our Hero.

As a first twist, we are going to spice things up is by having not just traps and treasures, but an arbitrary number of tile types. Each type of tile will have their own color and rewards, which will let us configure harder and simpler words to experiment with. As a bigger twist, instead of having the contents of a visited cell disappear, we will have a world entirely covered with tiles, where as soon as a tile is visited and "consumed," it is immediately replaced by a random tile. That way, while the board in our initial game became progressively empty, with nothing, this new world will keep changing and creating new states, so that we can play the game longer and still have something to learn. Once we have our game variation in place, we will incorporate the three modifications we discussed, and evaluate how much of a difference they make.

The main modification we want to implement is that instead of having an explicit discriminated union to represent cell contents, we will instead encode the contents of each tile as an integer, representing a state, and map that state to an array of rewards, and an array of colors for rendering. The first change that is required is in the Game.fs file, as shown in Listing 7-17.

Listing 7-17. Updating the Game file

```
// code omitted
type Board = int[,]

// code omitted

let tileValues = [| -100; -50; 50; 100 |]

let computeGain (board:Board) (hero:Hero) =
    let pos = hero.Position
    let cellType = board.[pos.Left,pos.Top]
    tileValues.[cellType]

let rng = System.Random ()

let updateBoard (board:Board) (player:Hero) =
    let pos = player.Position
    let updatedBoard = board |> Array2D.copy
    updatedBoard.[pos.Left,pos.Top] <- rng.Next(tileValues.Length)
    updatedBoard
```

In other words, the tileValues array defines how many tiles will exist in our world, and what they are worth; in this particular case, we will have four tiles, ranging from "very bad" (-100 points) to "very good" (100 points). We also now have a considerably larger number of possible states, with four possible values for a cell instead of three, which will make learning way harder. The updateBoard function simply creates a new board, replacing the tile the Hero just visited by a random new value.

Only two bits need to change in the Brains module: the State, where instead of a list of Cell option we now have a list of integers, and the tileAt function, which will now simply return the contents of the array, without any check required for whether there is anything at that position, because every cell will be filled in, as shown in Listing 7-18.

Listing 7-18. Updating the Brains file

```
type State = int list
// code omitted
let tileAt (board:Board) (pos:Pos) = board.[pos.Left,pos.Top]
```

In a similar fashion, we can now update the rendering code, by making the following modifications, using an array of colors to represent each tile, based on its index. Note that because we are now replacing the tile where the Hero was previously located, the render function can also be simplified, because only two tiles change: the new location of the Hero, and his previous location.

Listing 7-19. Updating the Rendering file

```
module Rendering =

    let colors =
        [|
            ConsoleColor.DarkRed
            ConsoleColor.Red
            ConsoleColor.DarkYellow
            ConsoleColor.Yellow
        |]

    let creatureColor = ConsoleColor.White

    let offset (pos:Pos) = (pos.Left, pos.Top + 2)

    let prepareDisplay size gameState =
        Console.SetWindowSize(size.Width, size.Height+2)
        let board = gameState.Board
        for x in 0 .. (size.Width - 1) do
            for y in 0 .. (size.Height - 1) do
                let pos = { Left = x; Top = y }
                Console.SetCursorPosition (offset (pos))
                let tileType = board.[x,y]
                Console.ForegroundColor <- colors.[tileType]
                Console.Write("•")

    let render (before:GameState) (after:GameState) =
        let oldPos = before.Hero.Position
        let newPos = after.Hero.Position
        // previous player position
        Console.SetCursorPosition (offset (oldPos))
        let tileType = after.Board.[oldPos.Left,oldPos.Top]
        Console.ForegroundColor <- colors.[tileType]
        Console.Write("•")
        // current player position
        Console.SetCursorPosition (offset (newPos))
        Console.ForegroundColor <- creatureColor
        Console.Write("•")
```

```
    let renderScore score =
        Console.SetCursorPosition(0,0)
        Console.ForegroundColor <- ConsoleColor.White
        printfn "Score: %i   " score
```

Finally, all that is left to do is to modify Program.fs a bit. There is very little that needs changing; we modify the board initialization, to fill in every single cell, and merge the two functions renderPlayer and renderBoard into a single render function, as shown in Listing 7-20.

Listing 7-20. Updating the Program file

```
let board = Array2D.init size.Width size.Height (fun left top ->
    rng.Next(tileValues.Length))

// omitted code
// world rendering
    let updated = { Board = board; Hero = player; Score = score }
    renderScore score
    render state updated

    Thread.Sleep 20
    loop (updated,brain)

// start the game
prepareDisplay size initialGameState
let _ = loop (initialGameState,Map.empty)
```

And we are ready to go. If you run the game at this point, you should see something slightly different from our earlier version, with the Hero moving on a board covered with colorful tiles. The final change we need to make is to update the Headless.fsx simulation script, which only requires a tiny modification of the board initialization, in a fashion similar to what we just did in Program.fs, replacing the original board initialization with

```
let board = Array2D.init size.Width size.Height (fun left top ->  rng.Next
(tileValues.Length))
```

Speaking of which, let's run a simulation, to see what impact our modification has on how our "crude brain" performs. I ran a couple of 500-steps simulations on my machine, and there wasn't much of a difference between taking random decisions, and using our brain. This is not entirely surprising, because of our expansion from three possible cell states to four. This might seem like a small change, but it really isn't. Each cell can now take four states instead of three, and the visible state comprises 8 adjacent cells, which means that we expanded from 4 directions x 3 x 3 ... x 3 states, to 4 directions x 4 x 4 x ... x 4 states—that is, 26,244 states to 262,144 states to learn. Given that our Hero has only 500 steps to learn that world, it should not be a surprise that he doesn't do too well. Let's increase the length of each simulation run to, say, 100,000 steps, which should give him a better shot at learning things. Obviously, this will take a considerably longer time to run, but that is the cost of getting a reliable result. On my machine, this is what I got:

```
>
Random decision
average: -703
Crude brain
average: 12480
```

Implementing Brain 2.0

Now that we have a good playground to test out how well our brain is doing, and measured a baseline to compare against, let's try out the three possible improvements we discussed earlier: reducing the number of states, looking forward further than just short-term gains, and leaving some space for exploration.

Simplifying the World

Given the point we just made regarding the large dimension of states, a reasonable first pass would be to start with simplifying the states, and removing the direction, transforming the visible state into what the Hero has in his line of sight instead.

That is not very complicated. The two things that need to change are the definition of State, which will contain only a list of eight integers (the eight surrounding cells), and the visibleState function, which extracts the state itself. What we need is to rotate the state: if the Hero is facing north, keep the State intact. If he is facing west, rotate everything 90 degrees clockwise, as if the Hero was facing north—and so on and so forth.

All this takes is a transformation of our offsets. For instance, the first offset in the list, the pair (-1,-1), represents the cell located in the top left corner of the current position (-1 from the top, -1 from the left). If the Hero was facing west instead of north, instead of retrieving the cell located at offset (-1,-1), we would need to grab the cell at offset (1,-1). Similarly, the cell located on the top-right position from the Hero, which is located at offset (-1,1) when facing north, needs to be transformed into offset (-1,-1) when facing west.

With a bit of mental gymnastics, we can figure out how the offsets need to be remapped, based on the current orientation. The rotate function in Listing 7-21 performs that re-alignment, and all that's now left to do is to inject that function into our visibleState function, so that instead of applying the original offset, we pre-transform it into offsets that reflect the current Hero direction:

Listing 7-21. Reducing the number of states by rotation

```
let rotate dir (x,y) =
    match dir with
    | North -> (x,y)
    | South -> (-x,-y)
    | West -> (-y,x)
    | East -> (y,-x)

let visibleState (size:Size) (board:Board) (hero:Hero) =
    let (dir,pos) = hero.Direction, hero.Position
    offsets
    |> List.map (rotate dir)
    |> List.map (fun (x,y) ->
        onboard size { Top = pos.Top + x; Left = pos.Left + y }
        |> tileAt board)
```

... and we are done. Let's run our headless simulation to see if that improves anything. On my machine, this is the result I got, which shows a very clear improvement. Of course, results will vary from run to run:

```
>
Better brain
average: 30220
```

Compared to our original random decision making, which scored -703 on average, and our crude brain, which scored 12,480, that approach seems to pay off.

Planning Ahead

Let's see if we can improve our results by making our Hero less short-sighted. First, before going into the actual implementation, how could considering more than a single step ahead improve our results? In its crude original form, our brain is really only considering whether moving straight, left or right will produce an immediate gain. In that frame, considering as an illustration the case where our Hero is facing north, the two states described in Figure 7-4 will be evaluated the same way, because in both cases, moving straight will yield an immediate gain of 100 points.

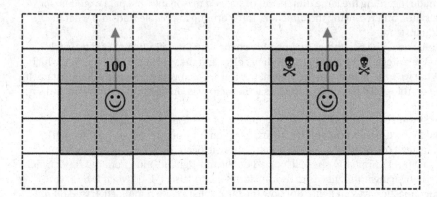

Figure 7-4. *Two states with identical short-term gains but very different end states*

There is an issue, though. Only three moves are allowed, straight, left and right, which makes the two situations very different. In the first case (displayed on the left), once the Hero has moved straight, he has two open paths, no matter what happens: one to the left, and one to the right. Even though there could be a trap in the third, currently unknown cell, he still has plenty of options.

The situation described on the right is much different. Once the 100 points are collected, there is no path open on the left or on the right no matter what. The only good situation is when the third cell, which he currently cannot see, is open, which might or might not be the case—and with a non-zero probability, the Hero will be left with absolutely no good move.

This illustrates where looking only greedily at the immediate gain would be an insufficient approach, because it would lead us to take the same decision in two situations which are very different, and should therefore be evaluated quite differently. This issue is directly addressed by including the γ term we described earlier, which will take into account not only what we gain immediately by taking a move, but also what happens next.

Let's implement that change, and see if theory and practice agree. Again, the only thing we need to change is the Brains module. What we need is two things: a function that will tell us what the value of the best move in a given state is, and to include that term into our learn function. This is a matter of a couple of additional lines (see Listing 7-22).

Listing 7-22. Adding forward-looking into the learning procedure

```
let alpha = 0.2 // learning rate
let gamma = 0.5 // discount rate

let nextValue (brain:Brain) (state:State) =
    choices
    |> Seq.map (fun act ->
```

```
        match brain.TryFind { State = state; Action = act } with
        | Some (value) -> value
        | None -> 0.)
    |> Seq.max

let learn (brain:Brain) (exp:Experience) =
        let strat = { State = exp.State; Action = exp.Action }
    let vNext = nextValue brain exp.NextState
    match brain.TryFind strat with
    | Some(value) ->
        let value' = (1. - alpha) * value + alpha * (exp.Reward + gamma * vNext)
        brain.Add (strat, value')
    | None -> brain.Add (strat, alpha * (exp.Reward + gamma * vNext))
```

So how does this work out? Only one way to find out—simulate. Again, results will vary from run to run, but on my machine, this is what the headless simulation produced:

```
>
Forward-looking brain
average: 38300
```

That's quite a nice improvement. We jumped from around 30,000 to 38,000 points—a 25% improvement over our greedy strategy.

Epsilon Learning

We have one avenue left to explore, ε learning. The idea behind the approach is to encourage exploration, by taking random decisions from time to time, even though we already have a known strategy with decent results. This one is a bit more counter-intuitive—in essence, it says that it pays off to take a careful amount of risk, in order to discover potentially better strategies, even though this will also at times result in bad decisions when a perfectly valid strategy was available.

The most straightforward way to implement this is to simply roll the dice every time we take a decision. In a certain proportion of cases, we will completely ignore everything we learned so far, and take a random decision—which is quickly implemented, again in the Brains module (see Listing 7-23).

Listing 7-23. Adding exploration to the learning procedure

```
    let alpha = 0.2    // learning rate
    let gamma = 0.5    // discount rate
    let epsilon = 0.05 // random learning

    // code omitted

    let decide (brain:Brain) (state:State) =
        if (rng.NextDouble () < epsilon)
        then randomDecide ()
        else
            let eval =
                choices
                |> Array.map (fun alt -> { State = state; Action = alt })
                |> Array.filter (fun strat -> brain.ContainsKey strat)
```

```
    match eval.Length with
    | 0 -> randomDecide ()
    | _ ->
        choices
        |> Seq.maxBy (fun alt ->
            let strat = { State = state; Action = alt }
            match brain.TryFind strat with
            | Some(value) -> value
            | None -> 0.)
```

Let's run our simulation again, to see if that pays off. With all the same caveats again, on my machine, this is what I observed:

```
>
```

```
Fully featured brain
average: 46500
```

Another nice bump: adding some exploration gave us a 20% improvement over our previous score, using q-learning. It seems that being adventurous and trying out to learn new things pays off quite nicely!

As a final summary, Table 7-1 recaps the average score each of our successive brains achieved, showing how much each of the learning features we added at each steps gained us.

Table 7-1. *Summary of Improvements for Each Added Learning Feature*

Brain version	Average score
Random decisions	−703
Basic learning	12,480
Reducing space	30,220
With q-learning (forward looking)	38,300
With epsilon-learning (exploration)	46,500

So, What Have We Learned?

In this chapter, we took a bit of a different direction from the previous ones. Instead of trying to build a model from a dataset, extracting features that represent "important facts" and combining them into equations that represent how a certain phenomenon works, we simply built a mechanism that feeds new experiences as they arrive, observes decisions taken and their outcomes, and reinforces behaviors that lead to positive results while avoiding strategies that do results in negative ones—without even attempting to understand the underlying causes.

The algorithm we derived is called *q-learning*, which uses one central equation:

$$Value(Strategy) \leftarrow (1-\alpha) \times Value(Strategy) + \alpha \times \big(gain + \gamma \times Value(best\ choice\ in\ next\ state) \big)$$

For each of the states our system can be in, and for each of the decisions we can make in each state, we progressively build and refine an evaluation of how much taking each possible move is worth, by balancing how much short-term gain the move brings, and how much value there is in the next state we end up with if taking that decision. We also included an element of exploration, via ε learning—even though we might already have a solid strategy for a given situation we are in, we still take some random decisions from time to time, to make sure we explore the space of all possible strategies.

A Simple Model That Fits Intuition

One of the aspects I find the most interesting in q-learning is how simple it is to explain in terms that map our understanding of what knowledge and learning are about. The basic idea underpinning q-learning is reinforcement; reward your donkey with carrots for good behavior, and punish bad behavior with a stick, and your donkey will progressively understand what you want him to do, and do the right thing. Similarly, q-learning lets the agent take decisions and adapt his behavior to maximize rewards and avoid penalties, without necessarily trying to understand what the task is really about.

Beyond that basic idea, we discussed more subtle aspects. Our initial algorithm was essentially blindly going toward the direction of immediate reward. It worked quite well, but we also saw how taking a less greedy approach, and taking into account not only the immediate rewards but also long term consequences, produced quite a significant improvement, and essentially emulated a planning behavior.

We also saw how, somewhat counterintuitively, including an element of randomness into our algorithm did produce another nice improvement. I find this idea particularly appealing. Our model is all about making rational, mechanical decisions, so it is a bit unexpected that introducing some chaos would make things better. However, it resonates well when you put in the perspective of human behavior. First, learning new things does require stepping out of your comfort zone, and trying out things which might or might not work out. Then, every acquired behavior is both a benefit and a hindrance: while good habits are a positive, some habits we form are actually negative, and will require us to unlearn if we want to progress, which is exactly what ε learning does. Another remark here is that while taking chances to experiment can result in either good or bad outcomes, the long-term consequences make it worth it, at least for controlled risks. If you try out something and it doesn't work out, you won't do it again. If it works great, you have now learned a lesson which can be applied over and over again, yielding a life time of positive rewards.

Finally, it might be worth pointing out that the underlying idea is somewhat related to the problem of over-fitting. One way of describing over-fitting is that it is the result of being very efficient applying one approach, but developing a blind spot in the process—a problem which can be overcome by introducing some randomness, for instance random bagging.

An Adaptive Mechanism

The other aspect I find interesting in this approach is its adaptive nature. We illustrated earlier on how applying a learning coefficient α to weight the previous knowledge against the new experience, and progressively updating our estimates, ended up converging to the correct value. An interesting aspect here is that this mechanism would also cope pretty well in a changing world. Imagine for a minute that midway through, we changed the rule of the game, and completely switched the effect of each tile, perhaps giving them new random rewards. The beautiful thing here is that our Hero would progressively adapt to this new world: as new experiences come in, his estimates for each state will gradually change, and so will his behavior.

In essence, if you consider how the learning rate works, what happens is, older memories become progressively less and less important, by comparison to the more recent experiences. This is quite a nice feature, because it allows us to create an agent that adapts his behavior to changes in the environment, without exactly knowing how it works. By contrast, building a model based on one dataset will be much more fragile: the recipe will work, as long as the world remains the same—and if it doesn't, your model will systematically behave incorrectly, without any correction.

Finally, you might wonder if this is actually useful. After all, our example in this chapter was a pretty silly game, something which is probably not very close to the type of code you write professionally. In my opinion, this is a very applicable approach to a variety of situations, and the simplicity of the underlying model makes it quite easy to tweak to the problem at hand. As an example, I recently ended up using a model extremely similar to the one we used here, in a totally different context (see https://vimeo.com/113597999 for more information). I needed to figure out how many concurrent tasks a machine could handle, a problem which is a bit tricky. It depends on the machine itself, how many cores and how much memory it has, and so on—and it can also vary over time, if for instance some other process is started on that machine. Rather than trying to figure out a complicated model based on what is actually happening in the machine, I simply ended up varying the number of tasks being processed, and measuring the throughput for each level of activity (my states), updating the estimates using a learning rate α and randomly trying out to increase and decrease the number of concurrent tasks with probability ε—which is pretty much exactly what we did for our game, except that instead of a silly game, I ended up with a server that automatically scaled itself for maximum throughput, without human intervention.

CHAPTER 8

■ ■ ■

Digits, Revisited

Optimizing and Scaling Your Algorithm Code

In Chapter 1, we explored together the digit recognizer problem, and wrote a classifier from scratch. In this final chapter, we are going to revisit that problem, from two different angles: performance, and useful tools. Chapters 1 to 7 were primarily focused on implementing algorithms to solve various problems, and discovering machine learning concepts in the process. By contrast, this chapter is more intended as a series of practical tips which can be useful in various situations. We will use the digit recognizer model we created in Chapter 1 as a familiar reference point, and use it to illustrate techniques that are broadly applicable to other situations.

In this chapter, we will do the following:

- Analyze the code we wrote in Chapter 1, and search for ways to tune it and improve performance, by making the code more efficient, and exploiting opportunities for parallel processing.

- Present Accord.NET, a .NET library which offers ready-to-use implementations of numerous classic machine learning algorithms. We will illustrate how to use three of them (logistic regression, support vector machine and artificial neural networks), and discuss some of their underlying ideas.

- Introduce m-brace.NET, a library geared toward running computations in a distributed manner on a cluster of machines in the cloud, from the F# scripting environment. We will demonstrate how that library can be used to process much larger datasets, while still keeping the ability to explore and design models with the rapid feedback FSI offers.

Tuning Your Code

Performance considerations are important in machine learning, probably more so than in everyday line-of-business applications development. Just like for any other piece of code, performance is usually not the first question to focus on; the first priority should be to design a model that is correct, and produces accurate results. Once that is done, if the model is too slow, it is time to consider tuning it.

In the words of Donald Knuth, "Programmers waste enormous amounts of time thinking about, or worrying about, the speed of noncritical parts of their programs, and these attempts at efficiency actually have a strong negative impact when debugging and maintenance are considered. We should forget about small efficiencies, say about 97% of the time: premature optimization is the root of all evil. Yet we should not pass up our opportunities in that critical 3%."

That being said, that 3% tends to be rather important in machine learning. The main reason for it goes back to our original description of what machine learning is: a program that will perform better, as it is fed more data. There is empirical evidence that, as the corpus of data used for training becomes large, simple and complex algorithms tend to have similar predictive power (see for instance Peter Norvig's talk "The Unreasonable Effectiveness of Data" for an example: https://www.youtube.com/watch?v=yvDCzhbjYWs). In that frame, regardless of what specific algorithm you use, you will probably want to learn from a larger volume of data if you can, which will mechanically slow things down. In that case, an ineffectively implementation can matter a lot, and have a direct impact on your productivity, or maybe even make an algorithm unusable in practice.

What to Search For

So what are we looking for, exactly? Improving the performance of an existing piece of code could mean a couple of things. The obvious one is speed: we want to get the same answer, but in less time. Memory footprint is another aspect to keep in mind: an algorithm that works great on small datasets might behave poorly as the data it needs to hold in memory increases.

If we inspect the nearest-neighbor implementation we wrote in Chapter 1, here is roughly what is does:

```
train a classifier =
        load 5,000 examples in memory
classify an image =
        for each of 5,000 examples in the classifier
                compute the distance between image and target, based on 784 pixels
        find the smallest distance
```

The structure alone is helpful in thinking through what behavior we should expect, and where it might sense to focus our efforts:

- As we use more training data, our predictions will slow down linearly

- Computing distance efficiently has a direct impact on speed

- The algorithm is memory hungry (we need to preload all training examples in memory)

On top of that, whenever we use cross-validation, we need to iterate over every one of the 500 validation examples. This doesn't impact the performance of the classifier, but it will have implications on our ability to evaluate variations efficiently. If we expanded both the training set and validation set by a factor of 10, we would expect validating the model to go roughly 100 times slower, because we now have two nested loops to process.

Another way to state this is, if we want to improve the algorithm performance by supplying a larger datasets, we should expect a significant degradation in speed, and potential memory issues as well. The algorithm we picked here has serious implications: if we want accuracy, we will have to pay a price in speed for any prediction we try to make. Whether it is an issue or not is entirely dependent on the business context. If making fast predictions is important, we should consider picking a different algorithm, where initial training is expensive, but a one-time cost only, with subsequent predictions being very quick.

We will take a look at some classifiers that have these characteristics in the next section; for the moment, let's assume that we are fine with potentially slow predictions, and start by exploring what we can do to improve our algorithm as-is.

The first and obvious direction is to make sure that our code is reasonably efficient. In general, as a first step, you should use a profiler to identify potential hot spots in your code. In this case, we will focus on the distance computation, which is where most of the work is taking place, to avoid anything costly or un-necessary. Typically, this involves making sure you are using the right data types and data structures, and possibly using an imperative style, mutating variables instead of incurring the cost of creating and allocating new data structures.

The second direction is to resort to parallelism. No matter how much we improve the distance computation, we will still need to compute 5,000 distances. The good news here is that we don't need to process these sequentially. The distance between two images is entirely independent from all the others, so in theory, we could get a speedup of up to 5,000 times by processing all of them simultaneously, without waiting for the others to complete. In a similar fashion, for the distance function we are using, we could theoretically speedup computations by up to 784 times, if we could process every pair of pixels in parallel.

Hoping for such massive speedups is not realistic, of course. However, the general thought remains valid: essentially, everywhere in your code you see a map, there is potential for parallelism.

Tuning the Distance

Let's begin with analyzing the distance function, and how we could possibly squeeze some performance out of it. We will start from Listing 8-1, the same script we ended up with in Chapter 1, using the same dataset, and experimenting with improvements.

Listing 8-1. Original Nearest Neighbor Model

```
open System
open System.IO

type Observation = { Label:string; Pixels: int[] }
type Distance = int[] * int[] -> int
type Classifier = int[] -> string

let toObservation (csvData:string) =
    let columns = csvData.Split(',')
    let label = columns.[0]
    let pixels = columns.[1..] |> Array.map int
    { Label = label; Pixels = pixels }

let reader path =
    let data = File.ReadAllLines path
    data.[1..]
    |> Array.map toObservation

let trainingPath = __SOURCE_DIRECTORY__ + @"..\..\..\Data\trainingsample.csv"
let training = reader trainingPath

let euclideanDistance (pixels1,pixels2) =
    Array.zip pixels1 pixels2
    |> Array.map (fun (x,y) -> pown (x-y) 2)
    |> Array.sum

let train (trainingset:Observation[]) (dist:Distance) =
    let classify (pixels:int[]) =
        trainingset
        |> Array.minBy (fun x -> dist (x.Pixels, pixels))
        |> fun x -> x.Label
    classify
```

```
let validationPath = __SOURCE_DIRECTORY__ + @"..\..\..\Data\validationsample.csv"
let validation = reader validationPath

let evaluate validationSet classifier =
    validationSet
    |> Array.averageBy (fun x -> if classifier x.Pixels = x.Label then 1. else 0.)
    |> printfn "Correct: %.3f"

let euclideanModel = train training euclideanDistance
```

As a first step, we need to create a benchmark. Let's activate the timer, and perform 5,000 distance computations. We don't really care about the output, and don't want to incur any cost that isn't directly related to the distance computation itself, so we will pick two arbitrary images, and add an ignore () statement to avoid clutter in the FSI window:

```
#time "on"

let img1 = training.[0].Pixels
let img2 = training.[1].Pixels

for i in 1 .. 5000 do
    let dist = euclideanDistance (img1, img2)
    ignore ()
```

On my workstation (a quad-core i7 with plenty of memory), this is what I get:

```
>
Real: 00:00:00.066, CPU: 00:00:00.062, GC gen0: 22, gen1: 0, gen2: 0
val it : unit = ()
```

First, note that this measurement will vary slightly from run to run. We are measuring fairly short times here, and there is very likely some noise polluting our observations. To mitigate that, we should at least run the test a few times, and potentially on more than 5000 calculations. It is also not entirely accurate; if you were to use the same code compiled into a dll, and not in a script, you might get better results, because of additional optimizations that might take place. However, this is a good starting point. The two pieces of information this provides are time (it took 66 milliseconds to complete, and 62 milliseconds CPU time), and garbage collection (22 garbage collections for generation 0 took place, none for higher generations). Garbage collection is interesting as an indication for how much objects we are creating; and higher-generation GCs are generally bad.

The first thing we could do is check whether we incur a cost by using pown. Let's simplify:

```
let d1 (pixels1,pixels2) =
    Array.zip pixels1 pixels2
    |> Array.map (fun (x,y) -> (x-y) * (x-y))
    |> Array.sum

for i in 1 .. 5000 do
    let dist = d1 (img1, img2)
    ignore ()

Real: 00:00:00.044, CPU: 00:00:00.046, GC gen0: 22, gen1: 0, gen2: 0
val it : unit = ()
```

242

Perhaps surprisingly, this is actually not negligible: we went from CPU: 00:00:00.062, down to CPU: 00:00:00.046. When predicting a single image, this would probably qualify as a micro-optimization, but this change would shave off about 11 seconds off the 33 seconds it takes to run the algorithm over 500 validation images.

We are still observing some GC taking place. The culprit is most likely the fact that we are performing a zip and a map, which each create a new array. Let's reduce that to one operation, map2, which essentially does the two operations in one pass, with one array instead of two:

```
let d2 (pixels1,pixels2) =
    (pixels1, pixels2)
    ||> Array.map2 (fun x y -> (x-y) * (x-y))
    |> Array.sum

for i in 1 .. 5000 do
    let dist = d2 (img1, img2)
    ignore ()
```

Real: 00:00:00.016, CPU: 00:00:00.015, GC gen0: 3, gen1: 0, gen2: 0

That's quite an improvement! We still have a bit of garbage collection going on, but it reduced considerably, from GC gen0: 22 previously, to GC gen0: 3; and we also reduced the computation time by around 75% from the initial version. Let's see if we can get rid of the GC altogether, by entirely skipping the intermediate arrays, and using recursion instead. We'll maintain an accumulator acc, and go over the pixels index by index, adding the differences to the accumulator until we reach the last one:

```
let d3 (pixels1:int[],pixels2:int[]) =
    let dim = pixels1.Length
    let rec f acc i =
        if i = dim
        then acc
        else
            let x = pixels1.[i] - pixels2.[i]
            let acc' = acc + (x * x)
            f acc' (i + 1)
    f 0 0

for i in 1 .. 5000 do
    let dist = d3 (img1, img2)
    ignore ()
```

Real: 00:00:00.005, CPU: 00:00:00.000, GC gen0: 0, gen1: 0, gen2: 0

We cut the computation time by 92% now, without any garbage collection along the way. The price we paid for this improvement is that our code is significantly longer, and perhaps harder to read. Last try: let's go all imperative, directly mutating a variable instead of passing an accumulator around:

```
let d4 (pixels1:int[],pixels2:int[]) =
    let dim = pixels1.Length
    let mutable dist = 0
    for i in 0 .. (dim - 1) do
        let x = pixels1.[i] - pixels2.[i]
```

```
        dist <- dist + (x * x)
    dist

for i in 1 .. 5000 do
    let dist = d4 (img1, img2)
    ignore ()
```

Real: 00:00:00.004, CPU: 00:00:00.000, GC gen0: 0, gen1: 0, gen2: 0

There is virtually no difference from the previous attempt. We are talking milliseconds here, so I would advise to run more computations before drawing conclusions. If you do so, and run, say, 1,000,000 iterations instead of 5,000, you'll see no obvious performance difference. At that point, the main distinction between the two versions is style, and picking one over the other is a matter of code readability rather than performance.

My general position on using mutable variables is two-fold. I tend to avoid it by default, unless there is a clear benefit to it. Mutation introduces complexity; the code usually becomes trickier to follow, and harder to parallelize. On the other hand, if your algorithm involves, say, large arrays (a common situation in machine learning), then using a map and copying arrays left and right will incur severe penalties. In this type of situation, I will then resort to mutation, but almost always do it in a way that is hidden to the outside world. In our example, while dist is mutable, all the changes happen within the scope of the function, and no other piece of the program could change it. In that case, mutation is an implementation detail: for anybody calling my function, everything appears immutable, because there is no shared state to tamper with.

▩ **Note**　There is another direction that could help speed up the algorithm. Using a different data structure, such as a KD-tree, instead of an array to store the examples should make it possible to search quicker for close neighbors. We will ignore that possibility here, because its implementation would require a bit too much code. However, keep in mind that using the right data structure for the task at hand is another way to speed up an algorithm, or make it more memory efficient.

Using Array.Parallel

Let's take a look now at the second angle, parallelism. Here, we are going to take a look at the evaluation function, which goes over 500 validation images, classifies the image, and compares it to the true expected label. The original implementation uses Array.averageBy, which combines two steps into one: first, it maps every image to a 1.0 or a 0.0, depending on whether the prediction is correct or not, and then, it averages the entire array. The map function is not immediately visible, but it is implicitly there.

Clearly, each image can be predicted independently of each other, so we should be able to perform that operation in parallel. What we would like is to divide-and-conquer the training sample, for example, splitting it evenly based on the cores we have available on our machine, running each chunk separately, and regrouping the results in one single array.

As it turns out, F# offers some interesting options out of the box, in the `Array.Parallel` module, which exposes a subset of the Array functions, implemented in a parallel fashion. First, let's measure how long our initial evaluation took, and where we are at after our distance tweaks:

```
let original = evaluate validation euclideanModel
>
Correct: 0.944
Real: 00:00:31.811, CPU: 00:00:31.812, GC gen0: 11248, gen1: 6, gen2: 1
```

```
let updatedModel = train training d4
let improved = evaluate validation updatedModel
>
Correct: 0.944
Real: 00:00:02.889, CPU: 00:00:02.890, GC gen0: 13, gen1: 1, gen2: 0
```

Now let's rewrite the evaluate function, breaking `Array.averageBy` in `Array.Parallel.map` first, and `Array.average`:

```
let parallelEvaluate validationSet classifier =
    validationSet
    |> Array.Parallel.map (fun x -> if classifier x.Pixels = x.Label then 1. else 0.)
    |> Array.average
    |> printfn "Correct: %.3f"

>
Correct: 0.944
Real: 00:00:00.796, CPU: 00:00:03.062, GC gen0: 13, gen1: 1, gen2: 0
```

The computation goes down from 2.9 seconds, to 0.8 seconds; note also the CPU time, which went from 2.9 to 3 seconds: the amount of work the CPU has to perform remains roughly the same. We divided duration by about 3.6; given that my machine has four cores, I could expect a four-fold improvement at best, so this is quite good, especially taking into account that it barely required any code change.

So why not use `Array.Parallel.map` everywhere? If you go back to our description of parallelization, there is a bit of overhead involved: instead of simply doing a single pass over an array, now we need to divide it, pass it to different threads, and regroup the results. As a result, you should expect a sublinear improvement in the number of cores: the speedup you will get from splitting the work between 10 cores (for instance) will be less (possibly much lower) than a factor 10. This will pay off only if the amount of work done in each chunk is significant enough that it offsets the overhead of splitting-and-merging. As a trivial example, consider this case, where we take an array of 1000 elements, each of them 10, and add 1 to each:

```
let test = Array.init 1000 (fun _ -> 10)

for i in 1 .. 100000 do
    test |> Array.map (fun x -> x + 1) |> ignore
>
Real: 00:00:00.098, CPU: 00:00:00.093, GC gen0: 64, gen1: 0, gen2: 0
for i in 1 .. 100000 do
    test |> Array.Parallel.map (fun x -> x + 1) |> ignore
>
Real: 00:00:00.701, CPU: 00:00:01.234, GC gen0: 88, gen1: 1, gen2: 1
```

In this case, splitting the array into chunks just to add 1 is not worth the effort, and the parallel version ends up being slower than the original version. In general, that strategy will pay off for non-negligible, CPU intensive task. In that frame, we could for instance use parallelism two ways in the classify function: we could use it on distance, computing pixels differences in parallel, or we could use it on examples, computing the classifications in parallel. The second direction is much more likely to be useful, because one classification does require a significant level of work, whereas computing the difference between two pixels is negligible.

NESSOS STREAMS

`Array.Parallel` implements a subset of the `Array` module functions in a parallel manner. If you find yourself needing more, take a look at the Streams library (`http://nessos.github.io/Streams/`). It contains additional functions in the `ParStream` module (for parallel streams), and offers other interesting possibilities. In a nutshell, the library distinguishes lazy and eager operations in pipelines, and will fuse together lazy operations, which can yield performance benefits.

Different Classifiers with Accord.NET

In the previous section, we discussed a few ways you can improve the performance of an existing algorithm. However, every algorithm has fundamental characteristics that define how your program will behave. In this section, we will take an entirely different direction, and take a look at Accord.NET, a popular (and good!) library that contains a wealth of machine learning and numeric analysis tools.

Our goal here is twofold. First, writing your own implementation is often not that hard, and comes with some benefits. In particular, you are entirely in control of the code, which offers some opportunity for tighter integration with the application that uses it, and maybe some room for optimization at a global level. However, developing a machine learning algorithm involves a lot of experimentation and trial-and-error, and sometimes, you just need to quickly check if a particular class of models works better than another. In that case, implementing the algorithm from scratch might be simply too much effort, and using an off-the-shelf implementation can speed up the elimination process. In that frame, knowing how to leverage a rich library like Accord is quite useful.

Then, we covered a variety of techniques in the previous chapters, but left out many other classic and potentially useful ones, too. We cannot realistically cover every algorithm in detail, but we will use this section as an excuse to provide a high-level introduction to some of them, and demonstrate how you could use the library.

Logistic Regression

In Chapter 4, we implemented a classic regression model, trying to predict a numeric value from multiple input features. One of the ways that approach is different from the nearest neighbor model is that there is a clearly distinct training phase in the process. The training set is used to estimate the parameters of a classifier function, which is much more compact than the original dataset. If I wanted to send someone my nearest neighbor classifier function, I would have to send the entire training set. By contrast, the regression model is just a function of the form $Y = a0 + a1 * X1 + ... ak * Xk$, and the only thing I would need to transmit is the values $a0, a1, ... ak$. Similarly, producing a prediction will be considerably faster: instead of computing 5,000 distances, all we have is one very simple computation. The price we have to pay for that is finding good values for $a0, a1, ... ak$, which is an expensive training operation.

Logistic regression is essentially the same model, adapted to classification. Instead of producing a number that can take any real value, its output is a value between 0 and 1, which represents the probability that an observation belongs to one of two possible classes.

For an observation with feature values X = [X1; ... Xk], the predicted value for Y is generated by the so-called logistic function:

$$f(X) = \frac{1}{1 + e^{-(a_0 + a_1 x_1 + \ldots + a_k x_k)}}$$

There is a visible relationship with the regression model: starting from X, we compute the result of a linear combination first, which give us a value z, and apply an additional transformation to z using the logistic function f:

$$[x_1; \ldots x_k] \to z = a_0 + a_1 x_1 + \ldots + a_k x_k \to Y = \frac{1}{1 + e^{-z}}$$

The reason for the last transformation is to resolve the following issue: if our goal is to produce a number that describes the probability for one observation to be or not to be in a certain class, the output better be in the [0 .. 1] interval. That is not the case with a linear regression, which can take any value between – and + infinity. However, if you plot 1.0 / (1.0 + exp (-z)), you'll see the shape in Figure 8-1; the function transforms any value into the interval [0 ... 1], with a value of 0.5 for z = 0. When the linear model predicts z = 0, the logistic will say it's a 50/50 chance between the two possible outcomes. Values further apart from 0 signal a higher confidence that the observation belongs to one class or the other.

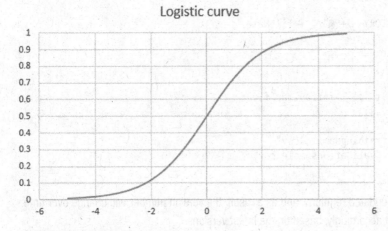

Figure 8-1. *Logistic curve*

In other words, the logistic function acts as an **activation function**. It receives an input value which can be anything, and transforms it into a binary signal: if the input value is higher than 0, we are in state 1, otherwise 0.

Simple Logistic Regression with Accord

Technically, estimating the parameters of a logistic function can be done in a very similar fashion to what we did in Chapter 4, using gradient descent with a slightly modified cost function. Implementing it is actually a fun exercise (and not overly complicated), but we will use Accord.NET's version instead.

As a starting point, we will leave aside for a minute the obvious issue that we have ten classes to recognize, while the logistic model can only distinguish two cases. We will work through a demonstration example first, creating a classifier that separates only two cases, say, 4s and 9s.

Let's add a new script file to our solution, logistic.fsx, and add the two NuGet packages we will use in this example and the following ones, Accord.MachineLearning and Accord.Neuro.

First, we need some data. We will proceed along the same lines as in Chapter 1, with two minor differences. First, we will parse the values as floats instead of integers, because that's what Accord expects; then we will simply use tuples to store the examples, the label being the first element, and the features the second.

Listing 8-2. Reading the Dataset for the Logistic Regression

```fsharp
#I @"../packages"
#r @"Accord.2.15.0\lib\net45\Accord.dll"
#r @"Accord.MachineLearning.2.15.0\lib\net45\Accord.MachineLearning.dll"
#r @"Accord.Math.2.15.0\lib\net45\Accord.Math.dll"
#r @"Accord.Statistics.2.15.0\lib\net45\Accord.Statistics.dll"

open Accord.Statistics.Models.Regression
open Accord.Statistics.Models.Regression.Fitting

let readLogistic fileName =
    let path = __SOURCE_DIRECTORY__ + @"/" + fileName
    path
    |> System.IO.File.ReadAllLines
    |> fun lines -> lines.[1..]
    |> Array.map (fun line ->
        let parsed = line.Split ',' |> Array.map float
        parsed.[0], parsed.[1..])

let training = readLogistic "trainingsample.csv"
let validation = readLogistic "validationsample.csv"
```

■ **Caution**   The Accord library is updated regularly, and as a result, the version number will change over time. Update the references in your script accordingly, based on the latest version!

Now that we have a dataset in memory, we need two things. Because we will learn how to recognize 4s and 9s, we will filter the dataset to retain only relevant examples. And because the Logistic regression expects outputs to be encoded as 0.0 or 1.0, we will create a small utility function to transform the labels appropriately. Finally, we will use this to create our new learning sample (see Listing 8-3).

Listing 8-3. Preparing a 4s vs. 9s Dataset for the Logistic Regression

```
let labeler x =
    match x with
    | 4. -> 0.
    | 9. -> 1.
    | _ -> failwith "unexpected label"

let fours = training |> Array.filter (fun (label,_) -> label = 4.)
let nines = training |> Array.filter (fun (label,_) -> label = 9.)

let labels,images =
    Array.append fours nines
    |> Array.map (fun (label,image) -> labeler label,image)
    |> Array.unzip
```

We can now start using the Accord Logistic regression model. Accord uses primarily an object-oriented style, and as a result, it follows a pattern along these lines:

1. First you create a model, a class defining how the prediction is made.

2. You pass it to a learner, a class that defines how to use training data to fit that model.

3. You then provide data to the learner, and "learn" until the fit is good enough,

4. You can now use the original model instance to make predictions.

In our case, we will use a `LogisticRegression` model, using 28 * 28 features, corresponding to each of the pixels of our scanned images, and use `LogisticGradientDescent` to learn, until the changes in our model become negligible. This is a good fit for a recursive loop (see Listing 8-4).

Listing 8-4 Training the Logistic Model

```
let features = 28 * 28
let model = LogisticRegression(features)

let trainLogistic (model) =
    let learner = LogisticGradientDescent(model)
    let minDelta = 0.001
    let rec improve () =
        let delta = learner.Run(images,labels)
        printfn "%.4f" delta
        if delta > minDelta
        then improve ()
        else ignore ()
    improve ()

trainLogistic model |> ignore
```

If you run the following code, you should see a series of numbers printing out in FSI, indicating how much the model parameters are changing at each step of the learning process; when the changes fall under minDelta, which defines how close you want the result to be to the optimal value, it stops. At that point, the model is ready to use; we can for instance run it against the validation set, filtering out anything that isn't a 4 or a 9, and check which predictions are correct (see Listing 8-5).

Listing 8-5. Validating the Logistic Model

```
let accuracy () =
    validation
    |> Array.filter (fun (label,_) -> label = 4. || label = 9.)
    |> Array.map (fun (label,image) -> labeler label,image)
    |> Array.map (fun (label,image) ->
        let predicted = if model.Compute(image) > 0.5 then 1. else 0.
        let real = label
        if predicted = real then 1. else 0.)
    |> Array.average

accuracy ()
```

On my machine, this produces 95.4% correct answers. One point of note here: `model.Compute` does not necessarily return a 1.0 or a 0.0, it returns a number between 0.0 and 1.0, which indicates the probability that the output belongs to class 1. This is why we check whether the value is above or below 50% to determine the classifier decision. While this might seem to introduce a bit of extra work, this is actually very valuable: instead of simply returning a label, the classifier also provides an estimate for how confident it is about its prediction.

One-vs-One, One-vs-All Classification

How can we use a binary classifier to distinguish between ten classes? There are two classic methods to approach the problem. In the first one, "One vs. All," you create one binary classifier for each label, trying to recognize each label against anything else. In this case, we would create 10 models: "is this a 0, or something else," "is this a 1, or something else," … and then run the ten models, and pick the answer with the highest confidence level. In the second approach, "One vs. One," you create a binary classifier for every possible label pair ("is this a 0 or a 1," "is this a 0 or a 2," …), run every model, and predict using a round-robin vote, selecting the label that gets the most picks.

Let's implement a one-vs-all model, mainly to illustrate the process. In our situation, we need 10 different models, "0 or not," "1 or not," and so forth… If we arrange the data in such a way that in each case, the digit we are trying to recognize is labeled 1.0, and the rest 0.0, then each trained model will return a number indicating how strongly it thinks the image is that particular label. In that frame, to classify an image, all we need to do is to run the 10 models, and pick the one with the largest output.

This is not overly complicated: in Listing 8-6, for each of the classes, we create a new training sample where examples are labeled 1.0 if they match the class we train for, and 0.0 otherwise. For each label, we train a logistic, just like we did in the previous section (with one small modification: we limit the learning process to 1000 iterations at most), and create a list containing all the labels and their models. The overall classifier function returns the label corresponding to the most "confident" model.

Listing 8-6. One-vs-All Logistic Classifier

```
let one_vs_all () =

    let features = 28 * 28
    let labels = [ 0.0 .. 9.0 ]
    let models =
        labels
        |> List.map (fun target ->
            printfn "Learning label %.0f" target
```

```
        // create training set for target label
        let trainingLabels,trainingFeatures =
            training
            |> Array.map (fun (label,features) ->
                if label = target
                then (1.,features)
                else (0.,features))
            |> Array.unzip
        // train the model
        let model = LogisticRegression(features)
        let learner = LogisticGradientDescent(model)
        let minDelta = 0.001
        let max_iters = 1000
        let rec improve iter =
            if iter = max_iters
            then ignore ()
            else
                let delta = learner.Run(trainingFeatures,trainingLabels)
                if delta < minDelta then ignore ()
                else improve (iter + 1)
        improve 0
        // return the label and corresponding model
        target,model)

let classifier (image:float[]) =
    models
    |> List.maxBy (fun (label,model) -> model.Compute image)
    |> fun (label,confidence) -> label

classifier
```

The resulting model is not particularly good; on my machine, I got close to 83% accuracy. We won't implement the other approach here, because the code isn't different enough to warrant it. On one hand, these two approaches are interesting, because they provide a simple technique to extend binary classifiers (which are the simplest classifier you could create) to handle an arbitrary number of labels. On the other hand, keep in mind that both of them are just heuristics: the approach is reasonable, but not guaranteed to work well. One-vs-all has the benefit of requiring fewer models (in our case, 10, against 90 for one-vs-one case), but both have potential issues. In the one-vs-all situation, we are lumping together many different situations in the negative case, which can make training difficult (for instance, you would expect that recognizing a 5 from a 0 or a 6 would be based on different features). Training a model to specifically recognize a 1 from a 6 (for instance) is easier than from nine different digits. Conversely, in the one-vs-one case, while training individual models might be easier, the final decision involves asking models trained to distinguish two specific digits to recognize something that is neither, which is arguably tricky (if you pass a 0 to a model trained to recognize 1 from 2, what answer would you expect?).

Support Vector Machines

The next model we'll take a look at, Support Vector Machines (SVM afterward), is another classic binary classifier. It has an intimidating name, and the algorithm is a bit more involved conceptually than the previous one. We will hand-wave the details of how it works, and limit our explanation to a minimum.

In essence, a SVM attempts to separate the two classes by a band as wide as possible, so that all examples of one class are on one side, all the others on the other side. Support Vectors are the examples that lie on, or "support," each side of the boundary. Figure 8-2 illustrates the idea on a simple example: the two dashed lines represent the boundaries of the separating band. Every observation that belongs to the same class (black or white) is on the same side, and three observations, denoted as squares, are the support vectors that define where the boundary is.

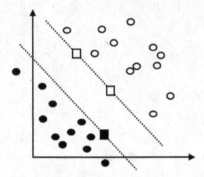

Figure 8-2. *Support vectors*

Just like the logistic regression, SVMs are binary classifiers. One difference with the logistic regression is that instead of 0 and 1s, the labels are encoded as –1 and 1, and the output is simply a class, and not a "confidence level." Let's see how we could use the Accord SVM to classify our digits. Conveniently, Accord has a built-in multiclass version of the SVM, which means that we can directly use it with 10 classes, instead of having to build an extra layer: it will handle the one-vs-one process for us.

For clarity, we'll put our SVM sample in a separate script, svm.fsx, including the same references we used for the logistic example. First, as usual, we'll read the dataset, but in this case we won't convert the label to a float (see Listing 8-7).

Listing 8-7. Reading Data for the SVM

```
let svmRead fileName =
    let path = __SOURCE_DIRECTORY__ + @"/" + fileName
    path
    |> System.IO.File.ReadAllLines
    |> fun lines -> lines.[1..]
    |> Array.map (fun line ->
        let parsed = line.Split ','
        parsed.[0] |> int, parsed.[1..] |> Array.map float)

let labels,images = svmRead "trainingsample.csv" |> Array.unzip
```

The training part requires a slightly more complex-looking setup than the logistic. Most of the complexity takes place in the algorithm function. If you inspect the code in detail, you'll see that it takes in a SVM, a dataset (inputs and outputs), and two values, *i* and *j*, and returns a learning strategy. This is the price you have to pay for handling multiple classes at once: the algorithm block will be used during training, to create the appropriate dataset and learning strategy for each of the one-vs-one classifiers that are generated behind the scenes; as a benefit, though, it makes it possible to configure and use different strategies for different pairs of labels. The rest of the code follows a logic similar to what we saw before: we create a model, a learner, and start the training, which is even simpler than in the logistic case, because it terminates by itself, and directly returns the error rate observed in the training sample (see Listing 8-8).

Listing 8-8. Training a Multiclass SVM Model

```
open Accord.MachineLearning.VectorMachines
open Accord.MachineLearning.VectorMachines.Learning
open Accord.Statistics.Kernels

let features = 28 * 28
let classes = 10

let algorithm =
    fun (svm: KernelSupportVectorMachine)
        (classInputs: float[][])
        (classOutputs: int[]) (i: int) (j: int) ->
        let strategy = SequentialMinimalOptimization(svm, classInputs, classOutputs)
        strategy :> ISupportVectorMachineLearning

let kernel = Linear()
let svm = new MulticlassSupportVectorMachine(features, kernel, classes)
let learner = MulticlassSupportVectorLearning(svm, images, labels)
let config = SupportVectorMachineLearningConfigurationFunction(algorithm)
learner.Algorithm <- config

let error = learner.Run()

let validation = svmRead "validationsample.csv"

validation
|> Array.averageBy (fun (l,i) -> if svm.Compute i = l then 1. else 0.)
```

That particular model classifies correctly 92% of the validation set, which is not too shabby. What can you do if you want to improve the result? A first lever you can use is the Complexity parameter, defined on the strategy. Its value is automatically set to a level that is typically close to 1, and should work reasonably well. Increasing it will force a better fit on the training sample, with two risks: it could overfit, or it could simply be too high, in which case the algorithm cannot find a solution, and will throw an exception.

The second lever you can use is the so-called Kernel trick. You have probably noticed that in the SVM setup, we passed in a Linear kernel. What this means is that we are searching for a clean, straight separation between the classes. If such a separation can be found in the dataset, there is no problem. However, it is quite possible that while examples from each class are nicely separated, that separation might not be a straight line (or hyperplane). At a very high level, the Kernel trick consists of applying a function to the observations, transforming the initial features into a new set of features in a higher dimension space, where the examples might actually be separable by a hyperplane. If that happens to be the case, we can then train a "standard" linear SVM to find that separation, and classify new observations, transforming them first by applying the same Kernel function.

If this is not entirely clear, fear not! The main practical implication is that if the default linear kernel doesn't work, you can try out other kernels, and see if this works any better. Accord has a quite a few kernels built in, which you can find by exploring the namespace Accord.Statistics.Kernels.

Neural Networks

The last classifier from Accord that we will take a look at is artificial neural networks (ANN afterward). The name is inspired by a loose analogy with the way a brain works. The brain is a large collection of interconnected neurons. When we receive a signal from the outside world, receptors send electrical impulses which activate neurons in our brain. Neurons that have received a signal strong enough will in turn send a signal to connected neurons, and in the end, our brain will (perhaps) make sense of the signal and recognize something.

The construction of an artificial neural network follows a similar general structure. They can come in different shapes, but the canonical ANN is a collection of neurons, organized in layers, each of them connected to every neuron in the next layer. The neuron itself is an activation function; it receives as input the output from every neuron connected into it, each of them with an individual weight, and if the weighted sum of inputs it receives is high enough, it will in turn send a signal forward.

Neural networks are a huge topic, which we couldn't possibly do justice within a single chapter here. In a fashion similar to what we did for SVMs, we will simply illustrate how you could go about building a classifier using the built-in tools in Accord, and highlight a couple of interesting points in the process.

In our particular situation, we have 784 pixels, our input signal, and what we expect is one of the 10 digits 0, 1, .. 9. In terms of neurons, we can represent this as a layer of 784 input neurons (which can each send a signal between 0 and 255), and a final layer of 10 neurons, each of them corresponding to one of the digits. The simplest possible network we could build would be to create a direct connection between each input neuron to each output neuron, as in Figure 8-3.

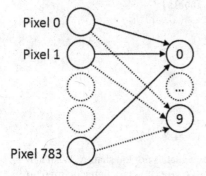

Figure 8-3. *Shallow artificial neural network*

What we would like is a model which takes an image, sends its input (each pixel value) into the network, and transforms it into a 0 or 1 value for each of the possible outputs. Whether we have hundreds of inputs or just two doesn't change the nature of the problem, so let's look at a simpler network, with just two inputs and one output, and explore how we could make that work. One possibility is to build a model where we activate a node if the weighted sum of the input signals is above a certain threshold, as in Figure 8-4.

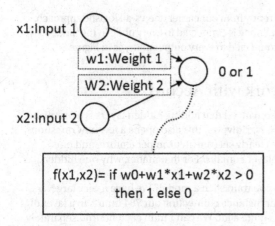

Figure 8-4. *A perceptron*

As it turns out, this model has a name, the **perceptron**. It is defined by three elements: the weights w1 and w2 assigned to each of the incoming signals (how important each input is), a threshold w0 (the so-called bias term), and a linear activation function f, which combines the input, and converts it into a 1 (a signal) if the input signal is higher than the threshold. Training such a classifier is very simple; we just need to find values for the weights and bias to minimize error—for instance, using methods similar to what we discussed in Chapter 4.

Note also that if we changed the activation function and used a logistic function in our nodes instead of a linear combination, we would have replicated our entire one-vs-all logistic model. The point here is that while a perceptron in isolation looks perhaps a bit simplistic, it forms a building block that can easily be composed into interesting and complex models.

So what's the problem, then, and how are artificial neural networks different? One key insight of ANNs is that if a simple linear model doesn't fit your data well, instead of using more complex components (creating new features, using nonlinear functions...), you can keep using simple perceptron-like nodes, but compose them into deeper models, by stacking one or more hidden layers between the inputs and outputs layers, as in Figure 8-5. If you are interested in the question, there is plenty of resources discussing modelling logic gates with a perceptron (see for instance http://www.cs.bham.ac.uk/~jxb/NN/l3.pdf); and as it turns out, while you can model AND, OR or NOT without problem, a XOR gate cannot be modelled unless you add a hidden layer.

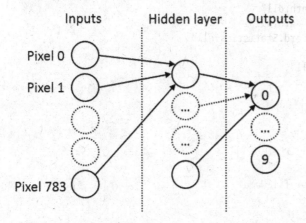

Figure 8-5. *Artificial neural network with one hidden layer*

In our case, if we wanted a model that we behaves differently from our earlier one-vs-all logistic approach, we would need to insert at least one hidden layer. Every input node is connected to every node in the hidden layer (but not to the next), and every node in the hidden layer is connected to every output node, as in Figure 8-5.

Creating and Training a Neural Network with Accord

With a lot of hand-waving, you are hopefully reasonably convinced that adding hidden layers is a promising way to compose simple perceptrons into powerful classifiers. However, this also opens a few new questions, too. First, while the size of the input and output layers are clearly set (one neuron per feature, and one neuron per class), how many neurons should the hidden layer contain? For that matter, why one hidden layer, and not two, three, or more?

A second and somewhat related question is, how do you train such a model? We have a very large number of parameters to estimate here. If you consider for instance connecting our 784 inputs to a layer of 10 neurons, we have to tune close to 8,000 weights. This is quite a lot. We can't train each neuron separately, because they are interconnected; if I change the incoming weights for one neuron, its output will change, and potentially require adjusting other neurons in the same layer. Finally, there is another subtle issue: how should we initialize the weights? If you started with weights of zero for every connection, because every neuron is identical, you would be at risk of learning the same parameters for every single neuron. Instead of capturing different features from the input set, every neuron would be producing the same output, and you would have a single model replicated multiple times.

Explaining in detail how to train an artificial neural network is a topic all by itself; we will limit ourselves to a very broad outline. The main approach for that purpose is called back propagation. In a fashion similar to gradient descent, you feed the network examples, and compare the desired value with the model output, and then go backward in the network, layer by layer, adjusting each neuron to reduce the error. To avoid the issue of identical nodes, the weights are initialized using some form of random procedure.

In practice, what this means is that training a neural network is a time-consuming affair. While expanding the network depth, and the number of nodes per layer, could in theory produce a finer model, it also has direct implications in how much time it might take to train it, not to mention the risk of over-fitting.

With that in mind, let's illustrate how one could create and train such a network using Accord, in a separate script (See Listing 8-9). As usual, we'll start by loading the required libraries, and writing a read function to prepare our dataset.

Listing 8-9. Preparing to Train a Neural Network with Accord

```
#I @"../packages"
#r @"Accord.Math.2.15.0\lib\net45\Accord.Math.dll"
#r @"Accord.Neuro.2.15.0\lib\net45\Accord.Neuro.dll"
#r @"Accord.Statistics.2.15.0\lib\net45\Accord.Statistics.dll"
#r @"AForge.2.2.5\lib\AForge.dll"
#r @"AForge.Neuro.2.2.5\lib\AForge.Neuro.dll"

open Accord.Statistics
open Accord.Neuro
open Accord.Neuro.Learning
open AForge.Neuro

let nnRead fileName =
    let path = __SOURCE_DIRECTORY__ + @"/" + fileName
    path
    |> System.IO.File.ReadAllLines
    |> fun lines -> lines.[1..]
```

```
|> Array.map (fun line ->
    let parsed = line.Split ','
    parsed.[0] |> int, parsed.[1..] |> Array.map float)
```

We can then set up our neural network, initiate the training phase, and validate the results (See Listing 8-10). The approach follows more or less the same pattern we have seen before, with a couple differences worth pointing out.

Listing 8-10. Creating, Training and Evaluating the Network

```
let trainNetwork (epochs:int) =

    let features = 28 * 28
    let labels,images = nnRead "trainingsample.csv" |> Array.unzip
    let learningLabels = Tools.Expand(labels,-1.0,1.0)

    let network = ActivationNetwork(BipolarSigmoidFunction(), features, [| 100; 10 |])
    NguyenWidrow(network).Randomize()

    let teacher = new ParallelResilientBackpropagationLearning(network)

    let rec learn iter =
        let error = teacher.RunEpoch(images, learningLabels)
        printfn "%.3f / %i" error iter
        if error < 0.01 then ignore ()
        elif iter > epochs then ignore ()
        else learn (iter + 1)

    learn 0

    network

let ann = trainNetwork (50)

let validate = nnRead "validationsample.csv"
validate
|> Array.averageBy (fun (label,image) ->
    let predicted =
        ann.Compute image
        |> Array.mapi (fun i x -> i,x)
        |> Array.maxBy snd
        |> fst
    if label = predicted then 1.0 else 0.0)
```

First, we need to transform the output, so that each of the digits becomes separate feature. In order to achieve that, we use `Accord.Statistics.Tools.Expand`, a built-in utility that expands a set of labels into a new representation, where each label becomes an individual column, with binary outputs encoded in this case as –1 or 1. We use that particular encoding because of the activation function selected, the `BipolarSigmoidFunction`: its values go from –1 to 1, where 1 would be a positive case ("this is a 1"), and –1 a negative ("this isn't a 1"). Alternatively, `AForge.Neuro` contains a couple of other built-in activation functions.

We create a network, passing in the activation function, the expected number of inputs (in our case, the 28 × 28 pixels), and the number of nodes per layer in an array, the last element of being the expected number of labels, here 10. Note also the usage of `NguyenWidrow`, which creates random but reasonable initial values for the network weights.

On my machine, the following code produces nearly 82% correct classifications (due to the randomization of initial weights, results may vary). This is not entirely terrible, but it is not great either. As you probably noticed if you ran it, it is also pretty slow. That being said, we limited the training to 50 iterations here, and the error (which prints out after each pass) is still regularly decreasing when we reach the 50th iteration. When I expanded the search to 500 epochs, I saw another decrease from 1775 to 1200, with 82.6% correct. In other words, the learning process slows down quite a bit, but is still producing improvements.

We will leave it at that on the topic of neural networks, and of Accord in general. The library contains a lot more than the algorithms we described here, as well as interesting samples which illustrate some of it capabilities.

Scaling with m-brace.net

Tune your code all you want, at some point, the bottleneck will be your machine. The reason this matters comes back full circle to our initial definition of machine learning. A good machine learning algorithm should mechanically become better at performing its tasks, if it is fed more data.

One of the implications here is that if more data is better, then you will want more, which explains in part the recent craze around "big data." And, as your datasets grow, both data exploration and model training using simple F# scripts will become slower, or even impossible, for instance if the dataset is too large to open or save locally. In this section, we will provide a brief introduction to m-brace.net, a library designed to address that issue, by sending code from the scripting environment to be executed in a cluster in the cloud.

Getting Started with MBrace on Azure with Brisk

If our limiting factor is the computer itself, one direction is to throw more computers at the problem. Just like "nine women can't make a baby in one month" (in the words of Fred Brooks), many computers will not always speed things up, depending on the problem. That being said, in general, any time we identify a map in our code, we should have an opportunity to apply a divide-and-conquer approach: break the collection we are mapping into chunks, run the map for each chunk independently on separate computers, and reduce all the chunks into one final result.

This is the same pattern we saw earlier in `Array.Parallel.map`. The framework we are going to discuss next, MBrace (`www.m-brace.net`), extends that idea much further: instead of simply processing chunks across cores on your local machine, it allows you to do the same, but across a cluster of machines in the Microsoft Azure cloud.

The beauty here is that all of this is possible while still working from the scripting environment. In essence, the goal of MBrace is to let you work with F# scripts in Visual Studio, so that you can keep a rapid design feedback loop, but seamlessly send that code to be executed remotely to your cluster. You can create a cluster on-demand, just for as long as you need large computation power or data, without being limited by your local equipment, and shut it down once you are done.

The easiest way to get started with MBrace is to follow three steps:

1. First, if you don't have one yet, get an Azure subscription. You can get a free trial version at http://azure.microsoft.com.

2. Then, register for a free account at www.BriskEngine.com. Brisk is a service that allows you to easily provision a cluster on Azure, fully configured with all you need to run MBrace, and delete it as soon as you are done. Brisk itself is free; you only pay for your Azure cloud usage.

3. Finally, download the MBrace Starter Kit from the MBrace repository on GitHub: https://github.com/mbraceproject/MBrace.StarterKit. That project contains a preconfigured solution with numerous examples illustrating how to use MBrace; you can simply download it, and add your scripts to it for an easy start.

At that point, you should have an F# project on your local machine that looks like Figure 8-6.

Let's deploy a cluster of machines on Azure first. To do that, simply go to BriskEngine.com, log in, and head to the Dashboard menu, where you can inspect what clusters you recently created, and create new ones. Let's create a new cluster, select {m} for MBrace, and choose where it should be deployed geographically. You probably want a location that is close to where you are, so that moving data back-and-forth between your machine and the cluster is as fast as possible; if you are going to access preexisting data, where it is located matters, too. Finally, let's pick a cluster size; you can go from a tiny four-cores cluster (two medium machines), for less than $0.50 an hour, all the way up to 256 cores for around $20 an hour.

Figure 8-6. *The m-brace starter project*

Let's go for 16 cores, which gives us solid horsepower, for about $1.50 an hour. The BriskEngine dashboard will indicate how far along the deployment is, and after 5 to 10 minutes you should have your own cluster ready to go (see Figure 8-7).

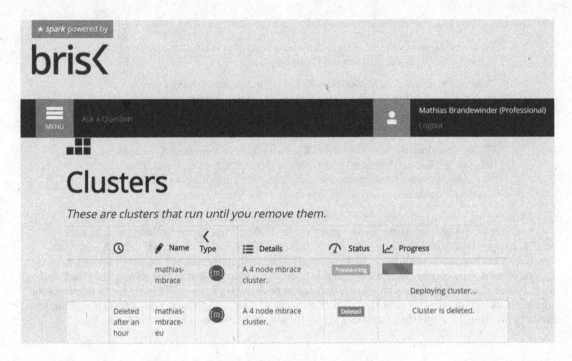

Figure 8-7. *Deploying a cluster on Azure via BriskEngine*

We are now about ready to start running code on that cluster; we just need to connect to it from our scripting session in Visual Studio. We will do that by providing MBrace with two connection strings in the credentials.fsx file. BriskEngine makes that simple: in your dashboard, once the cluster is active, you can click the cluster name, and copy the two connection strings into the credentials file.

Finally, let's add a new script, digits.fsx to the Starter Kit solution, with Listing 8-11.

Listing 8-11. Connecting to the Cluster

```
#load "credentials.fsx"

open MBrace.Core
open MBrace.Azure.Client

let cluster = Runtime.GetHandle(config)
```

Send that code to FSI, and … that's it, you are now connected to the cluster. You can check that by running the following line of code, which will display information about the workers you have running in your cluster:

```
cluster.ShowWorkers ()

>

>

Workers
```

```
Id                       Status    % CPU / Cores   % Memory /
--                       ------    -------------   --------------------
MBraceWorkerRole_IN_2    Running      2.3 / 4        13.5 / 7167.0
MBraceWorkerRole_IN_1    Running      1.4 / 4        14.1 / 7167.0
MBraceWorkerRole_IN_0    Running      1.8 / 4        13.6 / 7167.0
MBraceWorkerRole_IN_3    Running      1.5 / 4        13.6 / 7167.0
val it : unit = ()
```

So how do you send work to the cluster? By using the cloud computation expression cloud { ... }. The name might sound scary: don't let yourself be intimidated. Cloud computations are a very powerful mechanism in F#, usually designed to provide a simpler way to write and manage complex code workflows. They use a builder, which defines a "context" marked by { }, within which F# is extended, using keywords such as let! or return, hiding some of the less interesting side-effects of the operations, and emphasizing the structure of the overall workflow. As a result, while understanding how to write a new computation expression might be a bit of a mind-bending exercise, using an existing one is usually not complicated, because the whole point is to let you write simpler code to achieve your goals.

In the case of MBrace, executing code in your cluster involves two phases: you define the code you want to run in the cloud inside a cloud { ... } computation expression, and then send it for execution. As an example, try sending the following code line by line to FSI:

```
#time "on"
cluster.AttachClientLogger(MBrace.Azure.ConsoleLogger())

let localHello = "Hello"
let cloudHello = cloud { return "Hello" }
cloudHello |> cluster.Run
```

While localHello is instantaneously evaluated, cloudHello does nothing by itself: it is of type Cloud<string>, a piece of code that can be run in the cloud and will return a string. The moment it is sent to cluster.Run, a process is created and enqueued for execution; MBrace inspects the code that has been sent to FSI, sends the types and data needed to run your code on the cluster over the wire, and returns the result in FSI, as if it had all been a regular local script.

Instead of sending the code for execution and waiting until the result is available, you can also start a process, and await for its result, like this:

```
let work = cloudHello |> cluster.CreateProcess
cluster.ShowProcesses ()
>
Processes
```

```
Name                                        Process Id    Status     Completed   Execution Time
----                                        ----------    ------     ---------   --------------
       c93fa4d3b1e04a0093cbb7287c73feea     Completed     True       00:00:00.8280729
       c833d511623745e2b375f729be25742b     Completed     True       00:00:00.1129141
```

```
// ask if the work is complete yet
work.Completed
>
val it : bool = true
// when complete, ask for the result
Let result = work.AwaitResult ()
> val result : string = "Hello"
```

This allows you to send the work to the cluster for execution, and retrieve the result once it is available, without blocking FSI.

Processing Large Datasets with MBrace

In our initial example, all we got from MBrace was a performance hit compared to the local version of "Hello, World". This should not come as a surprise: we ran the same code we had on our local machine, with no gains to expect, but had to serialize everything in the process. Just like `Array.Parallel` might not pay off for small tasks where the parallelization gains don't make up for the coordination costs, MBrace typically won't be beneficial on small scale problems, because moving data and code between machines introduces overhead.

Fortunately, the digit recognizer constitutes a perfect example here. The "real" dataset used in the Kaggle competition contains 50,000 examples. The training set we have used in all our examples so far has been shrunk to 5,000 examples precisely because we wanted to be able to explore ideas from the scripting environment, and get rapid feedback on whether they seem worthwhile investigating. What would you do if you wanted to keep a similar workflow, but using the entire dataset? Let's start by outlining how the purely local code, operating on a reduced dataset, would look like. Starting from our initial model from Listing 8-1, I would take our optimized distance function, train a model and evaluate it, as shown in Listing 8-12.

Listing 8-12. Evaluating the Model on a Reduced Dataset

```
let optimizedDistance (pixels1:int[],pixels2:int[]) =
    let dim = pixels1.Length
    let mutable dist = 0
    for i in 0 .. (dim - 1) do
        let x = pixels1.[i] - pixels2.[i]
        dist <- dist + (x * x)
    dist

let optimizedModel = train training optimizedDistance

#time "on"
evaluate validation optimizedModel
```

Now imagine that we want to use the full 50,000 examples. As we do that, we only increase the dataset size by a factor 10, but our evaluation will now run about 100 times slower, because the number of operations required went from $1,000 \times 4,000$, to $10,000 \times 40,000$.

This type of scenario is fairly typical: your dataset becomes larger, which is a good thing in general, but your local machine can't handle it, and your development rhythm suddenly grinds to a halt. This is one scenario where MBrace shines; let's see how we could tweak our original code to handle the heavy lifting in the cloud, without sacrificing our scripting experience.

We have no reason to change the model itself. The first place where we need to change the code is in the data preparation section. We are now reading from a single large file, and we will need to split the data into training and validation. The evaluation function is where most of the changes need to happen. Listing 8-13 describes one way we could go about it. Let's start with the code, which we'll comment after.

Listing 8-13. Distributing the Evaluation in the Cloud

```fsharp
#load "credentials.fsx"

open MBrace.Core
open MBrace.Azure
open MBrace.Azure.Client
open MBrace.Store
open MBrace.Flow

let cluster = Runtime.GetHandle(config)
cluster.AttachClientLogger(ConsoleLogger())

let fullDataPath = __SOURCE_DIRECTORY__ + @"/large.csv"

let large =
    CloudFile.Upload(fullDataPath,"data/large.csv")
    |> cluster.RunLocally

let cloudValidation =
    cloud {
        let! data = CloudFile.ReadAllLines(large.Path)
        let training = data.[1..40000] |> Array.map toObservation
        let validation = data.[40001..] |> Array.map toObservation
        let model = train training optimizedDistance
        let! correct =
            validation
            |> CloudFlow.OfArray
            |> CloudFlow.withDegreeOfParallelism 16
            |> CloudFlow.averageBy (fun ex ->
                if model ex.Pixels = ex.Label then 1.0 else 0.0)
        return correct }
```

■ **Note**   At the time of writing, MBrace is still undergoing some evolution. As a result, API changes are likely to take place in the near future.

The code could be simplified a bit, but as it stands, it highlights a few interesting features. First, we create a CloudFile. We upload our entire dataset to the cluster, which allows us to read its contents using CloudFile.ReadAllLines, in a fashion similar to what we did previously with File.ReadAllLines. Note the usage of cluster.runLocally; the purpose is to have our local machine (where the original data file is located) perform the upload, rather than one of the worker roles on the cluster

The cloudValidation function is also similar to the original, purely local version. The main modifications are that first, we wrap the evaluation in cloud { ... }. As a result, the entire process will run in the cluster. Then, instead of using Array.averageBy to evaluate the model across the validation sample, we use a CloudFlow., which behaves essentially like a sequence, but distributes work intelligently across the cluster.

So... how well does this work? On a 16-cores cluster, the evaluate part runs in about a minute. Of course, we had to pay a cost for the initial data upload, but this is a one-time cost. At that point, we could start modifying our algorithm and testing the impact; and each evaluation of the modified code will take a minute, instead of over 5 minutes if I run it on my workstation without MBrace. This is very significant: over the duration of a day, running a dozen evaluations, I would gain an entire hour, not to mention the ability to just stay focused, instead of being distracted by 5 minutes breaks every time I want to try something out.

There is much more to MBrace than what we just showed in this rather simple example; however, I hope it gave you a sense for the type of scenarios it is useful in—essentially, use cases where you want to keep an interactive and flexible workflow, but need to significantly increase how much data you can handle. I want to specifically point out that while this example was entirely driven from the scripting environment, it is perfectly possible to acquire data from other sources. This is particularly important if you need to handle very large datasets; in that case, opening the data in the scripting environment might be impractical, or even impossible. Instead, you can access the data wherever it is located, from within your cluster, do the heavy lifting there, and simply send back the results of your analysis to your local environment.

So What Did We Learn?

This final chapter was fairly different from what we have been doing up to that point. Instead of focusing on one specific problem, and building a machine learning algorithm from scratch to address a question, we revisited the model we developed in the first chapter, and used it as a reference point to explore two directions: improving code performance, and demonstrating a couple of useful modelling techniques.

We started by analyzing the structure of our algorithm, to understand where improvements would be possible, and what performance we should be expecting as we increase the volume of data used for training and validation. In this specific case, we identified the function responsible for computing the distance between images as a bottleneck we could potentially improve. We isolated this function, and, by measuring its speed and garbage collection characteristics, we managed to adjust the code and improve both aspects, with a ten-time speedup. The price we had to pay for that improvement was writing more code, and perhaps more complicated code, using either recursion or mutating variables. This is not an uncommon trade-off. While coding in a functional style, favoring immutable data structures and higher-level functions, comes with its own benefits (clear and safe code that describes intent), it can also have drawbacks, notably from a performance standpoint. One of the strengths of F# is its hybrid nature: by default, the language tends to favor a functional style, but it handles perfectly well coding in an imperative style, which allows for simple local optimizations when they are needed.

We also explored parallelism as a way to squeeze out additional performance. One of the benefits of a functional style is that it helps spot places where such improvements are possible. Specifically, whenever a map is being used, we have a candidate for speedup gains, because a map signals an operation that can be run in parallel instead of sequentially. We illustrated that first with Array.Parallel.map, and later on with m-brace.net, which both exploit that pattern to divide-and-conquer work across resources, on the cores of your local machine, or across many machines in a cluster.

This is extremely useful in a machine learning context. Machine learning is about building predictive models that become better as they are fed with more data; and while increasing the volume of data used by your models is an important ingredient in making them better, this also creates a problem, because larger datasets require more computation power to be processed. But in many situations, that increase can be mitigated because its translation in code happens through a map, or a similarly parallelizable operation, which implies that the increase in volume can be divided across more resources. We saw a prime example here with cross validation: even though we needed to evaluate more observations, they can all be processed independently of each other, and as a result, we can handle larger volumes without much effort, simply by provisioning a large cluster and parallelizing the map operation.

The second main direction in this chapter was a brief introduction to Accord.NET, a rich .NET machine learning library. Writing your own algorithm implementation is a perfectly valid thing to do, and often easier than it seems. However, it is impractical at times. Being able to simply try out whether a particular algorithm works, and eliminate it quickly if it doesn't, can help avoid wasting valuable time that could be spent focusing faster on a direction that is promising. Accord.NET offers a wealth of well-implemented classification and regression models, and is a useful tool to master for that purpose. Also, while the R Type Provider offers another venue to try out off-the-shelf algorithms, Accord.NET has the advantage of being a .NET library, which makes its integration with a .NET code base simpler.

Finally, we used this introduction to Accord.NET as a pretext to present, at a very high level, a couple of classic classifiers which we haven't covered in previous chapters—logistic regression, support vector machines, and artificial neural networks—and how you would go about using them. Accord contains many other tools, and I would recommend taking a deeper look at the library. Our introduction to the library (and the three classifiers we used as examples) was somewhat superficial; it wouldn't be practical to attempt to cover everything in detail in here, but we hope that our focus on usage, illustrating the general patterns Accord.NET follows, will be helpful in digging further into the library!

USEFUL LINKS

- Accord.NET is a wonderful library, with numerous machine learning algorithm, as well as tools related to computer vision and numeric analysis: `http://accord-framework.net`

- MBrace, a library for scalable cloud data scripting: `www.m-brace.net`

- Brisk, a website that simplifies the deployment of MBrace clusters: `www.briskengine.com`

- Peter Norvig's talk "The Unreasonable Effectiveness of Data": `https://www.youtube.com/watch?v=yvDCzhbjYWs`

- Modelling logic gates with single-layer perceptrons: `www.cs.bham.ac.uk/~jxb/NN/l3.pdf`

CHAPTER 9

■ ■ ■

Conclusion

You made it through this book—congratulations! This was a long journey, and I hope it was also an enjoyable one—one from which you picked up an idea or two along the way. Before we part ways, I figured it might be worthwhile to take a look back at what we have accomplished together, and perhaps also see if there are some broader themes that apply across the chapters, in spite of their profound differences.

Mapping Our Journey

My goal with this book was to provide an introduction to the topic of machine learning in a way that was both accessible and fun to .NET developers. Machine learning is a large topic, which is—deservedly—attracting more attention every day. It's also a topic that is all too often presented in a somewhat abstract fashion, leading many to believe that it's a complicated topic best left to mathematicians.

While mathematics play an important role in machine learning, my hope is that, after reading this book, you realize that it isn't quite as complex as it sounds, and that many of the underlying ideas are actually fairly simple and applicable to a wide range of practical problems.

Let's take a step back and look at the ground we covered. At a very high level, we established something like a map of machine learning problems, making important distinctions. First, we introduced supervised and unsupervised methods. Each addresses a distinct problem, as follows:

- **Unsupervised methods** are about helping you make sense of data, when you don't know yet what question you might be after. This was the main topic of Chapter 5, where we took a dataset of StackOverflow questions and simply looked for patterns that would help us make sense of otherwise hard-to-interpret, unstructured data.

- By contrast, **supervised methods**, where we spent most of our efforts (Chapters 1, 2, 4, and 6), are about training a model to answer a well-defined question that matters to us based on labeled examples; that is, data for which the correct answer is known.

In that exploration, we covered a wide range of models, which have important differences. First, we distinguished between classification and regression models, which differ in the type of answer we expect from them. A **regression** model aims at predicting a continuous numeric value; in Chapter 4, we developed such a model to predict the usage level of a bicycle-sharing service based on various inputs. By contrast, **classification** models are about deciding which is the most likely out of a limited number of possible outcomes. We saw three examples of that type of model, from automatically recognizing which of ten possible digits an image represented (Chapter 1) to separating between ham and spam messages (Chapter 2), and predicting which passengers on the Titanic would survive their trip (Chapter 6).

We also explored a different approach using reinforcement learning in Chapter 7. The resulting model was a classifier that decided between a limited set of possible actions, with a key difference from previous models: Instead of learning one time using past data, we built a model that kept learning constantly as new observations were coming in, an approach generally known as **online learning**.

Throughout the book, we dug into a variety of real datasets and let the data guide our exploration. In spite of the apparent diversity of topics (images, text, numbers, and so forth), patterns emerged across problems. In most cases, we ended up applying **features extraction**—we transformed the original data into rows of values that were more informative or convenient to work with. And, just as the type of answer we were looking for in a model determined whether classification or regression was more suitable, we ended up with different approaches depending on whether features were continuous or categorical. We also saw how one could potentially transform a continuous feature into a discrete one by binning (age, in the Titanic example), or conversely how a categorical could be flattened into a series of indicator variables (day of the week, in the regression example).

Science!

Another pattern we saw emerge across the chapters involved methodology. We begin with a question we want to answer, we gather whatever data we have available, and we start to perform a series of experiments, progressively creating and refining a model that agrees with the facts.

In that sense, developing a machine learning model is fairly different from developing a regular line-of-business application. When you build an application, you usually have a set of features to implement; each feature has some form of acceptance criteria describing what it takes for it to be done. Developers decompose the problem into smaller pieces of code, put them together, and the task is complete once things work together as expected.

By contrast, developing a machine learning program is closer to a research activity that follows the scientific method. You don't know beforehand if a particular idea will work. You have to formulate a theory, build a predictive model using the data you have available, and then verify whether or not the model you built fits with the data. This is a bit tricky, in that it makes it difficult to estimate how long developing such a model might take. You could try a very simple idea and be done within half a day, or you could spend weeks and have nothing to show for your work except failed experiments.

Of course, things are not entirely that clear cut. There is some uncertainty involved when developing a regular application, and some failed experiments as well. However, the fact remains that with machine learning you won't know whether your idea works until you confront your model with the data. That being said, some software engineering ideas still apply, albeit in a slightly modified manner.

Just like it helps to have a clear specification for what feature you are trying to ship, it is crucial to think early on about how to measure success, and then set yourself up for that purpose. Correct code is only a small part of what makes a good machine learning model; to be valuable, a model has to be useful, and that means it has to be good at making predictions. In that frame, we repeatedly used **cross-validation** throughout the book. Put aside part of your data, don't use it for training, and once you have a model ready, test how well it works on the validation set, which simulates what might happen when your model sees new input in real conditions. In some respects, cross-validation serves a purpose similar to a test suite for regular code by allowing you to check whether things work as intended.

A habit that has worked well for me, both for machine learning and software development, is to build a working prototype as quickly as possible. In the context of machine learning, this means creating the most naïve and quick-to-execute model you can think of. This has numerous benefits: It forces you to put together an end-to-end process, from data to validation, which you can reuse and refine as you go. It helps catch potential problems early on. It establishes a baseline, a number that sets the bar by which to judge whether other models are good or bad. And finally, if you are lucky, that simple model might just work great, in what case you'll be done early.

Speaking of simple models, there is one point that I really hope I managed to get across in this book. Much of the discourse around machine learning emphasizes fancy models and techniques. Complex algorithms are fun, but in the end, it is typically much more important to spend time understanding the data and extracting the right features. Feeding a complex algorithm poor data will not magically produce good answers. Conversely, as we saw in a few chapters, very simple models using carefully crafted features can produce surprisingly good results. And, as an added benefit, simpler models are also easier to understand.

F#: Being Productive in a Functional Style

The vast majority of the code we wrote together was written in F#, a functional-first .NET language. If this was your first exposure to F#, I hope you enjoyed it, and that it will inspire you to explore it further! In a way, functional programming suffers from a problem similar to machine learning; that is, it is all too often described as being a theoretical and abstract topic. The reasons F# became my primary language in the past few years have nothing to do with theory. I have found it to be an incredibly productive language. I can express ideas with clear and simple code, and rapidly refine them and get things done faster. Plus, I simply find the language fun to work with.

In my opinion, F# qualities shine when applied to the topic of machine learning. First, the built-in scripting environment and a language with light and expressive syntax are crucial. Developing a machine learning model involves a lot of exploration and experimentation, and being able to load data once and continue exploring throughout the day, without the potentially distracting mental interruption of having to reload and recompile, is key.

Then, if you look back at the models we built together, you might have noticed a general pattern. Starting from a data source, we read it and extract features, we apply a learning procedure that updates a model until the fit is good enough, and we compute some quality metric with cross-validation. That general process is a very good match with a functional style, and our implementations looked fairly similar across problems: Apply a map to transform data into features, use recursion to apply model updates and learn, and use averages or folds to reduce predictions into quality metrics such as accuracy. The vocabulary of functional languages fits fairly naturally with the type of problems machine learning is after. And, as an additional benefit, functional patterns, which emphasize immutable data, tend to be rather easy to parallelize, something that comes in handy when working with large amounts of data.

While this point applies to other functional languages as well, F# has a couple of characteristics that make it particularly interesting. The first one is type providers, a mechanism we explored in Chapter 3. Most languages are either dynamically or statically typed, and each comes with its advantages or challenges. Either external data is easy to access, but we get limited assistance from the compiler, or the opposite is true. F# type providers provide a resolution to that tension, making data (or languages, as in our example calling the R language) consumable with very limited friction, and discoverable in a safe manner, with all the benefits of static typing.

Another distinct benefit of F# for that particular domain is its ability to be used both for exploration and for production. We have been focusing mainly on the first aspect throughout this book, exploring data in a rapid feedback loop and progressively refining models. However, once ideas become stable, promoting code from a script to a module or a class and turning it into a full-fledged library is rather trivial, as illustrated in a couple of chapters. You can expect the same level of performance you would from .NET in general—that is, quite good. And, at that point, you can just run that code in production and integrate it with a .NET codebase, regardless of whether that code was written in C#, VB.NET, or F#. There is real value in being able to use the same language from exploration to production. I have seen in many places a development process where a research team creates models using one set of tools and languages, and transfers it to a development team that is left with the choice of either rewriting it all (with all the problems that entails) or trying their best to integrate and run exotic tools into a production system. F# can provide an interesting resolution to that tension, and can serve both as an exploratory language for research and a production-ready language for developers.

What's Next?

So, are you a machine learning expert now? I am sorry if this comes as a disappointment, but this book barely scratches the surface, and there is much, much more to learn. That being said, if you enjoyed the topic, the good news is you won't run out of interesting material to learn from (as a starting point, I would recommend taking a look at the class with Andrew Ng on Coursera, and trying out some of the Kaggle competitions). Machine learning is developing rapidly, and that is one of the reasons I enjoy the domain so much.

Perhaps more important, you might not be an expert just yet—but then, few people are, because of the sheer size of the topic. At this point, however, you are likely to know much more about the topic than a majority of software engineers, and you should be able to start productively using some of the ideas we talked about together in your own projects. Most important, I hope I managed to convince you that machine learning is both less complicated than it might appear at first, full of really interesting problems for mathematicians and software engineers alike, and a lot of fun. So, go try it out, do great things, and have fun!

Index

Get the eBook for only $5!

Why limit yourself?

Now you can take the weightless companion with you wherever you go and access your content on your PC, phone, tablet, or reader.

Since you've purchased this print book, we're happy to offer you the eBook in all 3 formats for just $5.

Convenient and fully searchable, the PDF version enables you to easily find and copy code—or perform examples by quickly toggling between instructions and applications. The MOBI format is ideal for your Kindle, while the ePUB can be utilized on a variety of mobile devices.

To learn more, go to www.apress.com/companion or contact support@apress.com.

Printed in the United States
By Bookmasters